Pierre Bourdieu

Pierre Bourdieu

Education and Training

MICHAEL JAMES GRENFELL

Bloomsbury Library of Educational Thought
Series Editor: Richard Bailey

B L O O M S B U R Y
LONDON • NEW DELHI • NEW YORK • SYDNEY

Bloomsbury Academic
An imprint of Bloomsbury Publishing Plc

50 Bedford Square   1385 Broadway
London   New York
WC1B 3DP   NY 10018
UK   USA

www.bloomsbury.com

First published 2007 by Continuum International Publishing Group
Paperback edition first published 2014 by Bloomsbury Academic

British Library Cataloguing-in-Publication Data
A catalogue record for this book is available from the British Library.

ISBN: PB: 978-1-4725-1874-3
ePUB: 978-1-4411-3581-0

Library of Congress Cataloguing-in-Publication Data
Grenfell, Michael, 1953–
Pierre Bourdieu: education and training/Michael James Grenfell.
p.   cm. – (Continuum library of educational thought)
Includes bibliographical references and index.
ISBN-13: 978-0-8264-8401-7 (hardcover)
ISBN-10: 0-8264-8401-8 (hardcover)
1. Bourdieu, Pierre, 1930–2002.   2. Bourdieu, Pierre, 1930–2002 – Criticism
and interpretation.   3. Education–Philosophy.   4. Educational sociology.
5. Sociologists–France–Biography.   I. Title.

LB880.B6542G743   2007
370.1–dc22

2007018461

Typeset by Aptara Books Ltd
Printed and bound in Great Britain by Biddles Ltd, Kings Lynn, Norfolk

Contents

Foreword

The ambiguity of the social role of education has become widely known and well documented. On the one hand, it promises to liberate and to change lives and entire societies; on the other, it conserves and protects existing values and interests. Very few social theorists have provided greater insight into the dynamics of these processes and their underlying significance in modern societies than Pierre Bourdieu (1930–2002), the subject of the present work by Michael Grenfell.

Inequality comes in all shapes and guises, so pervasive in its characteristics and effects that it can escape categorization or slip by unrecognized. Yet, whether in the structure of organizations, the hierarchies of communities, or the experiences of everyday life, inequality is a familiar, as well as a resilient feature of human society. As such, it has of course attracted widespread attention and is a key reference point across the social sciences and humanities. Apologists, from Plato to Burke to Hayek, have sought to rationalize its role and to identify ideals and traditions to justify it. By contrast, critics such as Marx and Engels, Tawney and Gramsci have graphically demonstrated the conditions of inequality, and its causes and effects. A wide range of types of inequality have been identified, generating many detailed accounts of social class and status, gender and ethnicity, labor markets and global antagonisms. The work of Pierre Bourdieu has become internationally recognized as being among the most arresting, provocative and insightful treatments of this general set of phenomena.

Bourdieu conceptualized social inequality and difference in many different forms and forums. He also found a key explanatory framework for the pervasiveness and resilience of inequalities in the role of education. His conception of 'education' is itself very broad and varied, including schools and schooling, families and universities, and encompassing in its range the whole life course, the entire scope of society and culture, the dense fabric of social experience. His empirical work conveys the teeming detail of social life. His theoretical analyses are linked irrevocably to words and phrases such as *habitus*, *fields* and *spaces*, *social reproduction* and *cultural capital*, but these are merely entry points to a fuller and deeper understanding of Bourdieu's *oeuvre* and intellectual development.

Michael Grenfell's contribution to the *Continuum Library of Educational Thought* is to provide a full and comprehensive discussion to this influential yet often misunderstood scholar. There can be no doubt that such a treatment is entirely merited in terms of the depth and range of Bourdieu's ideas and their significance for modern educational thought. It is also very timely, in that it is able to review his life's work as a whole following his recent death, and at a juncture when there is increasing interest and curiosity about his ideas. Moreover, in keeping with the aims of the series as a whole, Grenfell shows how Bourdieu's own life and times shaped his approach to education, society and culture; indeed, that his work must be understood in terms of his own biography. National factors were clearly important in terms of contemporary changes in French society and politics and the influence of the French intellectual tradition. Nevertheless, international developments were also to the fore in influencing his thought as he himself assumed a growing presence on a world stage.

Not only was there a vital relationship between Bourdieu's life and his work, there was no less a significant interaction between his work and his audience. Grenfell's book also explores the dynamics of the reception to Bourdieu's thought among his contemporaries in the wider world. The 'Bourdieu industry' might be taken to constitute not simply his own books and papers which he has left behind, but the increasingly large and diverse body of material produced by others in response to his ideas, which continues to grow unabated. This splendid volume adds to the growing debate, and helps us to make sense of the work of Bourdieu as a whole.

Gary McCulloch
Brian Simon Professor of the History of Education
Institute of Education, University of London

Series Editor's Preface

Education is sometimes presented as an essentially practical activity. It is, it seems, about teaching and learning, curriculum and what goes on in schools. It is about achieving certain ends, using certain methods, and these ends and methods are often prescribed for teachers, whose duty it is to deliver them with vigour and fidelity. With such a clear purpose, what is the value of theory?

Recent years have seen politicians and policy-makers in different countries explicitly denying *any* value or need for educational theory. A clue to why this might be is offered by a remarkable comment by a British Secretary of State for Education in the 1990s: 'having any ideas about how children learn, or develop, or feel, should be seen as subversive activity'. This pithy phrase captures the problem with theory: it subverts, challenges and undermines the very assumptions on which the practice of education is based.

Educational theorists, then, are trouble-makers in the realm of ideas. They pose a threat to the *status quo* and lead us to question the common-sense presumptions of educational practices. But this is precisely what they should do because the seemingly simple language of schools and schooling hides numerous contestable concepts that in their different usages reflect fundamental disagreements about the aims, values and activities of education.

Implicit within the *Bloomsbury Library of Educational Thought* is an assertion that theories and theorizing are vitally important for education. By gathering together the ideas of some of the most influential, important and interesting educational thinkers, from the Ancient Greeks to contemporary scholars, the series has the ambitious task of providing an accessible yet authoritative resource for a generation of students and practitioners. Volumes within the series are written by acknowledged leaders in the field, who were selected both for their scholarship and their ability to make often complex ideas accessible to a diverse audience.

It will always be possible to question the list of key thinkers that are represented in this series. Some may question the inclusion of certain thinkers; some may disagree with the exclusion of others. That is inevitably going to be the case. There is no suggestion that the list of thinkers represented within the *Bloomsbury Library of Educational Thought* is in any way definitive. What is incontestable is that these thinkers have fascinating ideas about education, and that taken together, the *Library* can act as a powerful source of information and inspiration for those committed to the study of education.

Richard Bailey
Roehampton University, London

Acknowledgements

I especially acknowledge Cheryl Hardy for her support and encouragement while I wrote this book. She also read the initial draft and made numerous suggestions and comments to improve both the content and style of the text.

Introduction

Pierre Bourdieu was a French social philosopher. He was born in a tiny village in the French Pyrenees in 1930 and died in Paris in 2002. His professional life spanned the second half of the twentieth century – his first publications appearing in 1958. His family background was really quite modest financially. However, as a child he was sent to the nearest town as a boarder in a local school. This move was to begin an academic trajectory which took him to the very top of the academic establishment in France. From local schools, he went to a prestigious preparatory school in Paris, and eventually to one of the elite training colleges. After military service in Algeria, he was appointed to a research institution in Paris where he built a formidable career. He undertook a number of empirical research projects, the findings of which appeared in voluminous publications over the subsequent decades. His work was highly acclaimed and in 1981 he was nominated to a Chair at the Collège de France; an institution which includes only the cream of French intellectuals.

Bourdieu is now regarded as a key thinker in the social sciences. He is known first and foremost as a sociologist. However, his brand of sociology is very particular. He himself originally trained in philosophy. It is therefore unsurprising if his sociology is also highly philosophical. Issues of 'knowledge', 'reason' and 'truth' are at the centre of his concerns. Nevertheless, early experiences in his home region, and while in Algeria, stimulated his interest in the practical world which surrounded him. Much of his work therefore begins with direct observation of a particular social event or phenomenon. Bourdieu's own academic training included anthropology and, consequently, he employed a range of ethnographic techniques in his empirical studies.

For much of the 1960s, Bourdieu was simply 'just' another French sociologist. However, his work attracted increasing attention and, by the 1970s, translations began to appear in an English-speaking world. There were two major areas which interested him: education and culture. Yet, it was as part of the 'new' sociology of education movement of the 1970s that he first achieved a wider public attention. For many, he is still known primarily for the part he played in the development of new sociological perspectives on education; in particular, with a focus on classroom language, pedagogic discourses and the construction of knowledge. Bourdieu's interests expanded rapidly, however, and in the 1980s and 1990s he published analyses on a range of topics such as art, literature, the media, economics, politics, philosophy, language and the history of science.

For much of his early career, Bourdieu seemed happy to remain within the confines of his own academic world and eschewed public appearances. However, by the 1980s and 1990s, he increasingly took on the mantle of the 'public intellectual' and became involved actively in a wide range of social movements and governmental committees. Yet, his reputation rests on his published work. Many hundreds of texts – some large, some small – appeared throughout his life. Many of these are now translated into several languages. A veritable Bourdieu industry has grown up. In fact, he was the last of a generation of grand intellectual masters – many of them French – who strongly influenced thinking in the social sciences during the second half of the twentieth century.

This book offers a biographical account of Bourdieu's work on education. It is divided into four main parts.

Part 1 establishes an Intellectual Biography for Bourdieu. It describes his own life events in detail in the context of the socio-historical climate of the times. The ways these impinged upon Bourdieu and shaped his thinking are highlighted. Reference is made to the French intellectual tradition, how it characterized itself, and the differences and similarities Bourdieu shared with it. The roots of a sociological tradition dating back to the eighteenth century are presented as a way of locating Bourdieu's thinking within this developing discipline. Bourdieu's work is set alongside that of the founding fathers of sociology – Comte, Marx, Weber, Durkheim – in order to show what Bourdieu shared with these and how he modified their principal concepts.

Part 2 is a critical discussion of Bourdieu's thinking on education. As noted above, Bourdieu's was a sociology which was heavily infused with philosophy. Issues of epistemology are therefore present throughout the discussion. Part 2 begins by presenting Bourdieu's theory of practice. His approach is characterized by a set of conceptual 'thinking tools': for example, habitus, field, capital, etc. These are defined and their relationship to each other explained. How they are employed in empirical studies is also discussed, as is how this theory of practice is also a practice of theory. Salient sociological issues are addressed.

Part 2 is made up of seven chapters, which offer a chronological account of Bourdieu's major works on education. The first chapter begins with the educational aspects of his early work in the Béarn (his home region) and in Algeria. His analyses of university students and issues of studying are then addressed. The concerns of the 'new' sociologists of education are described in the context of their day. Bourdieu's seminal text – *La Reproduction* – is discussed in detail. This coverage shows what Bourdieu understood by 'the school' and how 'pedagogic authority' and 'symbolic violence' were embedded in its processes and procedures. The principal aim of Part 2 is to offer an accurate account of what Bourdieu wrote and how his ideas were shaped by the world of events and ideas which surrounded him. However, it also considers his theories in terms of their developmental nature and their continuing relevance today. This coverage is a critical enquiry into Bourdieu's studies of education. In the 1980s, Bourdieu published two major studies on the French academic field and elite training schools. Details of his field analyses are offered and the final conclusions to be drawn from them discussed. A further issue of the applicability of these studies and their conclusions to contexts other than France is also addressed. Finally, Part 2 returns to issues of policy and practice; in particular, the role that Bourdieu played in public committees on educational reform. Furthermore, there is discussion of the 'acts of resistance' (and the form they took) that Bourdieu mounted in opposition to what he saw as the dominant trends in education in the latter part of the twentieth century.

Part 3 focuses on the reception of Bourdieu's work on education and its influence. A number of critical responses are considered. Critiques are discussed in terms of Bourdieu's own theory of practice and the strength of the objections raised. Part 3 begins with a reconsideration of the new sociology of education; what characterized it and how Bourdieu's ideas fitted into this movement. Questions are raised about its evolution and about the issues that subsequently emerged. In many places, Bourdieu's perspective is contrasted with the work of other writers; some radical, some neo-conservative. Finally, Part 3 addresses 'social theory' itself. Bourdieu's own theories are compared with other theoretical developments in the social sciences and with the nature of 'fin de siècle' social theory. The question as to whether what Bourdieu offers is in fact emancipatory or a form of 'sociological terrorism' is posed.

Part 4 has two principal aims. First, to bring the critical reception of Bourdieu's work up to date by considering ways in which it has been discussed in the twenty-first century. A range of authors' critical responses and applications is quoted. One particular focus here is the structure of higher education, and how morphological changes in the field have shaped learning and teaching. Second, Part 4 aims to show ways in which Bourdieu's theory of practice has the potential to be employed in a variety of areas in educational research. Some of these topics do not explicitly address the usual sociological concerns – race, gender, class – but deal with other issues of teaching and learning. The theme of 'language' is used as a focus for this discussion. Part 4 looks at the language *of* educational research and contrasts it with Bourdieu's own. There are examples taken from classroom language to show how others writers' analyses of educational discourse can be developed to provide further illumination using Bourdieu's conceptual tools and empirical approach. Finally, Part 4 also addresses the nature of educational knowledge itself and the conduct of research studies. Reflexivity is a key concept here. Part 4 concludes with a consideration of how such reflexivity can be made operational in practice and the status of the resultant knowledge. Thus, reflexivity returns the book once again to epistemological issues of theory and practice.

A brief Afterword brings the book to a close.

The design of the book is intended to aid reading for those with a range of interests and motives. Part 1 offers details of Bourdieu's biography – both personal and professional – and shows the historical climate in which he lived his life and developed his ideas. Part 2 is a critical account of his works on education. Part 3 shows the way his work was received and the influence it has. Part 4 discusses the potential for extending Bourdieu's ideas in the future. There are then different ways of reading this book.

Bourdieu has taken his place in a line of major thinkers about education. The principal aim of this book is to show why.

Part 1

Intellectual Biography

Introduction

This first part of this book sets out an 'Intellectual Biography' of Bourdieu. It comprises five main chapters. The first chapter offers biographical details of Bourdieu's life and work. Bourdieu often made a plea that his ideas should be understood in terms of the times in which the various works were produced. The next four chapters attempt to provide the structure for such a 'socio-genetic' reading of his publications. First, a historical background is established, against which, second, details of the French intellectual tradition are set. These chapters cover the period from the Great Revolution of 1789 to the Second World War. Various philosophical, social, economic and historical trends are traced across this period. In particular, we look at the founding fathers of sociology and the way commonalities of ideas and concerns fed into the period which directly influenced Bourdieu. The next chapter deals in detail with Bourdieu and the post-war intellectual climate. We consider both what Bourdieu responded to and reacted against. Ideas and events are interwoven. The whole provides a historical and philosophical background to understanding Bourdieu's 'theory of practice', which will then be set out in detail in the next part of this book.

Chapter 1

Biography

Pierre Bourdieu was born on the 1 August 1930 in Denguin, a small village in the Béarn region of the French Pyrenées-Atlantiques, in the south-west corner of rural France. His father was an office worker cum postman for the French Post Office, although he had also worked as a sharecropper. Reputedly, the family was one of modest means and of limited education or training. His father left school before completing his education. Only his mother continued to the age of 16. Gascon, a now moribund regional language, was spoken at home, which posed few problems in an age before mass communication. This was a fairly isolated existence with outside contact being largely with local towns and markets. The nearest cities – Toulouse, Bordeaux, Montpelier, themselves still quite unmodernized in France between the wars – would be visited only occasionally. The major economic activities for the inhabitants of Denguin revolved around agriculture and rural crafts.

There are few published details of Bourdieu's early life. We can surmise that he was a gifted pupil, even at primary school, since he was subsequently sent to the main *lycée* in Pau as a boarder. He clearly succeeded academically as he went on to the Lycée Le Grand in Paris to complete his secondary education. This school was a renowned preparatory institution for pupils destined for the very highest and most prestigious French training schools. Two of these dominated as the very pinnacles of French education: the École Polytechnique (EP) and the École Normale Supérieure (ENS). Bourdieu went to the latter in 1951, graduating as an *agrégé* in philosophy in 1955.

After a brief period teaching in Moulins, he undertook his military service in Algeria where, eventually, he also taught at the Faculté des Lettres in Algiers. This period was marked by the appearance of his first publications; most noticeably *Sociologie de l'Algérie*, which was first published in 1958 in the famous French *Que sais-je?* series. Other articles on Algeria followed.

In 1960, Bourdieu returned to France. He worked as a 'teaching assistant' to Raymond Aron who at that time was one of France's leading intellectuals. Bourdieu progressed to teach at the University of Lille. He married Marie-Claire Brizzard in 1962, with whom he had three sons: Jérôme, Emmanuel and Laurent. In 1964, he was appointed as Director of Studies at the École Pratique des Hautes Études in Paris, where he took over the directorship of the Centre de Sociologie Européenne. In 1964, he also became editor to the 'Le Sens Commun' series of the 'Éditions de Minuit' publishing house. These academic and commercial positions provided Bourdieu with a base from which he was able to develop his research agenda. Empirical studies were undertaken on the French education system, museums and photography as he built up a research team around him. The outcomes and results of these studies were published in a series of books and articles; for example, *Les Héritiers. Les etudiants et la Culture* (1979b/1964), *La Reproduction* (1977a/1970) on education; *Un Art moyen* (1990a/1965) and *L'Amour de l'art* (1990b/1966) on photography and museums.

In 1968, France was shaken by a series of national strikes by both workers and students. By this time, Bourdieu was known as a sociologist in France but his reputation had not yet extended beyond its borders. He published a major treatise on sociology in which he set out his principal methodological concerns: *Le Métier de sociologue* (1991b/1968), which included illustrative extracts from key thinkers as a background to the approach described; for example, Marx, Weber, Durkheim, Mauss, Bachelard and Canguilhem. This book was then followed up by a major exposition of what he called his 'theory of practice': *Esquisse d'une théorie de la pratique* (1977b/1972), which itself also included further work on his Algerian studies. *Esquisse* was translated into English in 1977, the year in which *La Reproduction* also appeared in English. In 1971, *Knowledge and Control: New Directions for the Sociology of Education* had been published. This book was a collection of papers edited by Michael Young (1971) and was a seminal publication in defining a *new* sociology of education. Bourdieu had two papers included: 'Intellectual field and creative project' and

'Systems of education and systems of thought'. In fact, neither of these articles were written especially for *Knowledge and Control*. However, their appearance in this book brought Bourdieu's work to the attention of an English-speaking world. The publication of *Reproduction* and the *Outline of a Theory of Practice* consolidated his reputation as key sociological thinker – in education at least.

However, Bourdieu's next major work returned to questions of culture and taste. *La distinction* was published in 1979 (1984a/1979) and quickly became a sociological classic, to be cited next to such canonical works as Durkheim's *Suicide* and Weber's *Protestant Work Ethic and the Spirit of Capitalism*. In *La distinction*, Bourdieu set out to demonstrate what we might term the 'sociological construction of taste' and, by implication, aesthetics (see Grenfell and Hardy, 2007). His next major books, however, returned to educational matters. *Homo Academicus* (1988/1984) is a study of Bourdieu's own academic field and its mechanisms of self-reproduction and competitiveness; while *La Noblesse d'État* (1996b/1989) examines the forms of influence constructed and used by those involved with the French elite training schools, of which Bourdieu's own ENS was one. By this stage, Bourdieu was writing freely and extensively on a wide range of topics. Further methodological and, by implication, philosophical statements followed: most noticeably, *Le Sens pratique* (1990c/1980) (itself a reworking of his Algerian studies), *Questions de sociologie* (1993a/1980), and *Choses dites* (1990d/1987). *L'ontologie de politique de Martin Heidegger* (1991c/1988) offered a socio-historical reading of a key twentieth-century philosopher. He also published a major statement on language: *Ce que parler veut dire* (1991a/1982).

In 1981, François Mitterand won the French Presidential elections and, after the subsequent parliamentary elections, formed the first socialist government of the Fifth Republic. Bourdieu's most direct involvement in political power came in 1984 when he chaired a committee of the Collège de France commissioned by Mitterand to look at the future of French education. Subsequently, Bourdieu co-authored a report (1985a) which provided a set of guiding principles for education. Although, Bourdieu undertook a series of media events to explain and publicize the proposals, he eventually withdrew from active involvement with the Mitterand government when it became clear that few if any of their proposals were going to be adopted in any meaningful way.

If, by the last decade of the twentieth century, Bourdieu's profile was more evident in France, his reputation abroad developed to the point where he became a thinker and writer of major international status. His books appeared in English with shorter and shorter delays after their French publication. His influence spread beyond sociology and his main preoccupations, and now included such diverse disciplines as architecture, geography, art and literature, economics, and politics. In 1981, Bourdieu was named Chair in Sociology at the Collège de France; an institution, seen as an exclusive 'club', which groups together just 52 members drawn from the *crème de la crème* of French academia. His inaugural lecture was published in 1982, entitled *Leçon sur une leçon* (1982).

In 1993, Bourdieu was awarded the Gold Medal from the French CNRS – the highest accolade that can be bestowed on an intellectual in France. That same year, *La Misère du monde* was published (1999a/1993). In this book, Bourdieu and his team set out to catalog 'the weight of the world'; namely, the poverty of experience, both material and psychological, of various groups within French society. Its impact was instantaneous. More than 150,000 copies were sold, extracts were re-enacted in theatres, and its depiction of France in the late twentieth century was the subject of numerous media events. Bourdieu was now fast becoming the 'public intellectual', appearing on TV, radio and in the press. In 1975, he had complemented his editorship of *Le Sens Commun* by founding the academic review *Actes de la Recherche en Sciences Sociales*. *Actes* served as a publication output for Bourdieu and his team for the publication of topical papers, work in progress and initial reports. Its international perspective meant that it attracted a wide audience. It also offered a sociological perspective of political issues. *Actes* targeted an academic audience, but by the 1990s Bourdieu sought a medium through which he could address a larger public. In 1998, he founded *Raisons d'Agir*, a series aimed at the production of small publications accessible to a more general reader. His own contributions to the series – *Contre-feux* (1998a) and *Contre-feux 2* (2001b) – included a collection of Bourdieu's more polemical and journalistic texts. These texts targeted the neo-liberal world of market economics and argued for the formation of a new social movement in Europe. This mission and these publications were supported by his further interventions in the media, as well as his membership of several pressure groups seeking social and political reforms (for example, 1994a, 1994b, 1996c, 1998b, 1999b, 2000a, 2000b).

This activity can be understood as Bourdieu adopting a more public and political role, albeit on the margins of politics. Nonetheless, academic works continued to appear at frequent intervals. His principal analysis of the artistic field was published – *Les Règles de l'art* (1996a/1992) – and had, at its core, a study of the French nineteenth-century writer Gustave Flaubert. A further major artistic study of the 'Pre-Impressionist' painter Manet formed part of his ten-week *leçon* at the Collège de France in 2000. He addressed the issue of gender in *La Domination masculine* (2001a/1998). His critique of methodology and philosophy continued in *Réponses* (1992a), *Raisons pratiques* (1998c/1994), *Méditations pascaliennes* (2000a/1997), *Science de la science et réflexivité* (2001c).

He died of cancer on 23 January 2002 and was buried in the Père Lachaise cemetery, along with many of France's most illustrious scholars, artists and writers.

Chapter 2

French Historical Background

As noted in the Introduction to Part I Bourdieu asks for a 'socio-genetic' reading of his work (1993b: 263). He asks for this in order to offset the misunderstanding, objections and refutations that his work has traditionally attracted, and which arises as a result of commentators ignoring the 'social conditions' which have given rise to particular writings. From the last chapter, it is possible to see that Bourdieu's own biography was closely linked to his various projects and publications; and that these concerns were a response to contemporary events. The focus of the present volume is 'Bourdieu and Education' and, certainly, for much of his academic career, he was known mostly as a 'sociologist of education'. However, we shall see that in this context both terms are problematic. His 'sociology' was highly individual, and might equally be called 'social philosophy', 'anthropology' or 'ethnology'. And, if 'education' was one of his major preoccupations, this was only true in terms of the part educational processes played in the experiences of people and their life trajectories. The next two chapters of the book provide a 'socio-genetic' context to his work. In the first chapter, I shall consider France and the socio-political tradition which formed an important background to Bourdieu's writing. The next chapter will then look at the intellectual tradition in France.

Bourdieu was born in the 1930s, a pivotal period in French history. At this time, the Third Republic was some 60 years old; the longest any political establishment had survived since the Great Revolution in 1789. During these years, France had experienced almost continual social upheaval. Some claim that the forces unleashed by the Great Revolution were not really laid to rest until after the humiliation inflicted on France by the Franco-Prussian war of 1870–71 and the subsequent trauma of the Paris Commune. In pre-revolutionary times, the allegiance of Frenchmen was claimed by God and the King.

The Palace of Versailles was a perfect illustration of the aristocratic court in which French noblemen lived, while large portions of the rest of the population starved. The Revolution swept all this away in the name of Equality, Liberty and Universal Brotherhood. When the First Republic was born, the 'King' was dead, and 'God' along with him. However, the actuality of French life trailed behind such revolutionary rhetoric, and it was to experience a Second Republic, three Empires and attempts at the restoration of the monarchy before a stable republican system was finally established in 1871. Non-religious State education came later in the 1880s. The Church was finally separated from the State in 1905. Although, the principles of the Revolution were clear, they did not entirely purge the forces of patriotism and the ongoing nationalism of the men of the Left and Right. Napoleon Bonaparte rose as a revolutionary leader, but then had himself crowned Emperor. Ambitions to extend France's natural frontiers united, in spirit at least, both those who sought to export the Revolution and those with more traditional National-ist leanings. During the nineteenth century, national strength was often defined in terms of the procurement of foreign territory. For example, Algeria in North Africa was invaded in 1830 to back up the restored monarchy, and other overseas territories were quickly added (see Grenfell, 2006). 'Insecurity' is the watchword to understanding nineteenth-century France. Nothing, it seemed, defined the French view of themselves in the world as did the relationship between these internal and external forces.

By the beginning of the twentieth century, Frenchmen were criticiz-ing the record of the Third Republic in protecting national interests. Politically, the old monarchists and Bonapartist Right had moved to the Centre where, paradoxically, they joined those of the radical Left. The First World War was a defining moment in recasting the political landscape. The revolutionary Left, born of eighteenth-century Marx-ist communism and given a heroic twist by the Paris Commune, took the Russian Revolution of 1917 as a sign of the imminence of Inter-national communism. The broader Socialist Party was reformist. The new Right, however, was born out of extreme reaction to the Drey-fus Affair, which implicated the army in political corruption. This sense of outrage targeted what was regarded as a weak republican regime. Under the twin threats from without (invasion from Germany) and within (weak political leadership), the Right reverted to traditional themes of counter-revolution, the strength of traditional values, authority of the State, and even monarchy and Catholicism.

Victory in the First World War went some way to bolster French political rulers. However, growing economic problems together with an increasingly unstable international situation only added to the sense of inevitable catastrophe. Economic crisis was precipitated by financial crashes, unemployment and reports of corruption. The very system of democratic Capitalism was called into question and then directly challenged by the twin alternatives of Communism and National Socialism. This issue was not resolved until a Second World War was fought.

If the political situation in France was unstable, what of the French people themselves? The most noticeable phenomenon of the nineteenth century was the sluggish speed with which France became industrialized. Steady industrial advances were made, especially during the Second Empire and the Third Republic, but this was quite late in comparison to other European countries. What industry there was, was to be found in the north, in the traditional heavy industrial sectors and around Paris. By the time of the outbreak of the Second World War, some 40 per cent of the population were still employed in agricultural work compared to 5 per cent in the UK. The railways were also constructed comparatively late in France (1850s and 1860s). With industrialization, France increasingly experienced the type of 'rural exodus' other countries had undergone a century earlier. With new urban environments, lifestyle, habits and beliefs changed. A world which revolved around community and the Church was replaced by secular distractions and the anonymity of urban living. The phenomenon of 'de-Christianization' became more and more evident in the nineteenth century, developing into a contemporary crisis, provoking Christian missions and the formation of numerous Catholic youth movements by the Church. Certainly, by the 1930s, large areas of France – around Paris, the south-west and on the southern coast – were considered regions of 'minor' religious observance: with a high percentage of non-baptized children and only a minority of the population regularly attending Church.

If countervailing forces, which can be traced back to the Great Revolution, continued to exert influence on both the internal and external affairs of the French political establishment, then socially the twin forces of tradition and modernism seemed acutely opposed. The experience of the 1930s only heightened these tensions. Little wonder therefore, if, with German occupation during the Second World War, so many Frenchmen decided that coexistence with National Socialism offered a possible resolution of social, political and economic contradictions. In July 1940, the French Third Republic collapsed in the face of German invasion. Deputies and Senators voted for their own abolition, passing all powers over to Marshal Pétain. The defeat was called 'une étrange défaite' by Marc Bloch to refer to the way the French political and military establishment was old and tired. What Pétain in effect institutionalized was a system of full collaboration with Nazism. However, resistance was immediate and grew to a point where civil war virtually ruled between Frenchmen themselves. Increasingly, as the full implications of National Socialism impacted on French society, its people fought for their freedom from German oppression. In the early stages of collaboration, the choices were less clear cut. Thousands of photos of Pétain were sold and many Frenchmen, with the pain of the 1920s and 1930s very much in mind, welcomed the Vichy government with its call for a return to the traditional values of *famille, travail, patrie* (family, work and country).

We do not know how these events were seen through the eyes of Bourdieu at the time. He would have been ten when the Second World War began and an adolescent when it finished. What was life like for a school boarder in provincial France? Nevertheless, we can see that the issues embedded in the social and political structures of post-revolution France continued to shape the response of intellectuals to modern France. It is to the intellectual tradition in which Bourdieu was to take part that I now wish to turn.

Chapter 3

The French Intellectual Tradition

France, in particular Paris, has long been a centre for intellectuals of international significance. For much of the last 300 years, it has occupied a pivotal position in the world of ideas. Even in pre-revolutionary times, France produced some of the key thinkers of the Age of Enlightenment. Indeed, the organization of society based around the court partly favored the development of this tradition as men of letters, writers and would-be philosophers gathered in the Parisian *Salons* to discuss issues of the day. In mid-eighteenth century France, the *Encyclopédie* was compiled as a dictionary of the 'sciences, arts and trades'. Included in it were articles by such leading French writers as Voltaire, Helvetius, Diderot and D'Alembert. Generally, they took a skeptical view of religion in an age which increasingly looked to scientific knowledge to guide thought and action. 'Man' became the centre of this enquiry. He was unhappy, it was claimed, not because of God's will but because he did not understand nature. Hence, Man's project was to understand nature through knowledge based on experience, rationality and human thought. Scientific knowledge was grounded on empiricism, naturalism and materialism, not on religious doctrine. The Age of the Enlightenment was therefore also known as the Age of Reason. Reason and rationality showed men what to do and how to organize themselves. Society needed to be constituted through the moral needs of men, not the wishes of their rulers. There was then a need for an enlightened politics, which served the needs of society, not God and the King. The intellectual atmosphere of this age was therefore liberal and progressive rather than traditional. It would be wrong to depict such a spirit as uniquely active in France. Similar trends are identifiable across Europe. However, it was France which seemed to act as an intellectual focus for writers and thinkers of the age. The Great Revolution of 1789 can in many ways be seen as the logical precipitation of such ideas in overturning the old order, with its outmoded beliefs, in the name of human science.

We can trace some of the key currents in the French intellectual tradition to this age; for example, the founding principles of modern politics. Montesquieu (1689–1755) published *De l'esprit des lois* in 1748 in which he classified forms of government – he later also contributed to the *Encyclopédie*. For him, the principle of government is the spirit which animates it. So, monarchies are founded on 'Honor'; republics on 'Virtue'; and despots on 'Fear'. Montesquieu concluded (along with many others writers at the time) that society was unequal. However, unlike the revolutionaries, he did not believe that equality among the mass of the people could be a sovereign principle. Rather, he called for a political system, which would restrict the excesses of inequality and balance political power among the ruling bodies. It would therefore be wrong to conclude that Montesquieu provided the principles for the Great Revolution. However, he did contribute to a questioning of the existing systems which in effect acted to undermine them. The writings of Jean-Jacques Rousseau (1712–78), who was another contributor to the *Encyclopédie*, also had an influence in undermining traditional values and social structures.

In the case of Rousseau, we can see both enlightenment and rationality, and the main reaction to these – romanticism. Romanticism was at its height from the end of the eighteenth to the early nineteenth century and was another current which spread out across Europe. The Romantics – poets, artists and writers – reacted against the modern world with its rational thought, empirical obsessions and scientific world view. The Romantics celebrated the self and individual emotion and expression. They often looked back to the past and to a nobler age than the industrial, urban life which now surrounded them. Rousseau did this when he gave us the 'noble savage': the idealized view of man enjoying a 'pre-socialized' existence, until modern living ensnares him in insatiable desires and appetites. Education here amounted to the taming of these desires in terms of citizenship, defined as shared experience and consideration of the needs of the community. In *Discours sur l'origine de l'inégalité parmi les hommes* (1755) Rousseau argued that it is civilization which everywhere differentiates and distinguishes between one man and another. By its nature, this differentiation creates inequalities among them. However, Rousseau was not looking to traditional political structures to return us to this Romantic age. Rather, somewhat in a pre-Marxist mode, Rousseau argued for the 'volonté générale': the organization of society in which individual wishes were subjected to the 'general will'. Here, the collective view is sovereign and should be directed towards to the common good. Of course, this argument anticipates Marxism and the concept of the 'dictatorship of the working class', or 'party', to take its Leninist extension. Moreover, it is an antecedent of the Marxist aphorism, itself both romantic and rational: 'From each according to his abilities; to each according to his needs'. Rousseau had also written, 'man was born free, and is everywhere in chains'. Certainly, what he was proposing was meant to free him from such a condition. It is perhaps not surprising, therefore, if his ideas became key texts for the revolutionary Jacobins, or that he had to spend much of his later life outside France. This role to challenge the political status quo, everywhere apparent in the eighteenth century, became embedded in the French intellectual tradition. It is a mantle that we shall see Bourdieu taking on. It was, however, Augustus Comte who is accredited as the 'founder' of modern-day sociology – in fact, he is said to have invented the word.

Comte (1798–1857) studied the very way in which human thought had developed. For him, a certain type of society was dying; that characterized by the theological and the military – namely, that based on a 'transcendent' faith. The New World, on the other hand, was based on the scientific and industrial. Somewhat akin to Montesquieu, Comte saw the organization of society as 'animated' by certain principles or spirits. Just as in previous times, society embodied the principles of a transcendent hierarchy; it was now based around the principles of science and industry. To this extent, men had ceased to be preoccupied with war against each other, and instead had engaged with nature and how to turn it to their advantage. This approach in effect concluded that the way we think conditions the way we act and organize ourselves. Here, we have a principle which we will see was also central to Bourdieu's own thought: that ideas do change society. If we can effect an intellectual change, a change in the ideas which men hold, then society itself will change. Like Bourdieu, and many intellectuals before and since, Comte was essentially pessimistic about the world that surrounded him and thought that it was in crisis. For Bourdieu, we shall see it was the state of post-war France, together with imminent globalization and neo-liberal politics which threatened. For Comte, somewhat unsurprisingly in revolutionary times, it was the struggle between the old and the new order, typified by the theological-military and the scientific-industrial. For Comte, 'Sociology' was part of the New World in that it offered an interpretation of society which could be used to promote order. Two particular aspects of his work are to note: the 'law' of three stages; and the classification of sciences. The law of three stages states that men pass through three phases of intellectual thought. First, the human mind explains phenomena by associating them with aspects of man himself. In the second stage, metaphysics, abstract entities like 'nature' are used to explain phenomena. In the third stage, men are happy simply to describe things and the regularity of links between them. In this third phase, the search for transcendent principles is abandoned and men set about discovering the laws which underlie observed facts. This last stage was termed 'positive' and amounted to the systematic collection of facts and their interpretation through correlations. Indeed, Bourdieu followed on directly in this tradition; especially in his early empirical work. Observation is at its core. In a sense, therefore, this third stage was anti-metaphysical, and rather based itself on a defined limit to scientific enquiry. 'Science' was the means to understand the world. The name 'positivism' itself reveals its optimistic nature and coincided with the belief that through such an approach men could better understand themselves and the world, and in so doing, both gain freedom from its oppressions and act decisively in an informed way to shape it. In fact, Comte tried to turn positivism into a new 'religion', and have himself crowned Pope as ruler over it. In several countries, 'Positivist Societies' were established, and it is now possible to see in their derivation both the humanistic principles of the Revolution and the progressive spirit of the times. Comte saw the law of three stages existing in the way human knowledge had developed, but affecting the various disciplines in a differential manner. Thus, mathematics, physics and chemistry were more 'positivist' than the body of knowledge we would now call the human sciences – politics, history. Nevertheless, positivism would eventually take over these as well; indeed, his founding of 'sociology' was meant to announce this transformation. Sociology would study society in the same way that astronomers studied the stars. By discovering 'laws' of society, we could understand how it worked and thus solve the problems of crises it was experiencing. This approach presupposes a 'healthy' state, defined in terms of optimal functioning; in other words, that men should share common beliefs and act in their diversity according to the common good.

In this brief account of certain key figures in pre- and post-revolutionary France, it is possible to see the foundations of the modern French intellectual. There are common themes in the writings of Montesquieu, Rousseau and Comte which perhaps transcend their differences. We could quote other significant writers from this period; for example, Voltaire or Tocqueville. There is also Blaise Pascal (1623–62) from the previous century: a philosopher with whom Bourdieu strongly associated himself in *Pascalian Meditations* (2000a/ 1997). It would be wrong to claim that any one of these individual writers acted as a direct or decisive precursor for Bourdieu's work – too many others came in between. Nevertheless, it is important to note these influences as seminal providers of issues and arguments which continue to preoccupy all Frenchmen. For Bourdieu, we can recognize in these themes similar ones as those he confronted in his own contemporary 'crisis' of society: for example, the clash of the old and the new order; the impact of science and industrialization; attitudes to and the influence of the Church; the balance between society and the individual; the 'health' of society and how it functioned; and, consequently, how society might be better organized. There are also further questions concerning the actualization of revolutionary principles, and political organization and representation. Bourdieu addressed many aspects of these in his work to a greater or lesser extent, and in a contemporary sense. Furthermore, he claimed a relationship between ideas and how they might shape the material world, including how society is structured. Finally, there is sociology itself: how it is defined; its role in the world; its *modus operandi* and relationship to other scientific disciplines. Many of these issues are addressed later in the book in the context of education.

Above, we noted the international status of the French intellectual and their longstanding tradition. Clearly, this pre-dated the Great Revolution. However, the significance that this revolution took on in Europe and the world, not least in countries fearful that revolution would also happen there, amplified the intensity of intellectual thought both before and after it, anticipating and reacting to it. However, the word 'intellectual' itself did not really enter common parlance until much later in the nineteenth century. Before that period, the 'intellectuals' we speak of were known rather as writers, philosophers and authors. In 1898, however, Zola published his now famous open letter to the President of the Republic – *J'accuse* – in which he set out the case against the military, and by implication political corruption, in the handling of Captain Dreyfus who had been tried and convicted for treason. The 'Dreyfus Affair', as it became known, split not just the views of Frenchmen themselves but the political establishment. Indeed, it precipitated the kind of dilemma which has itself characterized French society both before and since, where a public issue forced them to decide and take up a position on either one side or the other of the debate. In this case, and apparently for the first time, French intellectuals acted en masse and defined themselves as an identifiable group. Bourdieu himself (1996a/1992: 341) later wrote of the way in which French intellectuals were often caught in a kind of 'pendulum swing' with regard to their relationship to politics; between commitment and retreat. The Dreyfus Affair forced them to get involved in a way which would characterize their involvement later in the twentieth century.

Culturally, intellectual life in the first third of the twentieth century remained characteristically aristocratic; the *lycées* were reserved for the Bourgeoisie, the intelligentsia was dominated by writers, and the mass media was in its infancy. Education for the masses did not go much beyond basic training in literacy and mathematics. For the elite, they were trained according to a philosophical tradition which heightened a sense of the need to comment on the society which surrounded them and its values. Following the Dreyfus Affair, writers in France became increasingly accustomed to signing declarations and petitions as the most effective means of social and political comment. This trend was taken one step further with a growing number of

'Revue' publications, conceived as periodicals publishing the French intelligentsia's writings. Such intellectuals faced the simultaneous appearance of three crises: that of society, upset by war and economic depression; that of the worker movement, divided as a result of the Bolshevik Revolution; and that of the Catholic Church, still searching for a place in the modern world. In nearly all aspects of French social and political life, therefore, the 1930s marked the end of an era, the 'death' of bourgeois society, in short, 'la grande crise'. French intellectuals were often grouped around three publications under the collective names of *Jeune Droite* (the Right), *Esprit* (a review of the Left to which Bourdieu later contributed and eventually decisively broke away from) and *Ordre Nouveau* (largely political abstention-sists). As previously noted, the political climate of the 1930s was itself ambiguous, and only the experience of eventual war would resolve the tensions involved. In effect, more seemed to unite these intellectuals than divide them in their rejection of bourgeois society. So, there was much talk of the 'désordre établi', seen as a direct consequence of the revolutionary principles of 1789, considered as abstractions and without contact with reality. The State was singled out for attack for its imposing influence on individuals, so that modern man, basing his life upon popular notions of freedom and equality, was no longer able to take responsibility for himself. Secular education was singled out for special criticism in the way it trained children in the secu-lar and profane. Liberal democracy was referred to as a 'un régime idéal de pourriture' (an ideal rotten system) and 'un système périmé d'institutions archaïques' (a system surrounded by archaic institu-tions). By supporting these structures, the function of the capitalist system was described as a subversion of human values, as the very basis on which the corruption of the State was founded. The character of the 'spirit of 1930' was therefore clear. The theories of these writers were philosophical and moral before being economic and political. The social order in their eyes was only the superficial consequence of the moral and spiritual disorder of man, of a misconception of his destiny (see Loubet, 1969). There were also influences by such writ-ers as the philosopher Jacques Maritain (1882–1973) who argued for the apostolic action of philosophy (and that sensation, reason, reve-lation and mystical union were different but equally significant forms of knowledge); and Charles Péguy, whose phrase 'Tout commence en mystique et finit en politique' (everything begins in mystery and ends up in politics) perfectly summed up the position of the 'Christian engaged in the temporal world'. As noted above, more seemed to unite these intellectuals than divide them in their spirit of moral revolution – in the early 1930s at least. Slowly, however, lines were drawn up in response to political events of the world stage: the rise of Fascism; the Soviet Union; the French 'Popular Front'; Munich; the Spanish Civil War; and, eventually, World War, and with it the choice between collaboration or resistance.

This, then, was the intellectual climate of which Bourdieu and his generation were the immediate inheritors. It included important elements which can be traced back to the Great Revolution and the writers of the Age of Enlightenment, and projected forward to the concerns which would face post-war France. To both developments the role and place of education was central. Many of the generation who were set the task of rebuilding France in the late 1940s and 1950s took their guiding principles directly from the ideas developed in the 1930s. These ideas were also used to animate worker and resistance groups in the war, when combat led to a temporary setting aside of such traditional social boundaries as class. The ideas form the intellectual backdrop of both Bourdieu's work and more generally education itself. It is time to consider Bourdieu's direct intellectual influences.

Chapter 4

Bourdieu and the Founding
Fathers of Sociology

In the above chapters, I have sketched out the general social, political and intellectual climate into which Bourdieu was born. I will now
consider more directly what shaped him intellectually, although we
shall also return to the issues of the 1930s which influenced him, and
the relation between the people and politics. I described earlier how
Bourdieu's own trajectory took a path considered the golden route
to academic success: going through highly prestigious preparatory
schools and becoming a student at *the* centre of academic training –
the École Normale Supérieure. The traditional discipline for non-
physical science graduates would be philosophy; Bourdieu himself
studied philosophy and graduated as a philosophy graduate. Philosophy at this time maintained its traditional role as the pinnacle discipline for any would-be intellectual; and philosophy, as it was included
in school programs, would set classical Greek thinkers at its core.
However, we have seen that a different sort of discipline – sociology –
had been developing in the nineteenth century and addressed the
more pressing contemporary concerns in the twentieth century. The
intellectual tradition which stemmed from the Age of Enlightenment
took society, science and politics as its central concerns. With Comte,
we saw the birth of the new 'science' of sociology. With the twentieth
century, the role of the intellectual as public individual grew, together
with their active involvement in events of the day.

If Bourdieu graduated as a philosopher, why did he choose sociology? At the time Bourdieu was ready to make this step, three principal 'founding fathers' of sociology were recognized: Karl Marx, Max
Weber and Émile Durkheim. Bourdieu often humorously referred to
the way various commentators tried to label him with one or other
of these: 'for Marxists, I am Durkheimian, for the Durkheimians, I

am Weberian, for the Weberians, Marxist' (Bourdieu and Grenfell, 1995b: 15. See also 1990d/1987: 27). However, behind this humor is a serious point: that the three have something common. Moreover, this commonality is found by working *against* them as much as *with* them (see 1990d/1987: 49). In other words, one proceeds by working *with* a particular thinker and in opposition to them at one and the same time. In this way, the original ideas are extended through critique. Bourdieu makes the paradoxical point that this approach goes against 'the classificatory logic' by which people establish a relation with past thinking. In one sense, Bourdieu's own theory of practice was born out of thinking Marx *against* Marx, Durkheim *against* Durkheim, Weber *against* Weber, as well as Marx *against* Durkheim, Marx *against* Weber, etc. What can we distil out of the interrelationship between these three sociological founders and Bourdieu himself? I am now going to discuss each in turn, including their key ideas about society and the individual.

The most obvious *point de départ* is perhaps the study of society in change. Many of the eighteenth- and nineteenth-century writers were, in effect, addressing the way the world was changing. Traditional society was dying; a new urban industrial world was being born. For Marx, this change came about through economic forces; put briefly, that a new form of economic system was created out of the exhaustion of the previous one. The traditional economy was based on rural communities and exchange economies in which money might not have a role to play at all; the New World was defined in terms of holders of *capital*: money wealth, material resources and labor – hence the title of Marx's magnum opus, *Das Kapital*. For Marx, feudal society was irreversibly being displaced by Capitalism. The reasons for this were fundamental laws of economic development – a kind of economic Darwinism (in fact, Marx originally wanted to dedicate *Das Kapital* to Darwin). Men were drawn away from their rural communities where they practised their traditional trades to sell their labor in exchange for money in the urban labor market. Such a move involved a radical restructuring of lifestyle – money and employment brought a certain degree of freedom. There was – for the first time for workers – leisure time and choice as to how to spend it, within the limits of one's wealth. But, other changes followed. A new structure of society was formed: the old aristocratic bourgeoisie were displaced as the leaders of society, squeezed out by the rise of a new industrial and commercial entrepreneurial class. Indeed, 'class' society was a modern world phenomenon. No longer were there simply land-owning lords and serfs. The industrial class structure included the owners of capital, a service class and, then, the labor force – the proletarian working class in Marxist terms. This very class structure shaped men's thinking as ideas developed in response to material conditions. In Marxist terms, the material *infrastructure* of society manifested itself in its ideological *superstructure*. Two further features of Marx's approach should be mentioned. First, there was the inevitability of economic crisis. Marx analyzed the capitalist system and saw that it was fueled by the production of surplus value. In other words, it is inherent in Capitalism that the product of labor created more value than it received in wages. It was this value that was taken by the holders of capital to finance their further capitalist ventures. But, it was a capital with value based on no material equivalence. As capitalists sought to continue to fuel their enterprise, the only way they could gain enough capital was by squeezing more and more surplus value out of the system; by working the labor force harder.

Marx was heavily influenced by Hegelian dialectics, which he reinvented in his own terms as 'dialectical materialism'. What such a philosophical approach amounted to was that social (economic) progress should be driven by the negation of existing material conditions, by which new material forms arose. This understanding was congruent with the 'law' of surplus value and also predicted imminent revolution, as economic crisis followed economic crisis and the material conditions of the working class worsened. A further essential feature of Marx's approach is rather more moral. Marx reasoned that as men's thoughts were shaped by material conditions, which were themselves based on a fundamental fault, their thinking must be similarly 'faulty'. In other words, their very thoughts, desires and wishes were not authentic in human terms – somewhat in the tradition of Rousseau's noble savage – but created in order to keep them in a way of thinking which led to their continued acquiescence to the capitalist system. Men were literally 'alienated' from who they really were and in a state of 'false consciousness'. Marx, or rather the polemical Marx, predicted that once revolution came, this false way of thinking would fail just as the capitalist system itself would fail and men would move into a state of reciprocality with their society in terms of what they contributed and received from it.

Of course, Marx was a major influence on thinking about philosophy, economics and politics, and acted as a defining element of sociology itself. Much of his language and predictions might now seem hopelessly simplistic or romantic in their view of men and society. Somewhat curiously, the mood of economic crisis and human alienation resonated with the philosophers of the 1930s. At that time, the state of financial collapse in Europe and human suffering in a secular world seemed very close to that which Marx had predicted; little surprise, therefore, if revolution – communistic, fascist and/or spiritual – was in the air. And, we will see that aspects of this mood continued to animate sociology in the decade after the Second World War when Bourdieu carried out his seminal works, and indeed for the remainder of the twentieth century.

Max Weber too offered an analysis of the social world in terms of a transformation from one state of organization to another: in his case, *Gemeinschaft* (community) and *Gesellschaft* (society). He saw the rise of a certain type of State rationality, enshrined in bureaucratic systems, as leading to a politically controlled economy for the benefit of the State rulers rather than capitalist ones; a prediction which was manifest in the communist regimes which were eventually founded. The capitalist system, he also saw, produced its own 'disenchantment' – which is the Weberian brand of alienation. However, unlike Marx, Weber did not see thinking and ideas as necessarily a mere epiphenomenon of material conditions. Rather, he argued that the way we think can also shape our material world. For example, in *The Protestant Work Ethic and the Spirit of Capitalism*, Weber argued that a particular form of ascetic thinking on the part of sections of Protestantism encouraged a certain way of being in the world which proved perfectly congruent with the capitalist way of operating. As such, he argued that these ideas, if they did not cause the development of Capitalism, certainly aided it. We shall return to Marx and Weber in considering the roots of Bourdieu's epistemology. However, before concluding this chapter on the founding fathers of sociology, it is necessary to look at a further key figure in French sociology, Émile Durkheim.

If Comte was the grandfather, then Durkheim (1858–1917) should be regarded as the father of modern French sociology. In many ways, and despite numerous differences of detail, his work echoes that of Marx and Weber. Like them, he offers a picture of the world in a state of change. Here, the contrast between traditional and modern urban society is presented in terms of *mechanical* and *organic solidarity*. The former gives rise to rather small homogeneous groups and communities. Although individuals often hold individually defined roles, there are close communal links between them, with common beliefs and whole aspects of living which are shared. In a sense, mechanical solidarity is akin to Marx's feudal community or Weber's *Gemeinschaft*. However, Durkheim is approaching this issue from a different direction. Indeed, at one point when reviewing Marx's work he writes of his position: 'we reached it before knowing Marx, by whom we have in no way been influenced' (see Lukes, 1973: 231). What was that position? In a country which had suffered so much socio-political upheaval, in which social institutions were still young and rather fragile, where traditional norms had been displaced in terms of secular principles, and in which the very health of society was at question (for example, the French birth rate was notoriously low compared with some other European countries in the nineteenth century, leading to a positive phobia about stronger more robust neighbors), it is perhaps unsurprising that Durkheim was interested in what binds a nation state together; in other words, what were its norms, agreed practices and representations.

Durkheim examined the ways in which associated individuals group and according to what collective representations. He used the term *collective conscience* to refer to this moral force. In a healthy state, this collective conscience formed a bridge between individuals and groups, and, groups and society at large. He saw it as a delicate balance. Durkheim argues, in a way reminiscent of Rousseau, that the individual must be represented in the collectivity, but then the collectivity must represent the interests of the individual. For Durkheim, the world was changing because of greater differentiation, which resulted in a different form of solidarity – organic. In the *Division of Labour* (1964/1933), he argued that society was becoming more organized and interdependent. Greater numbers of the population were involved and there was more contact between them. Durkheim did not see this as a bad thing. Nevertheless, where change and differentiation is too rapid, the collective norms which hold individuals together become diffuse, unclear or weak. A state of 'normlessness' results: *anomie*. This feature lay behind the phenomenon of *Suicide* (1952/1897) in society; simply, that there were insufficient social ties to balance the individual with the world and thus ground each individual in a *raison d'être* for living. For Durkheim, education had an important part to play in establishing this collective conscience. His aim was to found 'a pedagogy for the modern world'. Faced with the ills of modern society – especially that of the Third Republic – it was necessary to instill common norms and values for the new social context in pupils. Pupils must be educated to *be* in the world, the moral aspects of science and industry had to be rediscovered. In this way, individuals' needs, wants and aspirations could be balanced with the requirements of society. Anticipating Bourdieu's later formulation, Durkheim argued that education was only the 'image and reflection of society'. Education imitated and reproduced society in miniature, it did not create it. It was therefore also based on a cultural relative; namely, that each age and culture organized itself according to distinct principles. Durkheim's sociologized principles resulted in his conclusion that education had to instill the authority of society as its first aim. What Durkheim did not seem to conceive is that society, by its very nature, could be made up of 'competing' groups in conflict, and that education, in its formative role, could be partly responsible for this. For him, the functional health of its operation was inherently organic and thus groups needed to be understood as complementary.

As stated above, Bourdieu argued with and 'against' Marx, Weber and Durkheim in his own brand of sociology. However, before looking at Bourdieu's 'theory of sociological practice', it is necessary to consider one final influence on it: that of the immediate post-war intellectual climate.

Chapter 5

Bourdieu and the Post-war Intellectual Climate

We have seen that the 1930s and 1940s had precipitated a series of 'crises' and, as far as sociology was concerned, the background to this was a view of the modern world as dysfunctional. Both Weber and Durkheim's view of modern living is essentially pessimistic, while Marx only escapes from this pessimism by transcending it through the romantic terms of the greater man. The key question of the relationship between man and society was central to the intellectuals of the 1930s. Faced with a secular, dechristianized world, many of the Catholic intellectuals of the 1930s and 1940s were partly seduced by Marxist notions of unalienated man. The personalism of Emmanuel Mounier took the notion of '*l'épanouissement de la personne*' (the 'blossoming of the individual') as a guiding metaphor. Here, a man develops his spiritual sense of being in opposition to the individualism which now seemed to drive contemporary society. Such notions were to animate the resistant groups in the war when Frenchmen from different social backgrounds met and debated the shape of the New World. In the post-war years, a view of individual development underpinned ideas about the role that education should play. Groups such as 'Peuple et Culture' organized a series of 'foyers' and 'clubs' grouped around the study of music, art and literature – a kind of precursor of adult education. This view of the potential education had in 'forming' the common man was institutionalized by De Gaulle when he created the first Ministry of Culture in 1959. The first ministerial position was held by the writer André Malraux, who set about building a series of *Maisons de la Culture* as would-be 'temples of culture' with the aim of bringing culture to the masses. For Malraux, art was the 'means whereby the soul attains god'. The mixture of man's being with culture and spiritual experience was an important theme for intellectuals of the time. Indeed, we shall see that Bourdieu's own early interest in education went hand-in-hand with a consideration of the place of culture in contemporary French society. Both education and culture were seen as offering the possibility of offsetting the state of alienation, anomie and disenchantment which beset the modern world. These issues and the experience of modern living were at the heart of the existentialism which dominated the French intellectual field in the 1930s, 1940s and 1950s.

The word 'existentialism' is attributed first to Kierkegaard (1813–55), who wrote on the primacy of individual subject experience, often in the light of religious or spiritual experience. At heart, therefore, the origins of existentialism were religious. Many of the Catholic intellectual writers of the 1930s were deeply influenced by existentialism. By then, however, it had developed a rather more secular strand through such writers as Heidegger and Sartre. In a sense, existentialism is almost a form of Romanticism; it eschews rationality and any 'objective' abstraction of reality. Instead it focuses on the existence of man's 'being', defined in terms of his experience and acts in the world. That world is a lonely and potentially dangerous one, where man is free to choose what to do. In such choices he defines his existence and ultimately 'being'. Nothing is predetermined, only the inevitability of freedom and choice. Man therefore exists in a state of anxiety. The chief exponent of existentialism in France was Jean-Paul Sartre (1905–80). In essays, plays, novels and philosophical accounts, Sartre presented his form of existentialism: man is nothing at birth and at each point in his life has to define himself; he is condemned to be free; and must bear responsibility for his actions. For Sartre, man's 'being' was greater than the sum of any empirical description. In this sense, 'being' was transcendent. Sartre argued that existentialism was humanist and also complementary to Marxism. It is easy to see how this view of the world was indeed consistent with Marxist concepts of alienation and false consciousness. It is also easy to see how influential existentialism would be at a time of war when the choices that people made could literally be a matter of life or death. Moreover, the spirit of the age was 'existentialist' as individual men and woman sought to define their own identities. Existentialism was therefore significant in gender politics; for example, in the work of Sartre's partner, Simone de Beauvoir. This spirit continued well into the 1960s where it resonated with the Beat generation and the protest groups which sprang up at that time.

However, existentialism itself was based on a philosophy which went beyond a simple preoccupation with individual expression. The problem of existence was linked to questions about the relationship between the world and consciousness, which we might define in terms of objectivity and subjectivity. Sartre had been influenced by the German philosopher Heidegger (1889–1976), who is turn was a student of Husserl (1859–1938). Husserl was the father of phenomenology, a branch of philosophy which set out to study the 'essence of things'. In fact, this amounted to an analysis of consciousness in terms of human commonality rather than through individual particular experience. Therefore, this philosophy itself was against generalizations based on inductive extractions from experience – it was anti-rational. Rather, the essence of things was determined by states of consciousness which could include moods, desires, etc. Heidegger also took forward the phenomenological method. For him, similarly, there was no distinction between consciousness and the external world. What we know can only be sought through a consideration of human 'being' (*Dasein*), which transcends individual subjectivity and objectivity, and thus passes over this dualism. *Dasein* is seen as existing prior to the individual activity of objectifying thought and action. Time is an essential element of *Dasein*; Man is thrust towards a possibilizing future, fully in potential but actualized in individual choices and actions. In these choices lay authentic action. Education might then become the sum total about the characteristics of those choices and actions.

Bourdieu was to undertake a stunning critique of Heidegger's philosophy, showing how a socio-historical analysis of the work demonstrates the way in which the state of the German philosophy field, and Germany itself, can be seen as providing a system of thought which in effect separates the masses from the elite, and is perfectly congruent with the axioms of fascism itself (Bourdieu, 1991c/1988). He was also a lifelong critic of Sartre; although there was always a certain fascination for and attraction to a writer which provided Bourdieu with so much to 'think against'. Moreover, Bourdieu was a student of Maurice Merleau Ponty (1908–61), who founded the review *Les Temps Modernes* with Sartre and was, for a time, the leading phenomenologist in France. Thus, Bourdieu's thinking was grounded both with and against Sartre and Merleau Ponty.

In the late 1940s and early 1950s at least, Bourdieu considered himself a philosophy student. The first major academic study he refers to himself as undertaking was 'a phenomenology of affective life' (Bourdieu and Grenfell, 1995b: 2). Nevertheless, he states that philosophy at that time was not very impressive and existentialism seemed to him to be 'an insipid humanism' (1986a: 36). The people he does cite as being influential were of a quite different persuasion. Foucault (cited in Pinto, 1998: 21) writes of a split between a 'philosophy of experience, of sense and the subject, and a philosophy of knowledge and rationality'. If Sartre ruled supremely in the former, the latter is best represented by the likes of Canguilhem and Bachelard, and it is these names which Bourdieu refers to as being of direct influence on him.

Gaston Bachelard (1884–1962) was a key influence for post-war intellectuals, his work dealing with a wide range of philosophical themes including imagination. However, it is probably as a philosopher of science that he is best known; in particular, he was concerned with questions of epistemology. At this point, it is worth pausing to consider the word 'science'. In an English-speaking world, 'science' is most often assumed to refer to the 'physical sciences'. This assumption is much less strong in France at least, if not in other Latin-based language speaking countries. Here, 'science' is more often used to refer to 'systematized knowledge' and 'understanding'. Bachelard's approach to 'science' (and Bourdieu's) is in this broader sense. For him, science does not progress through the clarification of simple ideas and continuity but by assuming complexities and discontinuity. Somewhat anticipating Bourdieu, Bachelard wrote that complex ideas need complex explanations. That complexity involves understanding facts not as 'things in themselves' but as sets of relations. This is the basis of the difference between 'substantialist' and 'relational' thinking. Bourdieu later summed this up:

(The former) is inclined to treat the activities and preferences specific to certain individuals or groups in a society as a certain moment
as if they were substantial properties, inscribed once and for all in
a sort of biological cultural essence.

(1998c/1994: 4)

Seeing phenomena relationally, on the other hand, is to see them as
understandable in terms of social spaces, positions and relationships.
Science itself must be regarded in these terms. Therefore, scientific
knowledge (in the sense outlined above) was not 'truth' but simply
a certain way of looking at things. What we look at is always a representation not a real thing. For Bachelard, this issue is connected
to the distinction between rationality and realism. For him, rationality relates to a particular field of reason, while realism provides the
empirical objects for interpretation. Science was founded at the apex
of these approaches: a philosophy of science which balanced rationality and realism while considering phenomena in a relationalist mode
of thinking. Bachelard termed this way of thinking '*surrationalisme*',
which amounted to an invigorated view of the material world. For
Bachelard, theory was not enough – experimentation was also necessary, an idea which we can see echoed in Bourdieu's later concern
not to 'theorize' for its own sake but to engage with 'real' social facts.
This engagement also involved a process of 'objectification' by which
'scientific facts' are 'conquered', often in the face of orthodox ways
of thinking. In this way, 'science' was 'radical', if not 'revolutionary',
as it was frequently pitched against the continuity of the status quo.
We can see this approach applied in Bourdieu's later work where he
writes of epistemology and methodology in terms of 'rupture', 'the
construction of the object', and of an 'applied rationalism': the social
fact is 'conquered, constructed, noted (recorded)' (1968: 24).

In effect, what we can see in the 1940s and 1950s is a kind of academic generational shift. Sartre was still at his height; the Catholics
intellectuals of the 1930s were recovering or responding to the outcome of the world war, and their conduct in it. Philosophers such as
Bachelard were important for the new generation of post-war intellectuals who came to age, so to speak, during this period; acting as a

formative influence on what would be referred to as structuralists and post-structuralists, and those with a commitment to the philosophy of the history of science.

Georges Canguilhem was another such influence, representing the 'philosophy of knowledge and rationality' in contrast to a phenomenological and Sartrean 'philosophy of experience'. Canguilhem in fact succeeded Bachelard in the chair of philosophy at the Sorbonne and was later on the jury that examined the thesis of the post-structuralist, Michel Foucault. He followed the former in his view of science as relative to particular socio-historical conditions. Here, the aim was less to discover 'scientific' truth as to uncover the ways in which 'truth' and 'falsity' were constructed at a particular point in time. This approach can be understood as a pre post-structuralist opposition to the modernist notions of progress, truth and objectivity. There is no ultimate reality, only different ways of seeing it. In this case, the terms of that seeing are all important. Science then becomes not a closed system developing its concepts in a continuous manner towards an ultimate goal of progress, but rather characterized by openness and discontinuity. It is open because it is affected by its surroundings; it is discontinuous, since at any one stage it can be challenged in such a way that it has to reinvent itself. In this sense, 'science' is constantly being called upon to recreate itself.

Bourdieu cites these writers as being formative influences on him. In the case of Canguilhem, we can see the familiar theme of the social construction of knowledge. The terms used to articulate that construction are therefore crucial. These were for the most part philosophers, not sociologists. Even so, though influential, such writers were not regarded as intellectual leaders in philosophy. Sartre continued to dominate the field. Bourdieu himself makes the point that Bachelard and Canguilhem were not fashionable and they, along with others – Gilson, Gouhier, de Koyré and Cavaillès – had rather to be sought out. What of social sciences?

Bourdieu writes of the sociology of his day being 'averagely empirical' and 'lacking any theoretical or empirical inspiration', and of sociologists as 'failed philosophers' (1986a: 37). Durkheim had worked to found 'sociology' as an academic discipline independent from anthropology and, at this stage at least, this battle was yet to be won. Bourdieu's own route into sociology came through 'anthropology' and it is arguable that, methodologically at least, he remained an anthropologist of sorts, or at least an ethnographer, throughout his career despite his defense of and claims for sociology. The main anthropological influence in France in the 1950s was Claude Lévi-Strauss (1908). Although he trained as a philosopher, Lévi-Strauss later escaped persecution in France, as well as French philosophical orthodoxies, by going to the USA where he met the anthropologist Roman Jakobson. He subsequently developed an approach which he termed 'structural anthropology'. Ferdinand de Saussure had already laid the theoretical bases to social structuralism in his now famous work *Course in General Linguistics* (1907 and 1911). Here, he set out language in terms of a system of signs composed of *signifiers* (word or sound) and *signified* (concept). He also posed a distinction between *langue*, or the organized systems of structure of language, and *parole* (individual speech acts). Language was essentially structured because it worked through difference: 'in language there are only differences'. It could also be seen in terms of its *synchronic* nature – its state at a particular frozen point in time; and its *diachronic* nature – how it changes over time. Lévi-Strauss took a similar approach to the study of cultures. Here, as Saussure had done, he prioritized a 'synchronic' view of culture, as something that could be studied in terms of its inherent structures and signifiers. What those structures amounted to was transhistorical, and indeed, trans-cultural patterns of kinship, economic exchange, religion and language itself. Structures were not necessarily observable but were to be found in the differences set up within the social system. In effect, he argued, much in the same way that Chomsky would do later for linguistics, that there existed a 'universal deep structure' which could be found in all cultures to a greater or lesser extent; for example, in matrimonial patterns, myths and beliefs. Almost as some innate quality of the brain, structure, and deep structure in culture, were a kind of structural mirror held up to the brain by which individual and social thought and action were mediated. This perspective represented a radical break with previous modernist philosophies which placed individual man at the centre of social life (Sartre was in effect an extreme version of this, as the only history that mattered for him is that of a particular individual), and instead stressed the social context, background or structural map against which social action was generated and against which it should be read in order to interpret its meaning.

Despite his age, Lévi-Strauss was very much leader of a new structuralist generation, since the means by which culture could be 'read' in terms of its structure and signs was an attractive one to those looking for a more practical philosophy of man. In this sense, the philosophy of man became a philosophy of language. For someone like Louis Althusser (1918–90) that reading was in terms of structures which reflected the capitalist mode of production; for example, political, legal and cultural levels which need to be understood as prior individual action. Our articulations of this are themselves the symptoms of an ideology which assumes a fit between empirical facts and what we interpret them by. True science, on the other hand, needs to consider the construction of the object of knowledge itself. These are the intellectual ideas that confronted Bourdieu.

Conclusions

In his last lecture at the Collège de France on 28 March 2001, Pierre Bourdieu reflected on the 'auto-analytical' dimension of his work. In so doing, he brought to an end his formal academic career by making a direct link between the content of his work and his own personal background. This element in his work had been growing for some years. At one point, he talks about the distinction between the 'empirical Bourdieu' and the 'scientific Bourdieu':

> When I go to a meeting, I am like everyone; I am nervous, I am angry, etc. ... like everyone. When I analyse that, I put in place an (approach) which objectifies all that which understands why the empirical Bourdieu is angry. In life, one again becomes the empirical subject. But, it is possible to create a sort of subject torn away from social forces.
>
> (Bourdieu and Grenfell, 1995b: 29)

At another time, he writes of his own academic trajectory in personal terms:

> I spent most of my youth in a tiny and remote village in south-western France, a very backward place as city people would like to say. And I could only meet the demands of schooling by renouncing many of my primary experiences and acquisitions, and not only a certain accent.
>
> (Bourdieu and Wacquant, 1992a: 204)

Questions about his own cultural background led him eventually to study the community he came from in terms of the problems male farmers had in finding wives and adapting to the modern age. He states: 'Maybe my main discoveries I owe to my mother' (2000b: 19). It was his mother who taught him that kinship was more than genealogy: it had to be cultivated. At the same time, he writes about the usefulness of his approach as a form of 'socio-analysis': a tool by which individuals can understand, and therefore partly free themselves from the social forces which determine them and their lives. More academically, he wrote, in contradiction to orthodox attitudes, that the 'researcher's own experience should be used in order to understand and analyse other people's experiences' (*ibid.*: 7). Certainly, in the case of Algeria, it is clear that the shock of going there and seeing civil war at first hand had a profound and formative impact on his thinking. His response was highly personal, and Bourdieu writes that understanding the people he encountered there entailed him 'breaking' away from his own vision of the social world (2000c: 24). In effect, his own personal character is subsumed in the process of 'scientific' enquiry. Later, his own study and analysis of education were partly inspired by a wish initially to understand just this social phenomenon, 'students'. And, later still, as we shall see, both *Homo Academicus* (1988/1984) and *The State Nobility* (1996b/1989) were attempts, partly at least, to make sense of his own academic culture. However, it would be wrong to regard Bourdieu's work as best understood in 'biographical' terms; indeed, his posthumous account of his background and training – *Esquisse pour une auto-analyse* (drafted in the year immediately preceding his death and published in 2004) – has this sentence on its opening page: 'ceci n'est pas une autobiographie' (this is not an autobiography!).

This part of the book has set out the socio-historical and intellectual traditions which formed a background to Bourdieu's work. It would be a mistake to attempt to fit Bourdieu into any one particular current or connect him with an individual writer. Bourdieu himself always argued against such a reading of his work: '(He) says "market", that's marginalist – therefore from the Right'; or, he says 'there is capital, that's from Marx – therefore he is Marxist'; or, 'he says norms, therefore Durkheimian' (1995b:15). As noted above, he positively eschewed the terms Marxist, Weberian and Durkheimian. He claims not to have thought 'in those terms': 'the answer to the question as to whether an author is Marxist, Durkheimian or Weberian gives us practically no information about that author' (1990d/1987: 28). What we have instead, as we noted, is a process of 'thinking with these authors' and thinking 'against these authors' and against 'false incompatibilities'. We can take this to mean that Bourdieu was more interested in finding the usefulness of a range of writers than swearing theoretical allegiance to any of them. In the first chapter of Part 2, we look at just what that distillation amounted to. This part concludes with a brief reference to both the intellectual and socio-historical elements we have covered here and how they might be seen to be present in Bourdieu's own work.

Certainly, Bourdieu's own commitment to sociology is connected to an approach of which Comte offered a direct inheritance: sociology as a new discipline, with the power to explain and advise society; sociology as a kind of applied radical philosophy. In a way, sociology might be understood as akin to one of Montesquieu's 'spirit of the laws'; that to use language in these terms and to think in these ways implied a certain way both of knowing and being. There is a placing to one side of traditional aristocratic and religious ways of thinking and organizing the world. Bourdieu might be seen as echoing Rousseau in his view of society as based on inequalities. He might also share a view of society as changing from one system – feudal, traditional, community, mechanical – to another – capitalist, societal, organic. The fact that there is a relation between thought and the material world, indeed in the very way we think, gives us a theory of knowledge which can be connected with and across Marx, Weber and Durkheim; especially in the complementary view that ideas impact on what we do and how we organize our activities. There is also the recognition, albeit implicitly for Bourdieu, that the human condition is one that is disenchanted, alienated and anomic. Bourdieu accepted republican principles, but was similarly critical of the way they had been actualized in the modern State. In his sociology at least, Bourdieu was inherently secular but shared many of the criticisms of modern Capitalism articulated by the Catholic intellectuals of the 1930s. He recognized the need for a radical critique of its principles and effects. Bourdieu's own preoccupation with education can be seen in terms of what it and culture might offer to modern man, faced with the contemporary '*misère du monde*'. Bourdieu certainly thought 'against' Sartre and existentialism in general, and yet he was also an 'anti-materialist' in crude Marxist terms. He took inspiration from so-called historians of the philosophy of science. Best described as 'pre-post-structuralist', Bourdieu never succumbed to post-modernism, and yet many saw commonality of spirit at least between him and those who grew out of the same post-war intellectual generation; for example, Foucault, Derrida and Lacan. Bourdieu's own 'science de la science' offers a theory of knowledge that might best be easiest to understand in terms of 'reflexivity' and social constructivism, but in a highly cognitive way, deeply philosophical and phenomenological. His theory of practice was developed primarily in terms of a synthesis of and reaction to subjectivism and objectivism, which had its direct antecedents in structuralism (especially Lévi-Strauss) and existentialism (especially Merleau Ponty and its phenomenological aspects). Despite many misgivings, he recognized and, in the end, took on the role of public intellectual, acknowledging by this, that someone at least had to oppose the dominant orthodoxy by providing the intellectual 'thinking tools' for resistance. In a way, Bourdieu is saying 'I am all these things (and none of them) at the same time'.

This Part has set out the background to Bourdieu's work. It has taken his intellectual biography up to the 1950s and suggested that his formative years were shaped intellectually by the events and ideas which surrounded him. In Part 2, we shall see how much of his thinking on education was also shaped by contemporary events. In this respect, it is wrong to separate his work from the social world which produced it. We next present a 'Critical Exposition of Bourdieu's Educational Thought'. The focus is specifically on Bourdieu's work on education. However, we must keep in mind that, although this represents a major component of his output, his work also includes a wide range of other topics and themes. Where appropriate, we shall show that it is only possible to understand his educational thinking by direct engagement with, and in relation to, one or more of these other areas. First, however, it is necessary to set out the 'theory of practice' which underpins and illuminates all of this thinking.

Part 2

A Critical Exposition of Bourdieu's Educational Thought

Introduction

The second part of this book offers a discussion of Bourdieu's work on education. It includes seven major chapters. Across these, we see how Bourdieu's thinking about education developed over the course of his career. We see how early analyses in his home region of the Béarn in France, and his experiences in Algeria, laid the foundations for later studies on education. There is coverage of his principal works on education: the first, in the mid-1960s, looks at students and schooling; the second, published in the 1980s, concerns French universities and the elite training schools; the third deals with Bourdieu's own involvement in school and curriculum reform as a member of a governmental committee on education. This part extends the discussion to include broader issues of schools and training from the perspective of a range of work in the 1990s. In Part 1, we discussed Bourdieu's intellectual biography and the influences on his thinking. Here, in Part 2, we begin with an account of his analytical concepts, or 'thinking tools', which permeate the rest of the book.

Chapter 6

Theory of Practice

In 2003, a book was published By Christiane Chauviré and Olivier Fontaine entitled *Le Vocabulaire de Bourdieu*. This book represents an attempt to offer a potted version of Bourdieu and his work. (It was not the first. See also, Accardo, 1983; Accardo and Corcuff, 1986; Robbins, 1991; Jenkins, 1992; Corcuff, 1995 and 2003; Bonnewitz, 1998 and 2002; Lane, 2000; Grenfell, 2004a and Reed-Danahay, 2005.) In their book Chauviré and Fontaine provide a useful list of some 27 'key words' connected with Bourdieu's thinking: Action, Agent, Capital, Field, Class, Sociological Explanation, Body, Determinism, Disposition, Distinction, Domination, Doxa, Economy of Practice, Epistemology of Sociology, Social Space and Position, State, Habitus, Historicization, *Illusio*, Rule, Reproduction, Practical Sense, *Skholé*, Sociology of Sociology, Structure, Time and the Universal. But, this is not an exhaustive list. We could add: Connaissance/ Reconnaissance, Conatus, Construction of the Object, Double Bind, Externalization/Internalization, Hysterisis, Interest, Libido, Market, Microcosms, Objectivation, Objective/Subjective, Practical Rationality, Reflexivity, Reproduction, Socio-analysis, Strategy, Symbolic Violence, and Theory/Practice. Each of these words, and others, were used by Bourdieu, in his own particular way, which often gave a specific twist to them. For example, a common word such as 'field' has an exact connotation for Bourdieu, which sets it apart from its everyday usage. This vocabulary constitutes his 'thinking tools': the concepts he used in order to address and understand the social world and, in particular, education. He argues that these tools are, 'visible through the results they yield' (1989a: 50). Indeed, their worth can best be assessed in terms of what they reveal, as we shall see in the remaining chapters of this part of the book. They seem to represent an extensive and complex conceptual network and anyone approaching his work for the first time might be forgiven for thinking that his was a very intricate theory. Paradoxically, Bourdieu, while accepting that there is indeed a 'theory' in his work, declares himself against the 'conceptual gobbledlygook' that is so fashionable these days and claims that he never sets out to 'do theory' or 'to construct a theory' (*ibid.*) as such. Rather, he states that his intention is to engage with and explain actual phenomena in the social world, and that it is in the course of this undertaking that his concepts are developed. In other words, his is a practical project first and a theoretical one second.

Bourdieu never set out with a formal theory and then applied it to various projects. Rather, throughout his career, it was in and through these projects that we see the concepts emerging and developing. It *is* possible to identify certain concepts in his earliest work, but only in nascent form. Later, it is possible to see how these ideas developed and were integrated with others through working in education and other social domains. Further terms came comparatively late in his thinking. Bourdieu always maintained that he did not 'invent' a term for the sake of it. Rather, they were 'discovered' in the relationships and links he saw in empirical data, as they were needed in the course of studying the processes of social phenomena. What is also clear, however, is that each of his terms contributes to a coherent whole, which represents an integrated social theory. As stated above, much of Bourdieu's theorizing sits side-by-side with his analyses of empirical data. However, there are also major theoretical statements of his methodology, together with discussion of the philosophy of science which underpins them. The first of these was *The Craft of Sociology (Le Métier de sociologue)* which he first published with Jean-Claude Chamboredon and Jean-Claude Passeron in 1968 (1991b). The book is offered as a set of 'Epistemological Preliminaries', together with a series of selected illustrative texts. The latter are made up of some 45 extracts; including seven from Durkheim (as well as two from his close teacher, associate and nephew Marcel Mauss), four from Canguilhem, two from Marx, four from Weber, five from Bachelard, and one from Lévi-Strauss. There are also incidental extracts from Darwin, Panowsky, Polanyi and Wittgenstein. Other key figures are cited extensively through the text: Saussure, Nietzsche, Comte and Husserl. This selection illustrates the main points made in Part 1 of this book in connection with Bourdieu's own intellectual biography and his influences.

The Craft of Sociology probably sees Bourdieu at his most derivative. However, in *Outline of a Theory of Practice (Esquisse d'une théorie de la pratique)* (1977b/1972), he offers a much more original synthesis of his methodological stance and the epistemology that underpins it. It shows that his theoretical development was more than a straight borrowing of ideas and perspectives to create a unified theory. In its original form, *Esquisse* was also accompanied by three studies on Kabyle ethnology to illustrate what this theory gave us in terms of practical analysis. Issues of education and pedagogy are never far away in his accounts of the inculcation of children into dominant practices and ways of thinking. This work itself was extensively revised, reworked and extended in his next major methodological statement, *The Logic of Practice (Le Sens pratique* (1990c/1980). Further accounts about philosophy, theory and practice appeared along the way: for example, his own inaugural lecture given at the Collège de France in 1982 was in fact a lecture on his theory of knowledge, *Leçon sur une leçon* (1982); his methodological and theoretical discussions with Loïc Wacquant, *Réponses/An Invitation to Reflexive Sociology* (1992a); and collections of talks and interviews – *In Other Words/Choses dites* (1990d/1987), and *Practical Reason/Raisons pratiques* (1998c/1994). In 1997 *Pascalian Meditations/Méditations pascaliennes* (2000a/1997) was also published and represented a major summative statement from Bourdieu on epistemology and how it could be operationalized in practice.

Bourdieu's theoretical concepts and their developmental nature are not at the core of the concerns of this book. In subsequent discussions in later parts, I shall be drawing attention to the way particular concepts appeared or were developed. I shall also highlight the implications of individual terms, both in theory and practice. Moreover, the intention is to show that the whole approach itself amounts to a cohesive theory. The major part of the discussion will concentrate on Bourdieu, education and training. It will prioritize issues of educational practice rather than methodology. In order to do this, a number of the concepts listed above will be used in the course of the text, sometimes without reference to their specific content and justification (see Grenfell, 2004b for further discussion). What follows in the rest of this chapter is a brief version of Bourdieu's theory of practice as a theoretical 'point de départ'. It sets out his principal conceptual tools, their derivation and the significance they have in Bourdieu's method. It is somewhat of a synchronic, though integrated and workable version of his theory. I use this account as a basis to illustrate the discussion on education in the remainder of the book.

In Part 1, I drew a distinction between 'substantialist' and 'relational' thinking. I wrote that the distinction was important in Bourdieu's work, since he saw that the former – a way of inscribing people and things with 'substantial' essential properties – was quite contrary to his own method: that the properties of people and things are defined only in terms of their relations within other properties. This is a fundamental distinction for Bourdieu. The relational mode is essentially structuralist, albeit with Bourdieu's own phenomenological take on it (see below):

> ... the introduction into the social sciences of the structural method or, more simply, of the relational mode of thought which, by breaking with the substantialist mode of thought, leads one to characterize each element by relationships which unite it with all the others in a system and from which it derives it meaning and function.
>
> (1990c/1980)

Bourdieu notes the extensive work that was needed in the physical sciences (mathematics and physics, for example) for the 'relational mode' (or structural) of thinking to catch on and, therefore, what an achievement it is to extend this same mode of thought to the social sciences in the study of language, myth, religion, education and art. In so doing, he notes that he is 'overcoming', in the name of 'practice' rather than 'theory', the distinction established by Leibniz between 'the truths of reason and the truths of fact, in order to treat historical facts as systems of intelligible relations, and to do so in scientific practice' (*ibid.*). What is at stake therefore is a new form of *practical knowledge*. It is highly philosophical as it pertains not only to what we know, but what we *can* know and *how*. Here, Bourdieu is considering what is 'thinkable and unthinkable' (see 1971b) and, in so doing, establishing a distinction between personal knowledge and objective (scientific) knowledge. Bourdieu refers to this way of knowing as a 'conversion', to have 'new eyes', a 'new gaze', or *metanoia*: 'a mental revolution of one's whole vision of the social world' (1992a: 251). At one point, Bourdieu described his own 'conversion':

> I recall very well, it was in a seminar, it was an illumination to connect Husserlian's theories of doxa, with the doxic relation to the social world, and the analyses of the young Marx on praxis, practice, etc., and to draw out everything concerned with reflexion, opinion, and so many things normally kept separate.
>
> (Bourdieu and Grenfell, 1995b: 34)

What Bourdieu expresses here is not only a conversion to a certain way of thinking, but the synthesis of a number of strands of philosophical thought. This synthesis occurs with the concepts of '*culture*' and '*structure*' at its focus.

Bourdieu had written that the study of culture could be attributed to two traditions. The first saw culture as a *structured structure*, made up of signs signifying consensual meaning – an instrument of communication. Lévi-Strauss was the leading figure in this tradition with his studies of the universal meaning conveyed across cultures embedded in the structural forms of myth and language. The second tradition was 'functionalist' in its understanding of the interplay and relation between the material organization of society and its superstructure of ideas. Bourdieu is 'structuralist' inasmuch as he looks to use 'the analysis of symbolic systems (particularly language and myth) so as to arrive at the basic principle behind the efficacy of symbols, that is the structured structure which confers upon symbolic systems their structuring power' (1971b). However, he is at pains to argue that 'structure' in the structuralist sense of the word is simply too rigid and lacking in dynamism. It is not that society unfolds in terms of semi-permanent deep objective structures, but that structures themselves are always in flux, and are created and realized as immanent in human activity. This is why he opens *Outline of a Theory of Practice*

with a quotation by Marx, often overlooked in the cruder adaptation
of dialectical materialism:

> The principal defect of all materialism up to now – including that of
> Feuerbach – is that the external object, reality, the sensible world,
> is grasped in the form of *an object or an intention*; but not as *concrete
> human activity*, as *practice*, in a subjective way. This is why the active
> aspect was developed by idealism, in opposition to materialism –
> but only in an abstract way, since idealism naturally does not know
> real concrete activity as such (Marx: Theses on Feuerbach).
>
> (1977b/1972: vi)

So, if structuralism provides a certain 'objectivity' in enabling the
identification of generating structures, these structures themselves
also have to be understood as the product of individual 'subjectivities': 'one must remember that ultimately objective relations do not
exist and do not realize themselves except in and through the systems of dispositions of agents, produced by internalizing of objective conditions' (1968: 105). In other words, objective structures
only realize themselves through individual sense activity, *in thought
and word and deed*. This sense activity brings us to 'phenomenology',
which, as we have seen, was a precursor to existentialism. In Husserl's
philosophy, it is individual thought at any one particular instance
that sets up an 'inten*s*ional relation' between subject and object –
the 's' is included to draw attention to the fact that such a relation is inherently *structural*. Consciousness is forming and formed
as part of a dialectic between all that we know from experience
(*noema*) and individual moments of perceptions (*noesis*). Bourdieu
seeks to go beyond the duality between objectivism and subjectivism,
which he later refers to as the most 'artificial' and 'ruinous' in the
social sciences (1990c/1980: 25), and to found 'a science of dialectical relations between objective structures ... and the subjective
dispositions within which these structures are actualized and tend
to reproduce them' (1977b/1972: 3). Bourdieu echoes the epistemological position of Berger and Luckman (1971a/1967), who
incidentally had undertaken a theoretical journey similar to Bourdieu's in synthesizing Marx, Durkheim and Weber, in describing this

process as 'the internalisation of externality and the externalisation of internality'.

Bourdieu states that if he had to sum up his approach in two words they would be: 'constructivist structuralism' or 'structuralist constructivism' (1989a: 14). The approach was essentially 'structuralist', but not in the conventional sense of the word. To be concerned with structures is indeed to be concerned with qualities which act in a regulatory, generative and transformative sense. However, Bourdieu moves away from the trans-cultural description of universal synchronic structures found across societies (he charged Lévi-Straussian anthropology with committing this error). At the same time, he wanted to have nothing to do with philosophies which put individual subjectivities at the center of their theories (for example, Sartre and Personalism). Instead, he was looking for a 'theoretical third way'. However, this approach was not simply developed as an epistemological necessity. It also had a radical intent:

There was in my project ... a specific political intention ... capable of leading to a new way of doing social science, by taking the weapons of the adversary [notably statistics] ... and turning them against him, while reactivating European traditions which had been deformed and hijacked by their American translations [Durkheim, Weber, Schütz].

(2001c: 200; author's text in brackets)

It is therefore unsurprising if Bourdieu wrote of his method as being constituted by a series of 'epistemological breaks' from conventional forms of knowledge: from the *objectivist* mode, which 'constructs objective relations ... structure practice and representations of practice' (1977b/1972: 3); and from the *subjectivist* (phenomenological) mode, which 'sets out to make explicit the truth of primary experience' (*ibid.*). His epistemological third way represented a 'theory of practice', once referred to as, 'a science of existential structure and social meaning' (Dreyfus and Rabinow, 1993). However, how do you undertake it and what is the resultant knowledge?

True to the epistemological principles he inherited from Bachelard and Canguilhem, Bourdieu strongly argues for viewing the social world as a construct. There is a 'taken-for-grantedness' in empirical experience, and this is no less true for any single social agent than the would-be researcher. The world is 'socially produced', in and by 'a collective work of construction of social reality' (1992a: 239). To recognize this is one thing. It is another thing to have the conceptual tools available to 'deconstruct' this social construction in a way which reveals the dynamic relationship between the *modus operandi* (structuring structure) and *opus operatum* (structured structure), and the logic of differentiating practice which constitutes them. It is of the utmost importance for the would-be researcher to see his own scientific constructions, for what they are:

> The construction of a scientific object requires first and foremost a break with common sense, that is with the representations shared by all, whether they be the mere commonplaces of ordinary existence or official representations, often inscribed in institutions and thus present, often inscribed in institutions and thus present in the objectivity of social organizations and in the minds of their participants. *The preconstructed is everywhere.*
>
> (*ibid.*: 35)

Bourdieu looks to analyze this relationship by employing his own 'scientific' (sociological) concepts: *habitus, field, capital*, etc. *Field* can be seen as a structured space of social forces and struggles. In fact, the concept of *field* became a central part of his approach; so much so, that by the end of his career, he publicized his series of talks given at the Collège de France as 'explorations in Field Theory'. Bourdieu defines '*field*' thus:

> I define *field* as a network, or configuration, of objective relations between positions objectively defined, in their existence and in the determinations they impose upon their occupants, agents or institutions, by their present and potential situation (situs) in the structure of the distribution of power (or capital) whose possession commands access to the specific profits that are at stake in the field, as well as their objective relation to other positions.
>
> (1992a: 72, own translation)

A *field* is therefore a structured social space based on the objective relations formed between those who occupy it, and hence the configuration of positions they hold. It would be fair to say that for Bourdieu, *fields* were therefore quite heterogeneous: some could be very large and amorphous – the media, or education, for example; others could be very small and local – *microcosms*. There are in existence, therefore, *fields* within *fields*. For Bourdieu, this was the way to view the *social space* that existed. Concepts such as *field* and *social space* were superior to such Marxist constructs as 'class'. The latter, he claimed, suffered from the 'theory effect': Bourdieu liked to quote a statement that Marx used about Hegel, against Marx; namely, that there was an error in 'taking the things of logic, for the logic of things' (1992a: 123). In other words, Bourdieu warned against reifying dynamic social forces. Rather, *fields* needed to be seen as responsive and in a state of flux in relation to actual socio-historic forces. Several other Bourdieusian concepts logically follow on from this particular 'thinking tool'. For example, if a *field* is a network of dynamic forces, it is not surprising that struggle is inherent in it. Bourdieu reasons, on the basis of empirical investigations, that every *field* has a particular 'logic of practice'; in other words, it has a certain '*raison d'être*'. Its purpose is partly defined within the totality of social relations; although the ways it acts are particular to it at any one point in time and space. There are dominant factions in the *field* who fight to hold onto their position, while there are others struggling to displace them in the social ascendancy. The ruling principles of the *field* need to be seen as the 'consecrated' forms of orthodoxy, or 'legitimate' forms of social action. Orthodoxy, or *doxa*, implies acceptance of the dominant principles and products of the *field*. It is in effect a 'practical faith' (1990c/1980: 68) in the *field*. Entry into it depends on accepting, at least implicitly, the 'rules of the game'. However, this acceptance itself implies subscribing to the pre-existent forms of the *field*. Such acceptance, and the logic of practice implied by it, is therefore a kind of *illusion*, a kind of 'self-deception', but one which might still bring its rewards. This illusory thought is similar, but not the same, to Sartrean 'mauvaise foi', 'bad faith', or 'inauthentic thinking'. It is acting, thinking and speaking in ways because they have always 'been done that way' in this *field* (see 2000a/1997: 102). The *illusio* can also act as a form of *interest* in taking part in the processes and products of the *field* in order to accrue advantages from it. For example: 'It would be easy to show that Adam Smith's self interest is nothing more than an unconscious universalization of the form of interest engendered and required by a capitalist economy' (1992a: 116). In other words, the logic of practice of a *field* is partly internalized by individuals passing through it, and thus shapes their thoughts and actions in the *field* in order to profit from it. They have an *interest* in working to the *doxa*. However, heterodoxy is equally important. If *interest* and *illusio* are the affirming forces in the *field*, and constitute the *doxa*, then the *heterodoxa* is the denying force. Bourdieu explains in terms of social classes:

> Crisis is a necessary condition for a questioning of doxa ... In class societies, in which the definition of the social world is at stake in overt or latent class struggle, the drawing of the line between the field of opinion, of that which is explicitly questioned, and the field of doxa, of that which is beyond question and which each agent tacitly accords by the mere fact of acting in accord with social convention, is itself a fundamental objective at stake in that form of class struggle which is the struggle for the imposition of the dominant systems of classification. The dominated classes have an interest in pushing back the limits of doxa and exposing the arbitrariness of the taken for granted; the dominant classes have an interest in defending the integrity of doxa ...
>
> (1977b/1972: 169)

Within the context of social classes, this playing out of the forces between *doxa* and *heterodoxa* occurs at the level of the implicit and unconscious, often away from conscious knowledge and control. This characteristic of its nature makes its effectiveness all the more potent.

There are other issues which emerge from a consideration of the concept of *field*: for example, the means of entrance; the relative dependence and independence of *fields* to other *fields*; and the specific manifestations of its logic and practice in terms of actual materials, physical and ideological events.

A key function of *fields* is the way they provide a source of socialization for those who enter them. Using Bourdieu's epistemological approach, it follows that *fields*, as the 'objective' element of social action, act on individuals (the subjective) in constituting social action; in short, they form *dispositions* to think and act in a certain way: 'to speak of dispositions is simply to take note of a natural predisposition of human bodies ... a *conditionability* in the sense of a natural capacity to acquire non-natural, arbitrary capacities' (2000a/1997: 136). One of the biggest errors made in reading Bourdieu is to believe that he is therefore saying that we all act in a predetermined way, that there is no room for individual choice. In fact he is arguing the contrary. Dispositions are activated in particular *field* contexts as certain thoughts and actions, response and reactions:

> Dispositions do not lead in a determinate way to determine action; they are revealed and fulfilled only in appropriate circumstances and in relation with a situation. They may therefore always remain in a virtual state, like a soldier's courage in the absence of war...
>
> (2000a/1997: 149)

The issue of *disposition* offers a good example of the difference between *substantialist* and *relational* ways of thinking. Other writers before Bourdieu had used the term 'disposition'; for example, Aristotle, Hume, Bergson and Merleau Ponty. However, for many of these, dispositions were actual hidden entities within individual psychologies. For Bourdieu, 'dispositions' only exist in as much as they are part and parcel of social and psychological structures in their mutually constituting existence. They are best understood as 'energy matrices' that are constituted in the process of socialization of individuals and lay the structural generative schemes of thought and action, which are activated in particular social conditions, or *fields*. In other words, they only come alive when there is formed what might be referred to as an 'electivite affinity' between objective and subjective structures – something which occurs as a result of a resonance between the logic of practice predominant in the *field* and individuals who find themselves there. And, this resonance occurs through a matching and mapping of 'structural homologies' (structure in the sense defined above) between the two. Bourdieu is therefore replacing 'determinism' with 'dispositionalism'.

For Bourdieu, *fields* and *dispositions* need to be understood in terms of *habitus*, which is the second of his principal 'thinking tools': He defines it thus:

> The conditionings associated with a particular class of conditions of existence produce *habitus*, systems of durable, transposable dispositions, structured structures predisposed to function as structuring structures, that is, as principles which generate and organize practices and representations that can be objectively adapted to their outcomes without presupposing a conscious aiming at ends or an express mastery of the operations necessary in order to attain them. Objectively 'regulated' and 'regular' without being in any way the product of obedience to rules, they can be collectively orchestrated without being the product of the organizing action of a conductor.
>
> (1990c/1980: 53)

In fact, *habitus* too is not a concept original to Bourdieu. It has a history going back to Aristotle. Marcel Mauss used it to designate the 'apparatus' that individuals take from one field of activity to another. Husserl's phenomenology recognized that the 'noema-noesis' process was conditioned by a certain *Habitualität*. For Merleau Ponty too, phenomenological processes must be understood in terms of incorporated structures. There is something of all of these meanings in Bourdieu's use of the term. However, he integrates this general approach to individually constituted action into his particular epistemologically charged theory of practice. *Habitus* is 'relational'. It mediates between 'objective structures and practice'; it overcomes the 'alternative between consciousness and unconsciousness'; it is constitutive of a particular environment; is 'systems of durable, transposable dispositions, structured structures predisposed to function as structuring structures, that is principles of the generation and structuring of practices' (1977b/1972: 72). There are three important aspects to understand about *habitus*. First, in the same way as disposition, *habitus* should not be thought of as deterministic – indeed, Bourdieu partly adopted it in order to make a clear distinction between 'rule' and 'strategy' in social action. He associated 'rule' with structuralism, both in its Lévi-Straussian and Althusserian versions, which for Bourdieu were too static. Second, much in *habitus* operates at an unconscious level; while conforming to a logic of practice of a field condition, most of an individual's *habitus* may yet be occurring unselfconsciously. Third, we need to see *habitus* and *field* as being co-terminus. They are one and the same thing:

> The relation between habitus and field operates in two ways. On the one side, it is a relation of conditioning: the field structures the habitus, which is the product of the embodiment of immanent necessity of a field (or of a hierarchically intersecting set of fields). On the other side, it is a relation of knowledge or cognitive construction: 'habitus contributes to constituting the field as a meaningful world, a world endowed with sense and with value, in which it is worth investing one's practice'.
>
> (1989b: 44)

At one point Bourdieu refers to the relation between *field* and *habitus* as one of 'ontological complicity' (1982: 47). In a way, Bourdieu's epistemology *is* an ontology. *Habitus* is 'the reason of all objectivation of subjectivity' (1968: 706).

This picture is a complex one of social action being constitutive of the dynamic of a relationship between individuals and the social conditions – both material and ideational – which surround them. However, all is not neutral in *fields* – quite the contrary. For Bourdieu, *fields* also should be understood as networks of value, in that everything that occurs within them is valued according to the specific logic of the *field*, defined in terms of their orthodox or legitimate ways of doing thing. This 'ecology of fields' is also an 'economy of fields', in that practice within them is defined in terms of individual and group interest and investment. In other words, there is an assumption of profit. This is why Bourdieu often refers to *fields* as *markets*, as the place where social goods are exchanged. He employs the word *capital* to designate this 'energy of social physics' (1990c/1980: 122): 'capital is a social relation, i.e., an energy which only exists and only produces its effects in the field in which it is produced and reproduced' (1984a/1979: 113). It comes in three principal forms: social, economic and cultural.

Social capital is 'the sum of the resources, actual and virtual, that accrue to an individual or a group by virtue of possessing a durable network of more or less institutionalized relationships of mutual acquaintance and recognition' (1992a: 119). This capital is the value of social contacts with individuals and groups. *Economic capital* is in effect money wealth. *Cultural capital* is that capital which results from engagement in and with education and culture. It exists in three forms: embodied, objectified and institutionalized. The first of these are literally incorporated 'dispositions'; for example, of taste, expression, knowledge and culture – these can be expressed in such diverse practice as tone of voice, knowledge and general physical demeanor. The second form exists in the relationships which are established with actual material objects: paintings, dictionaries, books, machines and musical instruments. The third form is culture incarnated in specific institutions; for example, universities, schools, etc.

For Bourdieu, *fields* and *field* practices can be defined in terms of the configuration of their *capital*. So, in some fields, *economic capital* predominates; in others, it is *cultural capital*. However, all forms exist in all *fields* to a lesser or greater extent. The *field's* essential character is defined by its particular configuration. Bourdieu goes along with traditional economic theory to see *capital* as 'accumulated labor' (1986b: 241). In other words, *capital* results from 'investment' and 'return', some of which might be inherited. Whatever its forms, however, it has value to the extent that it supplies 'social energy', which can be used to 'buy' and make further investments in the *field*, thus working to establish preferential positions within it. However, he also argues that one seeks the 'maximization of profit' in terms of one's utility and *field* practices obey an 'immanent logic': '*practices form a economy*, that is, an immanent reason that cannot be restricted to economic reason, for the economy of practices may be defined by reference to a wide range of functions and ends' (1992a: 119). In other words, it is not simply a question of the 'mechanical reaction' for profit. Rather, it is reasonable action that is necessarily the product of a reasoned purpose or explicit calculation, conscious or not.

For Bourdieu, *fields* are dynamic, not static. They are constantly being redefined and revalued. What is legitimate and valuable is contested in the course of the history of the *field* and as a result of the dynamics of those who occupy positions within it, and which they are constantly acting to improve. Bourdieu uses a fourth descriptor for *capital* – *symbolic*: 'which is the form that one or another of these species takes when it is grasped through categories of perception that *recognize* its specific logic or, if you prefer, misrecognize the arbitrariness of its possession and accumulation' (1992a: 119). In other words, *capital* only has value to the extent it is *recognized* as having value. This is true of all forms of *capital*, and even *economic capital* is based on a consensus over the legitimate function of money, which is no more than a symbolic form of real products.

With *cultural capital* the process is more complex. Cultural products have value to the extent to which what passes as holding legitimate value is known (*connaissance*) and recognized (*reconnaissance*). Bourdieu makes the point that some groups within a *field* both 'know' and 'recognize' such value; for example, of specific forms of education – for others, while they recognize it in others, they do not 'hold' it themselves. Still others neither know nor recognize valued aspects within a particular *field*. This example is used by Bourdieu to show distinctions between 'upper', 'middle' and 'lower' social groups. An important aspect of this mechanism is that it occurs in a 'misrecognized' form; part of its power is that it is 'occulted', or at least not open to conscious control or acknowledgement. Indeed, Bourdieu would claim that it is the chief task of sociology precisely to name what has previously not been named.

Theory of Practice: Conclusion

In Part 1 of this book, I emphasized how Bourdieu's theoretical approach must be understood in terms of the socio-historical background from which it emerged. In the twentieth century, at least, as well as debates about Marxism and Catholicism, the intellectual climate could be understood in terms of philosophies of 'subjectivism' and 'objectivism'; most noticeably coalescing around the work of Sartre (and the existentialists) and Lévi-Strauss (and the structuralists). Subsequently, I have shown how both these traditions can be explained by focusing on 'structure' in its objectivist and subjectivist state. Bourdieu's is a social philosophy of practice that offers what he argued is an epistemology. It aims to escape from the previous limits of scientificity. The means of doing so is to apply his 'thinking tools' in their philosophically charged forms. In this chapter, I have set out his principal concepts: *field*, *habitus*, *capital* and *disposition*. Further associated and related concepts will emerge in the discussion of the following chapters. However, there is one further aspect of Bourdieu's work that should be highlighted before discussion of his treatment of education, and that is the character of the resultant knowledge that his method gives rise to. Above, I referred to Bourdieu's insistence that how we 'construct the object of research' is an important aspect of carrying it out. For Bourdieu, it was important to construct the object in terms of his own analytical tools. This approach entailed reconceptualizing the research object in terms of *field* and *habitus*:

1. To analyze the position of the 'field' *vis-à-vis* the field of power;
2. To map out the objective structure of relations between the positions occupied by agents who compete for the legitimate forms of specific authority of which the field is a site;
3. To analyze the habitus of agents; the systems of dispositions they have acquired by internalizing a determinate type of social and economic condition.

(1992a: 104–7)

In this way, we see a 'three level' analysis, albeit that Bourdieu often applied these simultaneously in his own accounts of the *field* he is studying. This approach, he has claimed, goes beyond the normal limits of objectivity and subjectivity.

There is a second feature of research which is important to apply – reflexivity. Bourdieu recognizes that his critique of scientific objectivity might be misinterpreted as another form of subjective philosophy:

The questioning of objectivism is liable to be understood at first as a rehabilitation of subjectivism and to be merged with the critique that naïve humanism levels at scientific objectification in the name of 'lived experience' and the rights of 'subjectivity'.

(1977b/1972: 4)

However, what he intends is something much more rigorous and scientific, and reflexivity is the key to this form of knowledge. The knowledge of scientists is just as much a social construction as any other. In fact, social scientists (and, in particular, Bourdieu-inspired philosophers) take a position with regard to knowledge which is wholly unselfconscious and unreflexive. In other words, it takes a privilege for itself that it will not grant others; to define what they have to say in universal, consecrated terms instead of as another social construction:

> One has to look into the object constructed by science (the social space or the *field*) to find the social conditions of possibility of the subject (*researcher*) and of his work in constructing the object (including *skholè* and the whole heritage of problems, concepts, methods, etc.) and so to bring to light the social limits of his act of objectivism.
>
> (2000a/1997: 120–1)

Bourdieu recognizes that scientists – social and physical – are 'self-aware' and cultivate a 'reflective' attitude to their work. However, he argues (*ibid.*: 10), that this is not enough and, indeed, believing that it risks developing an arrogant attitude to the 'omnipotence' of their thinking. We cannot, simply through being more self-aware, rid ourselves of the presuppositions inherent in the construction of our thinking. There is only one solution: 'the objectivation of the subject of objectification', or 'participant objectivation'. This amounts to: 'turning the instruments of knowledge that they produce against themselves, and especially against the social universes in which they produce them' (*ibid.*:.121). By doing so, 'they equip themselves with the means of at least partially escaping from the economic and social determinisms that they reveal' (*ibid.*). By 'instruments of knowledge', Bourdieu is thinking in terms of *habitus, field*, etc. In other words, the constructors of knowledge must apply these analytical 'thinking tools' to themselves in the very act of knowledge construction and interpretation.

What results is a form of 'relational knowledge' that Bachelard and Canguilhem had pointed towards, albeit given a structural phenomenological twist by Bourdieu, and mixed in with a theory of knowledge constituted from Marx, Weber and Durkheim and twentieth-century philosophy. It would, therefore, be wrong to claim that Bourdieu produced this approach *ex nihilo*, as it were, or in a fully developed form. Nevertheless, besides the theoretical synthesis and reconceptualization, it is important to emphasize that his is a theory of practice which emerged from a 'practical' engagement with practical problems. It is not simply a theoretical deduction applied to practice, but a slow clarification of theoretical dimensions arising from an investigation of practical phenomena. Bourdieu referred to the resultant knowledge as 'reflexive objectivity' or 'practical reason'. It is knowledge *of* and knowledge *for* social action, or praxis. What I have offered here is this theory in its later, more advanced, integrated and coherent form, developed in the course of a lifetime engagement with such research topics as culture, economics, art, literature, politics, language, media, etc. The remainder of this book addresses the application and animation of such a theoretical perspective to the *field* of education.

Chapter 7

Early Studies and Education

As previously stated, Bourdieu's work must be understood in terms of his own biography; in fact, he positively extolled the virtues of employing aspects of 'empirical habitus' for the ends of the 'scientific habitus' (see 1995b: 29). This chapter addresses Bourdieu's earliest work and considers the extent to which it can be seen as offering a foundation for his later preoccupation with education.

Bourdieu's own trajectory resulted in him experiencing a massive shift in lifestyle and environment: from remote rural village, to school boarder in the local town, to the 'royal' route of the educational elite in school at the very center of Paris. As referred to above, he describes how he spent most of his youth in a tiny and remote village in south-western France – a very 'backward' place, and 'I could only meet the demands of schooling by renouncing many of my primary experiences and acquisitions, and not only a certain accent' (1992a: 204). There are many strands to these remarks. First, there is recognition of the geographical move he made, and the way it necessitated a change in outlook on life. Second, a move towards a new lifestyle meant a certain 'renouncing' of a previous one and the values it represented. Third, there must be a hint of regret in such a renouncement. Fourth, there is the role that education played in accelerating the displacement of one set of ways of thinking by another. Finally, there is the depth to which this process personally affected one young individual; not only his accent was changed but his whole sense of being. Such a personal shift, from rural-traditional life to modern-urban, might be understood as analogous to the changes cited earlier to be found in the work of Marx, Weber and Durkheim – not to mention the profound changes which French society itself had undergone in the previous century and a half. Many of the emergent dichotomies of this period remained unresolved in the 1950s. And, it is this juxtaposition

between the old and the new which seems to be the common preoccupation in Bourdieu's earliest work.

Two subjects are the focus for Bourdieu's early publications. The
first is Algeria, a country in which France was fighting a fierce war in
the 1950s (see Bourdieu, 1958, 1963 and 1964a). The second is his
own native region of France – the Béarn – and the particularities of
peasant life there (see Bourdieu, 1962a). Bourdieu was a keen photographer, and both these topics were the subject of literally hundreds
of photographs. In another book on Bourdieu (Grenfell, 2004b), I
have suggested that considering the 'photographer's eye' (or 'gaze')
is a good way of understanding what acted as a generative force in ori-
entating his early work. Two images are paramount. The first is taken
in Algeria (see Bourdieu, 2003: 154 and 165, for example). It shows
a young male adult stood next to his bicycle, which also seems to be
acting as a 'mobile' shop, since it is covered with various ironmonger
goods. These individuals were a new phenomenon in urban Algeria. It is as if Bourdieu is asking, who are these men? What brought
them here? What knowledge and learning do they have? What social
conditions created them? The second image is of a Christmas dance
in rural peasant France. In the center of the photo are young men
and women dressed in modern clothes and dancing under festive
flags. However, on the edge of the photo is an older man. He is
dressed in his Sunday best complete with beret. He stands 'alone'
with hands behind his back looking at the dancers, but not dancing.
Other men, on their own, stand nearby – arms folded (see photos
7 and 8, also reprinted on the cover of Bourdieu, 2002a). It is as if
Bourdieu is again asking, who are these men? What brought them
here? What social conditions created them? We might argue that in
the answer to these questions of dislocation lays the whole basis of
Bourdieu's experience, his epistemology and consequent theory of
practice.

These are stark images, but what do they mean? In the case of the
Béarn, Bourdieu's focus was on the marriage strategies of the rural
peasant. In particular, he set out to discover what made a certain
category of peasant male farmer 'unmarriable'. How can this be so?
In successive papers, Bourdieu developed his argument (see 1962b,
72 and 89). At the heart of the matter were issues of social practice.

Bourdieu argued, against a strict structuralist view, and that social practice needed to be understood less in terms of adherence to marriage *rules* but as *strategic* action aimed at preserving the inheritance lineage of individual families. The locals now spoke of a 'crisis in society' because their customs no longer 'worked', leaving a certain group of them unmarriable because of their position in the chain of inheritance. They stayed single, suffering the personal consequences of loneliness.

Bourdieu developed an entire ethnography, including statistical analyses, to show the various permutations of age, gender and background, and their combined effects on the propensity to marry. However, he also showed how the background to all this was the challenging of one world view and lifestyle by another. In sum, people were adopting 'modern attitudes' as communities opened up and came under the influence of local towns. They dressed differently, formed more independent views, and looked to move into modern housing. Children went off to schools in local towns (as Bourdieu had done) and were inducted into a way of viewing the world which was quite distinct from that of the local environs.

The picture created by Bourdieu was one where education formed a key part in the opening up of closed communities. Nothing, he relates, more than education is capable of teaching the aptitudes needed by the modern economic and symbolic markets: for example, use of language, arithmetic, etc. He wrote that in many ways the force of the community was 'merciless' in directing individuals in how to behave. The traditional way of living eschewed education; what was valued was working on the land, lineage and inheritance. In this world, 'education' was not needed; indeed, there was positive resistance to it. Instinctively, community elders understood that broadening the minds of the young in the community could lead to a weakening of their influence over them. Bourdieu quotes many accounts from those involved, declaring one way or another, that the modern world is a threat. Women are seen as perhaps the most symbolically sensitive. They act therefore as veritable 'Trojan Horses' in importing modern values. In the past, they had gone to work in service in towns in order to earn some money for their trousseau. Now they are educated beyond primary level, they leave home when they want and there is no sense of returning (2002a: 64). Once, they were content to marry the 'son of a peasant', Bourdieu writes, now, they look for a 'handsome man'. Of course, these are clichéd images; although they are reported by individuals from the community. What they do is illustrate the very profound changes that were going on in society and the role which education had in such a process.

Until the twentieth century, French education had continued with the system it inherited from Napoleon. In effect, this amounted to a strict separation between primary and secondary education. Primary education was for the masses, while secondary was reserved for the sons and daughters (mostly sons) of the upper middle and ruling classes. In fact, this division continued up to and beyond the Second World War. Some form of education carried on beyond primary school; although this was invariably vocational. Politicians tended to follow traditional preoccupations: the Left wanted to broaden and lengthen education for the majority of the population; while the Right looked to vocational needs of supplying the skills and trades needed by society. On the land, this meant that most of the sons of peasants received training in the techniques needed to manage the farm, while daughters acquired the skills necessary to provide a support system for the home. Education beyond this potentially destroyed this close link between land, work and home life, and yet it clearly also offered an initiation into a whole world of learning, the result of which would impact on both the individual's personal and professional life.

The power of education had long since been understood by the French intellectual class, and strands can be found in writings throughout the eighteenth and nineteenth century. The 'non-conformists' of the 1930s, for example Emmanuel Mounier, saw education as a necessary antidote to the ills of modern living. As noted in Part 1, Personalism itself, with its guiding principle of 'l'épanouissement de la personne', argued that if modern man is to have a soul, then it will be through its animation by culture and education – both had the potential to develop the spiritual nature of men and women. The 'Peuple et Culture' movement in the post-war years had taken forward this agenda with its clubs and publications aimed at a form of 'éducation permanente' (adult education). And, De Gaulle used education in a sense to develop the minds and spirit of French people, founding his *Maisons de la Culture*. Informal educational 'communities' of this type were developed alongside changing patterns of formal education and schooling. The Béarn peasant culture provided Bourdieu with a living example of the way education had featured in a changing world, and how it might still further do so.

Algeria offered Bourdieu a second example of education as a social phenomenon with a profound role to play in society. France had proved itself to be an enthusiastic occupier. Algerian territory was 'assimilated' into that of the French – in effect making it a part of France. When crises at home led to economic penury for large portions of the populace, large numbers of Frenchmen were encouraged to settle there. The French language was promoted and, with it, French culture. The subsequent ruling elites were either French or Algerians heavily acculturated into French customs and ways of doing things. By the aftermath of the Second World War, the indigenous population occupied an inferior position vis-à-vis the colonialists by virtually every social indicator. The Algerians revolted against this state of affairs on several occasions before a general insurrection in 1954 led to the so-called Algerian War of Independence. Almost a decade of hostilities followed before modern Algeria, 'free' from France, was founded. Bourdieu first went there in 1955 when he was 25, in order to do his military service. Initially, he worked away from the capital, Algiers, before taking up administrative duties there in the General Government. The General Government held one of the country's best stocked libraries, and it is clear that Bourdieu drew on it avidly. What resulted was *Sociologie d'Algérie* (1958). Bourdieu claimed that he undertook this work more as a kind of service. Frenchmen, he stated, understood poorly what Algeria was as a social phenomenon (Bourdieu, 1995b: 2). On the very first page of *Sociologie d'Algérie* Bourdieu questioned if Algeria was itself a 'social construction'; in other words, 'Algeria' itself did not exist as an 'objective identity', but rather as what had been made of it by researchers. The book then offered a social topography of the economic and social structures of Algeria, an analysis of which was needed to reveal his main themes: the clash between indigenous and European cultures. A number of other early publications on Algeria followed (for example, 1961, 1962a, 1963, 1964a).

It is important to again place Bourdieu's own responses in its time. By the 1950s, fascism had been thoroughly defeated as a viable alternative to Western Capitalism, but criticism continued of the socioeconomic conditions which had led up to war in the first place. Fascism was dead. However, communism was alive and kicking. The Soviet bloc had actually expanded as a result of the war. In China, there was a major world power which based its political and economic system on ideas derived from Marx and Lenin. Defeat of fascism only gave an added spin to communism among the major European intellectuals at that time. Existentialism was at its height and, with it, its leading international exponent, Jean-Paul Sartre. Bourdieu's own response to the times was more empirical than philosophical. What was offered in *Sociologie d'Algérie* is a close and detailed structural map of Algeria as it presently stood – the 'reality' of a colonial country with all its inherent contradictions and ambiguities. This view stood in contrast to that of Left-wing intellectuals who were keen to seize on the romance of revolutionary rhetoric to explain events in Algeria. For example, Sartre (1963/1960), and with him the supporter of violent insurrection, Fanon (1961), set out to represent the colonized people as 'heroic' overthrowers of the Imperial regime. For them, revolution was at one and the same time a political liberation and an 'assumption of consciousness'. Those repressed were the harborers of the New World. The only thing in dispute was whether the revolutionary class was the peasantry or the industrial working class; in other words, the choice between the Chinese and the Soviet route to communist society (see Bourdieu, 2000d: 8). For Bourdieu this was to replace facts with a theoretical fiction. What he described in its place are both the traditional structures of Algerian society – and with it the socio-cultural as well as domestic and land patterns of its indigenous people (the Kabyles, Shawia, Mozabites and Arab-speaking people) – and the displacements that had taken place as a result of colonization and revolutionary war. The land of the indigenous peoples had been largely occupied by the colonizers, resulting in evictions. Many had combined patterns of work, which involved their own smallholdings, work for the occupying farm managers, and what they could pick up in the towns when there was little work elsewhere. The photos Bourdieu placed in *Travail and Travailleurs* demonstrate the homogeneous character of Algerian society: young and old; male and female; beggar and entrepreneur; peasant and industrial worker. Changes in Algerian society resulted in the appearance of 'new' groups of individuals, such as the street sellers mentioned above who carried their shop on their bicycles. It was socio-historical conditions which created them and dictated the limits of their personal action, both social and economic. Many native Algerians lived in a twilight world of 'camps' created for them by the colonizers. Others existed half in and half out of towns. Others, still, moved permanently to urban dwellings, taking up residence in apartments and squats. Here, as in the Béarn, there was the clash between the modern and the traditional, the town and the country, and, ultimately, the way they impacted on individuals' lives and thoughts. The similarities between Algerian and French peasant society are striking: the breaking of traditional community links; new patterns of employment; the replacement of agricultural market practice with financial banking systems; domestic locale and the structure of the home dwelling; the role of women and the young. As in the Béarn, the opening up of isolated societies brought with it the broadening of personal horizons. People were better informed and free to make their own choices. The family structure was weakened: the young were influenced by the contemporary world, which came to them through commerce and modern communication systems; women acquired a degree of emancipation.

By the 1960s, the destruction of traditional Algerian society was a fact. Bourdieu undertook (1963: 383ff) a structural taxonomy of the contemporary division of labor in Algeria, basing his analysis on four differentiating criteria: the economic sector, professional stability, type of activity and qualifications. He distinguished between six major categories. The first was *sub-proletariat*. These were workers without permanent work and without qualifications, and included the unemployed, small merchants/artisans and laborers. The second were the *proletariat*. These were skilled manual workers with a permanent job – the modern industrial workers. There were then those in the *traditional sector* – forming quite a heterogeneous group in terms of material conditions but sharing, according to Bourdieu, the 'same cultural universe'. There was the *semi-proletariat*, existing on the margin of the capitalist economy. The *traditional bourgeoisie* was then made up of the inheritors of industrial and semi-industrial firms. And, the *new bourgeoisie* were investors mainly in the new textile, clothing and food industries. In blatant opposition to the line taken by intellectuals with Marxist sympathies, Bourdieu argued that the traditional revolutionary line was insufficient. He agreed that the way people experienced the world was a product of their social conditions. However, he was not able to accept that such conditions and the outcome for social action should be simply interpreted in terms of the economic contradictions of Capitalism. For example, individuals' experience, in a deep phenomenological way, was subject to an ontological state of being which itself was the result of conditions of space and time. It is important here to recall the earlier discussion on the relationship between *habitus* and *field* as situated in *social space* with defining *logics of practice*, which are to be seen in terms of the underlying generating structures (both structured and structuring). In traditional communities, farming was geared to consumption. Increased production was, therefore, thanks to past efforts, an end in itself, not the means (often artificially supplied through a credit loan) to future profit. Here, the relationship with time is all-important: 'the peasant spends in relation to the income derived from the last harvest, and not the income expected on the next' (1979a/1977: 9). In contrast, in the capitalist economy, production cycles are larger and longer. The result is that those involved no longer have a grasp of the production cycle as a whole. This is the contrast between the traditional craftsman and the modern technical worker. In the modern economy, production time itself becomes abstract and disconnected with the experience of labor. In this sense, the 'organic relationship' between worker and work product is broken and, with it, a certain relationship to time. Indeed, a capitalist form of production depends on this 'cycle of reproduction' being broken. It is education, here technical and vocational, which can again provide the means for this rupture. In such an analysis, there are implications which go beyond the case of Algeria. What is being described is common to the modern economic conditions.

This relationship to time extends to the contemporary class structure. Bourdieu argued that in order to have 'revolutionary' plans, individuals must have sufficient material conditions to allow for a forward projection in time – action now with a future pay-off. For example, in Algeria at the time, the 'sub-proletariat' had security or stability. For them, unemployment was a fact of their life's very existence (1963: 303). Members of the 'sub-proletariat' could not therefore indulge themselves in future plans in the way that employed industrial working class did. It was material conditions which provided the conditions for rational calculation towards the future. Therefore, Bourdieu argues, it is possibly to the more affluent sections of society to which we must look for a progressive plan for the future. In two articles, 'Révolution dans la révolution' (1961) and 'De la guerre révolutionaire à la révolution' (1962c) Bourdieu challenged political leaders to break both from their colonial past and the rhetorical exigencies of the revolutionary war of independence: 'How to substitute revolutionary objectives for the objectives of a revolutionary war' (*ibid.*: 5). He later summed up what happened instead:

> The Algerians became masters in retrospective revolution which often acted as an alibi for establishing conservatism . . . the Algerian army repeats what the French army had done . . . with the same phobias, mania, the same primitive reflexes of barbaric militarism . . . the socialist rhetoric is used to mask and support the perpetuation of lineage privilege.
>
> (2002b: 321)

Bourdieu predicted that the mass of the dispossessed would not be able to go beyond the misery of their present condition to assert one future over another. What of the more well-off, the 'petite bourgeoisie'? This group included the non-manual workers of the modern industrial economy. They were reasonably well-educated and affluent. They were also steeped in French culture, reading French newspapers and literature. However, as if often the case in revolutionary times, the new had only partially displaced the old and, in effect, these individuals were able to hold traditional values alongside a modern lifestyle. In other words, the revolution was partial and incomplete. The situation resulted in a world outlook which was both progressive, embedded in contemporary structures, and yet highly reactionary. Bourdieu asks:

> The modern middle class, middle management of the public or private sector, members of liberal professions or teachers, will it be satisfied with this half-revolution ... which will allow it to dominate or will it produce a revolutionary intelligentsia, the only ones capable in such a context, to define revolutionary aims in rational terms, and to bring together the sub-proletariat of the towns and the *proletarised* peasants in a work of radical transformation, by putting charismatic *prophetism* to the service of rationalism?
>
> (1963: 389)

But, how should this be brought about? For Bourdieu, the only way to reconcile the cultural and economic demands of a modern Algeria, and to do so in a way which founded a stable political system, was a broad education which would be 'total and entire' and defined in terms of clear specific, but realistic, aims. The needs of the individual and those of society as a whole must be brought together in an education which fed personal growth and development; all while providing the necessary skilled and educated men and women to service the modern economy. For Bourdieu, this would not come about by a highly centralized, top-down driven education agenda. In place of 'arbitrary exercises, defined abstractly for abstract subjects', what he called for was a more particularized, creative approach defined in terms of the individual's context and adapted to specific people:

> It is in the permanent confrontation between the expectations of the peasants and the demands of the elite, responsible for the choice and continuous bringing into being of rational ends, that an authentic culture can be developed; systems of models of social and economic behaviour which are at one and the same time coherent and compatible with objective conditions.
>
> (1964a: 177)

In this quotation, we see the interpenetration of culture, economics and politics, and the key to this 'authentic culture' was education.

Both the Béarn and Algeria were examples of the same preoccupations which Bourdieu had held with regard to the changing nature of society. The emergent issues had been acknowledged for some decades, and continued a critical discourse which came to a height in the 1930s. Although the Béarn and Algeria were vastly different contexts, many of the underlying phenomena were essentially the same: the contrast between the new and the old; the displacement of individuals; the rise of new social groups; the opposition of traditional and modern economic systems; 'folk' education and technological and commercial training; the management of change. Bourdieu used these issues to develop his particular theoretical practice, which set out to link the individual with the social structures that surrounded them and the personal cognitive structures which guided their thoughts and actions. Although this approach intimately involved a phenomenological view of subjectivity, the political implications of his analysis were already very much to the fore. And, it is a politics in which education featured as a strong and determining influence on those who experienced it in its different forms. No wonder then that as soon as Bourdieu returned to France, education became his prime focus of work. It is to these initial studies on students and their learning that we now turn.

Chapter 8

Students and Studying

It has been stressed how important it is to understand Bourdieu's early work on education in relation to his own professional trajectory. He returned to France to work at Lille University in 1960 and became teaching assistant to Raymond Aron, commuting between Lille and Paris. In 1964, he was appointed as Director of the Centre de Sociologie Européenne (CSE) in Paris. These were clearly active and formative years; in fact, they seemed to have set an agenda for Bourdieu for the rest of his academic life. He continued to publish articles and books based on his field work in the Béarn and Algeria. He also initiated two extensive research projects – on education and photography – both of which were elements in a general enquiry into culture and its effects in human praxis. In photography and education, Bourdieu collected a team of researchers around him who undertook extensive empirical research, involving questionnaires and interviews, as well as detailed statistical analyses. In a sense, what he did was apply a similar approach to education as he had to the Béarn and Algerian; in other words, constructing a social topography of the space which formed the object of study. The results of this research on education can be seen in *Les Etudiants et leurs études* (1964b), which Bourdieu co-authored with Jean-Claude Passeron with the help of Michel Eliard. This first report from the CSE contains mainly statistical analyses with brief commentary. The data was collected between 1961 and 1964 in Paris and Lille and a number of other provincial universities: Rennes, Bordeaux, Toulouse, Dijon and Lyons. Clearly, quite a team was mobilized for work which often involved standing on the steps of university libraries and engaging with students as they left. A longer commentary on the same statistics – *Les Héritiers* – appeared the same year. This field work was carried out at the same time as other early projects on culture and photography (for details, see 1990a/1965: 176, 196 and 203; and 1990b/1966) and based at the CSE in Paris. Why education?

Bourdieu explains his change of orientation at the time but later was quite dismissive about the reasons for his choice of subject matter:

> I continued to work on my phenomenological research, then I slowly abandoned phenomenology for ethnology. I continued to do ethnology up to' 65–66, and the work of the sociology of education that I undertook was more or less for the same reasons which had pushed me to do work on the sociology of Algeria. I undertook to do research on students, first of all to better understand what is this phenomenon 'students', and also to introduce a little clarity in various confused debates at the time.
>
> (Bourdieu and Grenfell, 1995b: 2)

In fact, education occupied center stage in the French socio-political arena. There were four main components to this interest in education. First, was the question of the role of education in the New World. Second, there was a comparative element across countries. Third, there was education for individual fulfilment, both professional and personal. Finally, there was the emergence of a genuine sociology of education. The role of education in society had long since been recognized. If the world was changing, if traditional society was being replaced by modern living, that New World would need a different sort of education system. For Durkheim, the shift from mechanical to organic solidarity necessitated 'a pedagogy for the modern world' in order to instill group norms and values in individuals. In this case, education was seen as a 'moral' force, as a way of bringing about cohesion within social groups by establishing consensus around values and practices. Bourdieu was arguing similarly in his conclusions on Algeria society, but his was more radically forward thinking. Durkheim's views looked back to the past and to the continuation of established values. Indeed, for him, values and practices had to be integrated with modern living. For Bourdieu, on the other hand, a 'rational pedagogy' would 'methodically neutralize' the influence of socio-cultural factors. In the case of Algeria, this approach amounted to a sort of 're-education', a break with both colonial thinking and anti-colonial thinking; especially the latter which, although apparently emancipatory, was still conditioned by the 'old ways'. He challenged the new Algerian middle classes to grasp this re-education in their emergence from the war of independence. New Algeria would need a skilled and educated workforce, trained and socio-politically mature. Only education could prepare for this.

Of course, this was true not only in Algeria but in many other countries as part of their reconstruction which followed the devastations of the Second World War and its subsequent political upheavals. In 1964 and 1965, the CSE organized conferences in Madrid and Dubrovnik, specifically to compare education systems across countries. The subsequent publication (Castel and Passeron, 1967), to which Bourdieu contributed, sets out a range of issues drawing on countries such as Algeria, Hungary, France, Greece and Yugoslavia: education and social stratification; education and tradition; education and contact with the modern world. Clearly, there was an interest in learning lessons from other countries as well as establishing an optimal norm of operations when faced with cultural diversity.

As noted, in France at least, education also had a strong tradition as a means for personal development. Education was seen as 'enriching the soul'. Bourdieu was in fact quite critical of personalists and the intellectuals of the 1930s who espoused this theme and, as we have seen, it was one which permeated the whole cultural policy of the Fifth Republic. However, Bourdieu did clearly recognize the impact education had on his own life and, to this extent, saw it as a force for emancipation. It is therefore perhaps unsurprising that much of his educational research was done side-by-side with his early studies of culture. It is almost as if Bourdieu was testing education and culture, both of which had been traditionally associated with personal emancipatory roles for individuals in society.

Finally, sociology of education was itself growing in prominence at this time. In an Anglo-saxon world, sociologists such as Musgrave (1966) and Banks (1968) were producing statistics which demonstrated the iniquitous nature of education in terms of social differentiation and outcomes. The same topic featured in a conference organized by Bourdieu and Darbel for the Cercle Noiroit, which took place in Arras in 1965. In the subsequent publication (Darras, 1966), what is offered is a social topography of the changes which had take place up until this time in France since the Second World War with a special focus on the unequal distribution of benefits and profits from education. Bourdieu's own contribution to this publication deals with the inequalities of school and culture, indeed with the links between the inequalities of schooling and culture.

Education was therefore very much a part of the zeitgeist – social, political and academic. It offered Bourdieu a focus for issues connected with each of these dimensions of the modern world, an encounter which any young aspirant sociologist would relish.

While this early work on education offered Bourdieu a medium to develop his own approach and methodology, the CSE provided him with an institutional base. There was also considerable importance for him, as a young new director of the Centre, to acquire financial resources to develop its research program. Some of the research on photography was sponsored by Kodak, for example. The work on education was supported by an understanding on the part of politicians that it held the key to the future success of the New World which they were building. Bourdieu's way of working also lent itself easily to a synthesis of theoretical philosophy and practical ethnography.

Bourdieu developed an original mix of ethnography, anthropology, philosophy and sociology. Given that each of these disciplines represents a wide range of practices and perspectives, it is complex to track Bourdieu's own route through them. The discussion so far has sought to situate him both theoretically and practically. His developing method has been referred to as 'existential analytics', although the term 'social philosophy' might also describe his highly philosophical approach to social phenomena. Paradoxically, for a writer who is often seen as abstract if not obscure, Bourdieu repeatedly makes the point in his interviews that he rarely 'theorizes' for its own sake. Indeed, he claims to eschew theory (see 1989b: 34); rather, he seeks an engagement with 'practical' problems – to explain and understand them. In this sense, 'theory' comes after the event. Certainly, it is apparent that Bourdieu's initial enquiries into Algeria and the

Béarn were undertaken with this openness in mind. In the light of these field experiences, and the theoretical insights described earlier, it is clear that a specific theory of practice was indeed solidifying by the early 1960s. This approach involved the deployment of thinking tools such as *habitus*, *field* and *capital*, albeit as yet in their nascent forms. Nevertheless, Bourdieu maintains that he was constantly on guard against theoretical reification: 'As soon as we observe (*theorein*) the social world, we introduce in our perception of it a bias due to the fact that to study it, to describe it, to talk about it, we must retire from it more or less completely' (*ibid.*: 34). This is why he eventually saw that it was necessary to 'build into' the analysis the fact that it originates from a 'detached position'; that of the 'theoretical gaze' of the 'contemplative eye'. He makes the point that when an anthropologist constructs a genealogy, he does so in a way that is very different from a Kabyle head of clan who is faced with the very real practical problem of finding an appropriate mate for his daughter. Similarly, he extrapolates that when sociologists of education look at schools, they do so with a set of problems which differ from those of a father looking for the best school for his children. This perhaps explains Bourdieu's reassurance that what drew him to education was the need to understand a practical problem. Given the way in which education was indeed a central feature of the social, political and academic arenas, it is possibly unsurprising that he should undertake such a study.

His method itself, however, deserves further consideration. In his first article on the Béarn peasant farmers' marriage strategies, Bourdieu had written: 'Surely, sociology would not be worth an hour's trouble ... if it did not give itself the job of restoring to people the meaning of their action' (2002a: 127). In both this statement and the previous discussion, there is the issue of the interpretation of the social world. We saw previously how at that time (and indeed any time), different theories of social practice were offered: for example, existential, structural, Marxist. Each of these is a break from everyday, naïve knowledge and experience. Each claims to uncover the processes or underlying features of what really constitutes human praxis. Bourdieu's sociological account similarly implicitly claims to reveal the underlying state of social genesis. It is literally revealing, uncovering the generative nature of social phenomena. Bourdieu knows that all of us, including sociologists, pass most of our lives in a state of naïve lived experience. We go to school and send our children to school out of practical exigencies. However, to take on a sociological perspective is immediately to see beneath the surface of every day life and to understand its generative mechanisms. Such an issue is at the heart of a philosophical tradition which stretches back into time. However, in the 1950s, the major claims to philosophical legitimating came from structuralism, and various forms of phenomenology and hermeneutics (of which existentialism was a branch). If old-fashioned empiricism and nominalism had lost their places as focal points of scientific enquiries, in social sciences at least, there was still a struggle between various forms of metaphysics. Existentialism, for example, went beyond the world of simple appearances, to see existence in terms of action. In other words, the essence of man was in what he does:

> The appearance does not hide the essence, it reveals it; it is essence. The essence of an existent is no longer a property sunk in the cavity of the existent; it is the manifest law which presides over the succession of its appearance, it is the principle of the series.
>
> (Sartre, quoted in Robbins, 1991: 15)

'Essence' here should be understood as the fixed and timeless nature of certain things which makes them what they are. For a philosopher such as Locke, there was, even so, a distinction to be made between real essences (the unknown constitution of things which produce their properties) and nominal essences (what is known about a thing that gives it its name). For a writer such as Sartre such essence was basically defined in terms of what things are by virtue of what they do. However, for Bourdieu, when he actually encountered real-life situations, such as those in Algeria and the Béarn, there were no 'essential' Algerians or French peasants, any more than there were 'essential' causes of what was happening there. What was happening did not have an 'essential' cause but a multiplicity of generative structures determining outcomes. Bourdieu was moving towards a position where essential cause might best be expressed in terms of a certain 'logic of practice'. It was the 'logic of practice' which acted as the generative source of social phenomena, on its own and, more commonly, in encounters with other 'logic of practice'. His early work on education was consequently asking what was the essential cause behind this phenomenon called 'student' and indeed, behind the education and training which constructed them?

In order to undertake such an enquiry in practice, Bourdieu deployed both qualitative and quantitative resources, framed by what we know from philosophy. It was necessary to enter the *field* and collect empirical data, and this could be both qualitative (ethnographic) or quantitative (statistical). It was then necessary to analyze these for patterns and relationships; finally, taking the results of that analysis back into the data from which they were derived:

> The subjectivist intuitionism that seeks a meaning in the immediacy of lived experience would not be worth attending to for a moment if it did not serve as an excuse for objectivism, which limits itself to establishing regular relationships and testing their statistical significance without deciphering their meaning, and which remains an abstract and formal nominalism as far as it is not seen as necessary but only a purely temporary moment of the scientific process. It is true that this detour via the establishment of statistical regularities and formalization is the price which must be paid if one wishes to break with naïve familiarity and the illusions of immediate understanding, it is also the case that the properly anthropological project of reappropriating reified meanings would be negated by the reification of the reappropriated meanings in the opacity of abstraction.
>
> (1990a/1965: 2)

Here, Bourdieu was working on a method which began with detailed analysis of his research object, including statistics, from which relationships were discerned, which were then taken back to the original object of analysis. In this way, he was putting relationships back into the actuality of the experience. No wonder it has been called 'a science of existential analytics'. And:

> In other words, the description of objectified subjectivity refers to the description of the internalization of objectivity. The three moments of the scientific process are therefore inseparable: immediate lived experience, understood through expressions which mask objective meaning as much as they reveal it, refers to the analysis of objective meanings and the social conditions which make those meanings possible, an analysis which requires the construction of the relationship between agents and the objective meanings of their actions.
>
> (*ibid.*: 4)

The fact is that Bourdieu did not differentiate between the application of this perspective to the object of research, and both those who carried out the research and its product. In *Les Etudiants et leurs études* (1964b), and its companion commentary, *Les Héritiers* (1979b/1964), there are further examples of this approach to research, begun and refined in the Béarn and Algeria, and now extended to the world of education.

Les Etudiants et leurs études is divided into two parts: the first is entitled 'Students, schools and scholastic values'; the second deals with 'Students and their culture'. The first includes the analyses of questionnaires, which set out to provide details of the student population: social background, nationality, age, qualifications, experience in education, parental origins, political affiliation, and their attitudes to various academic disciplines. The second covers issues of art and culture in more detail; for example, knowledge and tastes in music, literature and art, as well as further asking them about their attitudes and ideas for university life. Clearly, there are several ways that the results of such work could have been presented. In the Introduction, Bourdieu and Passeron (p. 10) make it clear that their defining base category was 'social origin'; in other words, all other themes will be presented in terms of this one main theme since this was the 'principal differentiating factor' emerging from their statistical analyses. This is an example of the methodological approach quoted above;

that Bourdieu identifies a key relationship and then takes it back into the context as a way of illuminating the rest of the analysis. In this way, both the most obvious – for example, material life conditions – and the most hidden – the implicit attitudes of students – are highlighted. The book begins with the question of age. What they find is both explicit and implicit. For example, 64 per cent of philosophy students, at the time, were less than 21 years of age; while for sociology the figure was only 38 per cent (p. 15). The point made is that 'agedness' in the academic world is really an indicator of scholastic failure: for example, the need to repeat a school year was common practice in France, or, material demands delaying entry into university. A traditional subject like philosophy offered clear career structures for those 'on their way', while a new subject like sociology attracted a wide range of 'failures' from other disciplines. A further discovery was that sociology students held onto the traditional values of the intelligentsia, which they interpreted as obeying a certain intellectual consensus. The inference is drawn that holding onto 'traditional values' was a way of neutralizing the influence of their social origins. Of course, behind these straight facts about age and social origin, and attitudes to work in various academic disciplines, stood the shadow of issues already highlighted in work in the Béarn and Algeria: the changing world, the juxtaposition of young and old, traditional and modern, differing attitudes with respect to the future, and the scope for individual choice. There were paradoxes (sociologists were both older and more traditional) but these could be explained by uncovering the logic of practice of the *field* and the way this shaped individual choices, themselves constitutive of more general trends.

A further chapter in the book considers differences between female and male students. Female students had slightly less chance of going into higher education (8 in 100, as compared to 10 in 100 for males), and were more likely to follow arts subjects and education, while men were more apt to study sciences (p. 23). A higher percentage of girls were Catholic than the men. Women were also less inclined to affiliate themselves with the political Left. All of which reinforced a traditional view of feminine characteristics. However, Bourdieu and Passeron uncovered further associated themes; for example, this traditional image is dissipated once one considers these issues in terms of an indicator of independence such as living away from home. Here, such female students were more likely to be affiliated to the Left, were more actively political, and more likely to join a union once they were living away from the parental home. Curiously, living in university residence seems to make them more radical than having their own home (p. 33).

Geographical position was another factor. Parisians were wealthier than their provincial counterparts. Yet, students were not always better off in Paris. For example, Paris was an intellectual capital, but was characterized by a system where numerous students had little contact with their lecturers. There was, however, more opportunity to be a 'free thinker' here. In the provinces, a particular academic could still exert an intellectual hegemony, all while being more in touch with students.

The second part of *Les Etudiants et leurs études* considers students and their culture. Bourdieu and Passeron begin this part by suggesting that, with modern mass communication, it might be believed that cultural inequalities were less evident among the student population. Furthermore, that school was no longer the main source of culture for students. The study addresses these issues from a number of directions. Students' own knowledge of individual writers, painters and musicians was investigated (themselves categorized as classical, modern, 'avant-garde and 'boulevard'), as well as their cultural practices – frequency of trips to the theatre, cinema and concert hall, number of books read, etc. The main socio-economic classification was correlated against this data and their social origins (occupation of their father); for example, 'ruraux', 'manual workers', 'white collar workers', and liberal and managerial groups (lower classes, middle classes and upper classes). They concluded that students became notably more 'cultured' as their position in the social hierarchy rose. Generally, they knew more and were more culturally active. New styles of music and art had done little to define a new 'common culture', which might have democratized aesthetic taste. Rather, Bourdieu and Passeron conclude: 'inequality before School locks in the principle of all inequalities before culture' (p. 75). The argument followed that school in fact represented a certain type of culture, and students from higher social groupings were more likely to be initiated into it through their home background, indeed the home and academic culture were in a sense homologous. In contrast, there was a much narrower fit between scholastic and domestic cultures as one descended the social hierarchy. It follows that those who were socially advantaged (culturally) were more likely to be scholastically advantaged since they were already inducted into a culture which resonated with what was being asked of them academically. The opposite also applied: those without the requisite culture found they were disadvantaged since they did not possess the cultural attributes necessary to facilitate their academic thinking and ultimate performance. Bourdieu and Passeron conclude that the power of this phenomenon is that what is 'social' in effect appears as being 'natural': 'Blindness to social inequalities, so frequent among both students and teachers, condemns and allows the explanation that all inequalities of academic success are natural inequalities and inequalities of talent' (p. 123). They further make the point that even when the 'privileged classes' admitted that schools sanction inequalities of social origin, they were able to find legitimation for their privileged position by explaining it in terms of personal talent and individual style. They finally conclude that the task is to institute a 'sociology of cultural inequalities' in place of a pedagogy defined, as it was to a large extent up to the 1960s at least, in terms of 'psychological abstraction'. *Les Héritiers*, published the same year, set out a more comprehensive account of such a sociology.

Bourdieu and Passeron begin *Les Héritiers* (1979b/1964) with a quotation from Margaret Mead's *Continuities in Cultural Education*. In it, she describes the practice among North American Indians of using visions as a social *rite de passage*. A vision conferred on the visionary the right to start a business, to hunt and fight in war. In the case of the Omaha Indians, all young men had the potential for visions. They would go out alone into the desert, fast and return to tell stories of the visions they had experienced. The elders of the village would then explain to some of them why theirs was not a real vision. Mead noted that this designation of authenticity acted as a form of social selection: 'genuine' visions were most common among the sons of the ruling, elite families. In other words, membership of the groups nominating the chiefs, tribe doctors and army generals was controlled in order to preserve the privileged inheritance of certain families. This epigraph is offered without comment. However, the analogy between the nature of modern education and primitive society is clearly implied. Like traditional communities, the modern world had established institutionally based routes through which everyone had to pass. In schools, there was a claim to meritocracy: education is available to all. Yet, one function of the education process was social selection: to legitimate and replicate the dominant factions within the social hierarchy. Since this selection function went largely unacknowledged, and therefore unrecognized, it was all the more powerful and pervasive. In primitive societies, magic is an exemplar of this moral energy, connecting nature and culture, and giving symbolic power to totem and taboo, as well as rites and rights. Bourdieu connected the 'old' world with the 'new' by stretching the analogy to the mechanisms of the contemporary world. For him, magic is still essentially present in the ways certain individuals are symbolically consecrated; their position and title giving them power to endow individuals with rights and to legitimize systems, symbolically configured, who then act in mutual self-regard and support. In education, the same magic acts of power and legitimacy are bestowed on those who gain academic awards. Such awards give them the right to speak with authority, to join the establishment and perpetuate it, to adopt the magical language of the culture they now share. They make themselves stronger by excluding the *masses* and controlling who is, and is not, *one of us*. *Magical* is the appropriate word to describe this process because it is unrecognized, accepted, unchallenged within the social group as a whole. It derives its power from within the social group, it is not imposed. Schools are not simply places where individuals prove their innate worth but a mechanism by which elites are perpetuated and transformed. Bourdieu and Passeron described the ideal French *Homo academicus*:

> The philosophy prizewinner in 1964 as the son and grandson of teachers, and intended to aim for the Ecole Normale Supérieure, take the *aggrégation* there, and become a philosophy teacher; while the winner of the first prize in Latin translation had 'read the whole of French literature by the age of 15 years 2 months,' and was 'fiercely individualistic' and 'astonishingly precocious.' Only hesitated between research and teaching (newspapers, June 1964).
>
> (1979b/1964: 43)

The title of the chapter in which this quotation appears is 'Games Students Play'. In brief, the argument went as follows: students were involved in a game of several facets. They read the latest 'avant-garde' writers of the time – Camus, Malraux, Valéry, Kafka and Proust – while asserting the 'values that are celebrated in obituaries' (*ibid.*). They involved themselves in the typical student game of 'distancing oneself from all limitations ... difference for difference sake', while passing over in silence differences which derive from social origin (p. 47). All the while, differences deliberately expressed in opinions and tastes were manifest and manifested. This is a 'game' of signifiers, where what is signified is only partially acknowledged. In other words, differences are recognized but not the social derivation of which they are an expression. This phenomenon was omnipresent. Even where differences of economic background and its effects on scholastic outcome were recognized, and even when this led to an overt political aim of rectitude, it did so in such a way as to mask the cultural processes which continued to ensure the social reproduction of privilege: 'The educational system can, in fact, ensure the perpetuation of privilege by the mere operation of its own internal logic' (p. 27). This is the 'logic of practice' referred to above. That logic is one of 'differentiation', and it is operated by an entire system of strategies of exclusion and inclusion. Even the decisions which are made by representatives from different social categories are made in terms of the 'objective future' of that category. Bourdieu and Passeron write of the way in which the 'reality' of why students are studying is often 'denied', concealing 'self-interest' and thus disconnecting the present from the future, as a way of asserting an 'eternal autonomy', which is a valued prerequisite of the 'educated man'. The important principle here is that we need to distinguish between the function an educational system performs and the means by which it performs them (p. 66).

Academic success is acknowledged in terms of 'talent' and inherent scholastic gifts. This 'charisma ideology' (p. 71) is even accepted by those from the 'lower classes' in a way which directs them to a sort of academic and social fatalism. In a way, they are 'consenting victims':

When a pupil's mother says of her son, and often in front of him, 'He is no good at French,' she makes herself the accomplice of three sorts of damaging influence. First, unaware that her son's results are a direct function of the cultural atmosphere of his family background, she makes an individual destiny out of what is only the product of an education and can still be corrected, at least in part, by educative action. Secondly, for lack of information about schooling, sometime for lack of anything to counterpose to the teacher's authority, she uses a simple test score as the basis for premature definitive conclusions. Finally, by sanctioning this type of judgement, she intensifies the child's sense that he is this or that by nature.

(pp. 71–2)

Even the victims of what is being perpetuated in the name of democratic schooling collude (unknowingly) in the process by which 'what' you are is conflated to express 'who' you are in terms of scholastic talent. All the while, 'clumsy teachers' impose their 'essentialist definitions' by which they imprison individuals. But, this 'imposition' does not operate in terms of a simple inculcation of knowledge and control. Rather, it is inherent in the practice of cultural transmission: *cultural capital*. Even here, it is not that *cultural capital* can be taken simply as 'cultural requisites' or content. Rather, imposition is expressed in the very form that culture takes. Nowhere is this more evident than in the language of education. In *Rapport Pédagogique et Communication* (1994c/1965) the issue of scholastic language is explicitly addressed. The currency of education is language and it is *the* medium of knowledge transmission. Language has two basic levels of expression: form, or structure, and content. Both form and content may exist in a way which favors certain ways of thinking and expressing that thinking. Moreover, they both may act as a mechanism for cultural transmission, which itself advantages and disadvantages those who encounter it, depending on their background and the affinities (or not) this sets up when they enter a scholastic *field*. Bourdieu writes of the importance of language in the *academic discourse* and how it operates in education. If academic discourse is predicated on an assumption of communication between the teacher and the taught, this relationship is fraught with faulty signals:

> There are, in fact, two systems of contradictory demands that ped-agogical communication needs to satisfy, neither of which can be completely sacrificed: first, to maximize the absolute quantity of information conveyed (which implies reducing repetition and redundancy to a minimum); second, to minimize the loss of infor-mation (which, among other measures, may imply an increase in redundancy).
>
> (Bourdieu, Passeron and de Saint Martin, 1994c/1965: 6)

The paradox of language in the pedagogic relationship is that it cannot satisfy these contradictory demands. Moreover, the demands are intensified by the social origins of learners and teachers, repre-senting as they do, more or less, differing world views and ways of expressing them. Bourdieu argues that, 'the aim of maximizing the output of communication . . . goes directly against the traditional rela-tionship to the language of teaching' (p. 6). He offers evidence of this 'misunderstanding' everywhere in his empirical studies of language in education:

> . . . the traditionalist professor can slide from the *right* to demand that his students learn . . . to the *fact* of making this demand when he has withheld from them the means of satisfying it.
>
> (p. 8)

> The world of the classroom, where 'polished' language is used, contrasts with the world of the family.
>
> (p. 9)

> . . . the teacher's self-assured use of professional language is no more fortuitous than the student's own tolerance of semantic fog.
>
> (p. 10)

Student comprehension thus comes down to a general feeling of familiarity . . . technical terms and references, like 'epistemology', 'methodology', 'Descartes', and 'sciences', shoulder each other up. He can quite naturally refrain from seeking clarification of each one of these ... for his system of needs is not, cannot be, and up to a *point* must not be, analytical ... the student is able to put together an essay which is apparently written in the same language of ideas, but in which the sentence 'Descartes renewed epistemology and methodology' can only be an impressionistic restoration. For outside this sentence, many students associate nothing with the word 'epistemology'.

(p. 15)

These are evocative and telling observations. Bourdieu's thesis on academic discourse is clear. First, that the linguistic background of the family influences the student's ability to deal with both the content and form of scholastic language. Second, there is an implied interest in perpetuating this misunderstanding as it shores up social selectivity, misrecognized as such as a collective act of *mauvaise foi*. Third, the way we think and speak betrays a whole relationship to language and conceptual modes of thought. Fourth, the location of particular disciplines in the institutional hierarchy of studies is a structural homology of these differences most apparent in differentials of performance according to social class.

Based on their engagement with empirical data and the conclusions drawn, Bourdieu and Passeron conclude *Les Héritiers* with a series of statements about the nature of education. Individuals and families adopt different strategies (as in Algeria and the Béarn) to ensure reproduction of their social heritage. When society and the economy are changing, as they were in France, the nature of those strategies itself changes. Thus, for example, in an economy where there was a shift from industry to commerce, it is not surprising that the nature and configuration of *capital* held by different social groups was also changing: *economic capital* was replaced by *cultural capital* as the main currency of social differentiation. The competition for *cultural capital*, most explicitly expressed in terms of academic qualifications, leads to a downgrading in their value. There is 'qualification inflation': the same certificates 'buy' you less. The disparity between aspiration and reward is a 'structural reality', it is a product of the logic of practice of the *field*. Moreover, the disparity is itself experienced differentially by individuals according to their social origins and through the 'objective opportunities' available to them. If this 'competition' for qualifications strikes one as a 'market', that is precisely how it operates – and perhaps, so it should in a capitalistic economic world. It is the actions individuals undertake – to gain qualifications, to compensate for lack of them, and to catch up or 'regain' their social trajectory – which transform social structures. In other words, the dynamic of change *is* change; in this case, actualized in scholastic practice but resonant with broader structural logics of practice in society and its economy at large. But, what can be done about it?

Just how pernicious and insidious the education system is was summed up by Bourdieu in an address he gave to a 'Week of Marxist Thought' in March 1966 (see 2002b: 55). The main thrust of his talk was to attack a policy of 'egalitarianism', which Bourdieu identified as being at the heart of Jacobin ideology. Jacobin thinking was at the core of the political philosophy of the Great Revolution of 1789, best expressed in terms of its principles – equality, fraternity and liberty. Bourdieu states that to argue for 'equality' is in effect to sanction 'inequality': 'by treating all learners, so different as they are, as equals in terms of rights and duties, the school system is in effect led to give sanction to initial inequalities in front of culture' (1966: 167). Paradoxically, the competitive style of entrance examinations to better schools and universities was established by Jacobin thinking as a way of avoiding privilege – 'we are all equal before the competition'. However, we are not all equal when the culture which saturates the competitive exam and the schooling it represents has affinities and disaffinities with the culture of those who enter the race. Privilege re-expresses itself in a 'misrecognized' form. The ideology of the 'gift' or 'talent' only reinforces this misrecognition by adding mystification to a social phenomenon. The fact that a few exceptional individuals from the underprivileged classes do succeed only adds to this mystification by demonstrating that it is possible for anyone to pass into the privileged environs of the academic system, thus neutralizing not only opposition but even consciousness of what might be opposed. In this way, inequalities of 'fact' are transformed into inequalities of 'merit'. For Bourdieu, the agents of this process were teachers who, for him at that time, still came from and disseminated a culture which could be called 'aristocratic': 'affinities of style', 'values', 'lifestyles', etc.

In place of this situation, Bourdieu and Passeron called for the foundation of a 'rational pedagogy' – a term which is mentioned three times in the last paragraph of *Les Héritiers* (1979b/1964). What this amounts to is a system which acts to 'neutralize' the effects of social factors on cultural, and thus, educational inequality. Such a 'rational pedagogy' cannot be expressed simply in terms of ensuring that all pupils will have equality of access to culture and education, as the logic of the field of education will continue to operate and result in the reproduction of social hierarchies. Neither can it mean that all pupils are given the same cultural and educational requisites – some are more able to receive them than others. Rather, it has: 'the unconditional goal of enabling *the greatest possible number of individuals to appropriate, in the shortest possible time, as completely and as perfectly as possible, the greatest possible number of the abilities which constitute school culture at a given moment*' (p. 75, italics in the original).

This argument almost seems like one of 'positive discrimination', that those underachieving should be given extra help so that they can catch up. However, it is clear that Bourdieu and Passeron intended more than a form of cultural compensation. In fact, they were targeting an entire different world view for both learners and teachers. They were arguing that it is not enough to impose an idealized form of pedagogy; the conditions for such must first be established. And, the major condition, they argued, was the founding of a 'sociology of cultural inequalities' (*ibid.*). This is an important distinction. The response of Bourdieu and Passeron to inequalities in educational outcome is based on the proposal that inequalities of culture had first to be addressed. Here, we can see the influence of the immediate post-war period France, when culture was charged with this democratizing function. Bourdieu and Passeron were arguing that there is something 'essential' about the nature of 'schools' and 'schooling', which meant that the solution to the inequalities of outcome could not simply be found in the structure, form and content of the system itself. Rather, a different way of viewing schooling and the way it intersected with society at large was required. Bourdieu's next major publication – *La Reproduction* (1977a/1970) – examined both the empirical and theoretical detail of this thesis in greater depth.

Chapter 9

Reproduction and the New Sociology of Education

The previous chapters addressed how Bourdieu's thinking developed from the mid-1950s to the mid-1960s and the way education was a focus for his early preoccupations with changes in the post-war social world. Bourdieu was developing a reputation as a sociologist of education, and yet education per se seems almost to have been incidental to his concerns. As noted, at the time, there was a growing body of sociological evidence which catalogued the inequalities of educational outcome in terms of social provenance; crudely put, pupils and students were more successful academically, the higher their position in the social class hierarchy. Bourdieu's early work on education added further evidence to this conclusion. However, this was only one aspect of his project. If he was interested in studying education as part of the democratic processes of contemporary France, and the inequities they implicitly gave rise to, he was equally concerned to study the part that 'culture' played in these processes. Pursuing these topics and themes was as much about developing a new kind of social science research as about the results that the method gave rise to. In 1970, Bourdieu published *La Reproduction*, which he co-authored with Jean-Claude Passeron. The original French edition was subtitled '*Eléments pour une théorie du système d'enseignement*', but it is probably the English translated version which best describes its content: *Reproduction in Education, Society and Culture* (1977a/1970). It is this book more than any other which established Bourdieu's reputation and it is still among the most-cited of his works. This chapter first describes the background to the book, both in terms of the social climate of the times and Bourdieu's theoretical thinking. It then deals with *Reproduction* and the part it and Bourdieu played in the 'new' sociology of education.

The 1960s were times when the gloom of war and economic penury were at last swept away for a large proportion of the European and American populations. The 'Beat' generation of the 1960s culminated in 'flower-power' and 'hippy-dom'. Optimism was probably at its highest point of the last century. Individual expression burst out in student protests and social riots across the globe (for example, 1968 in Paris – see chapter 11). It would be a mistake to conclude that such optimism was equally prevalent in the world of academia. Indeed, much of the writing produced in the 20 years after the end of the Second World War could be read as being quite pessimistic about the contemporary world. Nevertheless, that pessimism itself was often covered by a sweeter coating. If existing socio-political systems were found to be wanting, critique of them was carried out in terms of how they might be replaced – implicitly at least. This was certainly true in education generally, and the sociology of education in particular. Bourdieu was one of a number of sociologists who had analyzed education systems and found them lacking. For many sociologists, the issue was one of malfunction. Functionalism was still a powerful sociological force, and with it the view that there was indeed an 'optimally functioning' social system. All that needed to be done was to undertake corrective measures to ensure its improved operation. Education was a case in point. So, problems found in such areas as selection, streaming and management could all be refined. Bourdieu joined others in defining schooling as essentially a 'conservative force' (see 1974/1966) in the way it tended to support the continuation of established social structures. However, what was original in his own approach was the way he connected this observation with culture in general and, in particular, the way the reproduction of social hierarchies was mediated by the processes of knowledge formation themselves.

As early as 1966 (1971c), Bourdieu had published 'Champ intellectuel et projet créateur' ('Intellectual field and creative project'), which was later translated into English, appearing in *Social Science Information* in 1968). The focus here was on the relationship between social structures and the nature of thought itself. A similar focus was given in 'The Thinkable and the Unthinkable' (1971b) where Bourdieu addresses literally what can and cannot be thought. The answer in both papers is that the limits of thought are defined by individuals' positions within a particular *field*. The argument is circular: because an individual is at a particular position in the *field*, they think in a certain way; and because they think in a certain way, they are in a particular position in the *field*. In 'Intellectual field and creative project' the 'knowledge field' is described in terms of it being the reflection of a certain form of society. Bourdieu's immediate concern was to show how the products of artists and intellectuals must be understood in terms of affinities between their creative project and the social world which surrounds them (see also Grenfell and Hardy, 2007). It is important here to stress that Bourdieu is not arguing for a kind of mechanistic determinism, that there is somehow an instrumental fit between society and thinking as expressed by artists and intellectuals. It would be better to describe it as one 'conditioning' the other along certain lines or tendencies. But, these lines and tendencies are themselves characterized in terms of their proximity of identification with orthodox and non-orthodox ways of viewing the world and expressing oneself. Schools, the educational system, institutions, academies are all directly implicated in propagating a particular world view; one that is 'consecrated' and 'legitimated', but one which finally has to be understood as arbitrary in that it is relative to a particular way of doing things – one that advantages certain sections of the populace. Bourdieu's analysis is full of irony and allusion. He writes of 'Prophets, Priests and Sorcerers' in referring to the 'magical' effect of consecration bestowed on individuals. He also writes of the 'cultural unconscious' – a hybrid allusion to both Durkheimian 'collective conscience' and Jungian 'collective unconscious' – of both designating a moral force in individuals, which directs what they think and do. Bourdieu writes:

> The school is required to perpetuate and transmit the capital of consecrated cultural signs, that is, the culture handed down to it by the intellectual creators of the past, and to mould to a practice in accordance with models of that culture a public assailed by conflicting, schismatic or heritage messages – for example, in our society, modern communication media. Further it is obliged to establish and define systematically the sphere of orthodox culture and the sphere of heretical culture.
>
> (Bourdieu, 1971c/1966: 178)

Behind this analysis is the issue of the symbiotic relationship between *habitus* and *field*, and the *ontological complicity* found in the *elective affinities* set up as any 'thinking person' enters a 'knowledge field'. In other words, not only the intellectual, but even a school pupil, enters the *field* already saturated with categories of thinking, codes and dispositions, which then act as primary *points de départ* in shaping their responses to what they find there. Inevitably, institutions win out and they either stay and are molded by it, or leave. Consequently: 'Men formed by a certain school have in common a certain cast of mind' (*ibid.*: 182).

Bourdieu drew on the work of Erwin Panowsky who had analyzed the relationship between Gothic art and the Scholasticism apparent in training schools. Such scholasticism emphasizes 'the principle of clarification', 'the schema of literary presentation', 'the order and logic of words', and can be seen as the defining principles for the architectural designs for Gothic cathedrals – with their symmetries and correspondences. In short, it is a 'mental habit', a way of doing things, which should be understood, not in terms of instrumental replication, but of genuine 'cause and effect'. Schools, Bourdieu insinuates, operate thus:

> As a 'habit-forming force', the school provides those who have undergone its direct or indirect influence not so much with particular and particularized schemes of thought as with that general disposition which engenders particular schemes, which may then be applied in different domains of thought and action, a disposition that one could call the cultivated *habitus*.
>
> (*ibid.*: 184)

In this way, the 'collective heritage', which itself is in a constant state of flux, is transformed into an individual's unconscious, which nevertheless is held in common with others. In effect, this analysis is to connect culture with education and the individual with society as a whole, and it is a relationship that is at the heart of the education system.

In another article from 1967, Bourdieu developed the relation between 'Systems of education and systems of thought' (1971a/1967). Bourdieu begins this article by addressing the ethnologist himself – in this case, Claude Lévi-Strauss – posing the question of the extent to which one can be objectively conscious of the patterns of thought which guide thinking. He then draws links between the patterns which predominate in French education and those which direct the behavior of so-called primitive tribes; for example, the Bororo Indians. He then asks:

> Do the patterns of thought and language transmitted by the school, e.g. those treatises of rhetoric used to call figures of speech and figures of thought, actually fulfil, at any rate among members of educated classes, the function of unconscious patterns which govern the thinking and the productions of people belonging to traditional societies or do they, because of the conditions in which they are transmitted and acquired, operate only at the most superficial level of consciousness?
>
> (*ibid.*: 190)

Bourdieu is asking whether it is a certain way of thinking that creates the world – in this case the scholastic forms of classification and thus thinking – or whether it is the structure of this world itself which creates a certain way of thinking. His answer is to see 'culture' as the medium of the relationships between these two. In other words, culture does not provide a 'common set of codes' or answers to recurrent problems in the social world. Rather, culture offers a set of previously assimilated 'master patterns' which are brought to bear on immediate problems as a sort of 'art of invention' in directing how to act and think. He uses an analogy to music: a fixed set of scales, etc. around which improvisations can happen in response to the current situation. Bourdieu sought to create a 'theory of knowledge' which was dynamic, fluid but also stable enough to be of practical analytical use. Part 1 of this book showed how Bourdieu was responding against various theoretical alternatives of the day. First, for example, he saw these patterns as being distinct from codes which might be seen as directing thought and action in a much more instrumental and predetermined way. Second, they were not 'rules' – they are never followed explicitly. Third, they were not even 'conscious' – indeed, part of their power was that they might govern and regulate mental processes without being consciously controlled. Fourth, the patterns were not static either – indeed, they are in a constant state of flux in response to the cultural (ultimately) economic conditions of the day. Bourdieu returns us to the notion that 'school' is instrumental in creating a 'habit-forming-force': a scholastic *habitus* – both as a general disposition and in terms of specific content, which are then active in various areas of thought and action. In short, the function of schools is to transmit the master patterns of the culture. It is culture which then differentiates; to separate out and divide individuals according to the extent to which they have acquired the necessary attributes, exposed in the way they act and think, and thus their dispositions to be a certain type of individual. But, for Bourdieu, that culture is itself enshrined in the institutional conditions of schools; for example, the way they organize themselves, the way the curriculum is delivered, and the way knowledge is classified. The whole takes place as part of a cycle of reciprocity:

> Having to prepare their pupils to answer academic questions, teachers tend to plan their teaching in accordance with the system of organization that their pupils will have to follow in answering those questions; in the extreme case, we have those prose composition manuals providing ready-made essays on particular subjects.
>
> (*ibid.*: 196)

Having established this relationship between culture and educational knowledge, and embedded it in the structure of schools and academic institutions, Bourdieu goes on to discuss the changing nature of the relationship between them over the course of the history of contemporary France. He sees how different types of scholastic culture have indeed existed side-by-side, and thus how this has led to a sense of 'uneasiness' when one intellectual 'clan' existed alongside another. In classical times, there was less of an issue: wealth and social prestige did not depend on education and training but on inheritance. However, in the contemporary world, schooling was increasingly used by society as a way of distributing social distinction and, ultimately, of positioning within the social hierarchy. In France, the *lycée* or *collège* had been reserved for the 'middle classes', while elementary or primary school was for the common people. In effect, this system resulted in producing a class distinction of cultural 'haves' and 'have nots'. 'Academic culture' is reserved for those who have the long discipline of schooling; 'popular culture' is for those who have been excluded from it. Thus, it is 'academic culture', and the cultural attributes inherent in it, which is highly valorized in society. This distinction of individuals in terms of the degree to which they express such culture is implicitly asking one section of the populace to act in a way which is alien to it. Indeed, 'scholastic knowledge' and 'academic culture' express themselves not only in terms of what you know, but a whole relationship to knowledge itself. This can be expressed not solely in terms of how much you know – 'vigour and brilliance' – but 'ease, elegance, and qualities of style'.

Bourdieu next offers a picture of what characterizes the French education system:

> (that) for several centuries, young Frenchmen had been taught that the very essence of thought was to abstract and generalize ... (to overlook) the substance of knowledge and only value style and talent ... the idea that human nature is eternal, immutable, independent of time and space ... (and, quoting Renan) the École Normale has, on the arts side, been a school of style, not a school where things are learnt ... (which is why) it has produced delightful journalistic writers, engaging novelists, subtle intellects in the most varied lines – in short, everything but men possessing a sound knowledge of languages and literatures.
>
> (*ibid*.: 201–3)

Bourdieu concludes that, finally, the distinguishing features of say 'English positivism' in contrast to 'French rationalism' must really be understood in terms of the peculiar 'tricks' and 'mannerisms' of their schools. The point is not only that certain schools, through the content, style and structure of the scholastic culture they propagate, give rise to thinking in a certain way but also, perhaps more pertinently, that way of thinking, that culture, is arbitrary. What is essential in education is the social function it performs: one of distinction and social differentiation as a way of perpetuating a social hierarchy. It is

necessary to stress that Bourdieu is not arguing that the social structure of society is static and never changing – far from it. Everything
exists in a state of constant flux and competition. Bourdieu was thus
consequently able to see that the social structure of French society
had changed its topography in the course of contemporary history. If
the 'modern' world was characterized by the rise of a new capitalistic
industrial class – the owners of industry, who based their position on
money wealth (*economic capital*) – in post-war France this group had
been eclipsed by a different social class, those emerging from the
new middle classes (bureaucratic, public service workers, communications and the media). With little money wealth, they based their
social prestige of education and training (*cultural capital*). For example, the École Normale d'Adminstration (ENA) was created after the
Second World War precisely to train a new class of 'super bureaucrats' to manage the French economy and political system. The ENA
quickly rivalled both the École Polytechnique and the École Normale Supérieure as a leading training school for the political elite in
France.

With these articles, together with early studies on students, academic discourse and culture, Bourdieu was ready to make a summative statement about education in general and schools in particular.
This statement came in 1970 when *La Reproduction* was published.

The first thing that is noticeable about *La Reproduction* is its structure. It is divided into two 'books' of similar length. The second of
these includes analyses based around the kind of research which Bourdieu and his team had undertaken up to that date. With an overall
title of 'Keeping Order' ('le Maintien de l'Ordre'), various themes
are included, for example, the morphology of the student population,
the systems of selection and examination, language and communication. But, it is the presentation of the first book – under the title
of 'Foundations of a Theory of Symbolic Violence' – which is perhaps the most shocking. Here is listed a series of propositions, almost
aphorisms, about the nature, function and processes of the educational system. These are offered under four further subcategories:
'The Twofold Arbitrariness of Pedagogic Action'; 'Pedagogic Authority'; 'Pedagogic Work'; and 'The Educational System'. Within these,
there are further categories and subcategories. In their Foreword to

the French edition, the authors of *La Reproduction* – Bourdieu and his collaborator Jean-Claude Passeron – make the point that the second book might be seen as an 'application' or exemplification of the first. However, the opposite is true: while the two books should be seen as the outcome of a process of 'mutual rectification', the analyses of book II were actually the starting point for the propositions in book I. These propositions were an attempt to provide a set of principles which could be organized in a way that was 'amenable to direct empirical verification'. In other words, what Bourdieu and Passeron had done was to deduce a series of 'logically required' statements to explain their findings in a way which gave rise to principles which could be both empirically verified and applied to contexts other than France.

A further striking feature of *La Reproduction* is the prominence given to two key notions: 'violence' and 'arbitrariness'. The centrality of the term 'violence' is attested to by its position in the title of book I. There is also a 'zero' proposition before education is addressed directly: 'Every power to exert symbolic violence, i.e. every power which manages to impose meanings and to impose them as legitimate by concealing the power relations which are the basis of its force, adds its own specifically symbolic force to those power relations' (1977a/1970: 4). This statement refers back to the way knowledge is representative of a particular group in society and their ability to impose their own definitions of what counts as legitimate; in short, it is a principle of a theory of sociological knowledge. In terms of the school system, it refers to the homology between its 'monopoly of legitimate symbolic violence' and 'the State's monopoly of the legitimate use of physical violence'. Ultimately the power of the State sanctions and legitimizes the power of the education system to impose its own ways of knowing and acting. Bourdieu and Passeron connected such a proposition with the main founding fathers of sociology: Marx, Durkheim and Weber. However, they seemed to wish to distinguish their own take on 'symbolic power' from each of these, all while taking on board essential elements from them. These elements included issues of class domination, the problem of social order and constraint, representations of legitimacy, and the way that social functions are fulfilled while being misrecognized in power relations.

The second prominent theme in Part 1 is 'arbitrariness'. The first proposition states: 'All pedagogic action (PA) is, objectively, symbolic violence insofar as it is the imposition of a cultural arbitrary by an arbitrary power' (p. 5). The notion of 'arbitrariness' had a prominence in the social sciences ever since it had been adopted by Saussure in his recognition that in language any signifier is relative and therefore fails to perform fully its signifying function. Meaning is a rough consensus. The logical conclusion of this understanding, one which later underpinned all post-modernist philosophy, was that language itself is arbitrary: in principle, any word can theoretically signify anything, and nothing is ever wholly signified. What remains is an approximation based on arbitrariness. But, Bourdieu and Passeron distanced themselves from such 'neo-Saussurian' perspectives, and with them 'para-Chomskyan' discussions, which are referred to as the 'dreariest of topics'. For them, the term 'arbitrary' is logically needed in order to explain, 'the question of the institutional and social conditions enabling an institution to declare its pedagogic action explicitly as such, without betraying the objective truth of its practice' (p. xx). Here, they are referring to the way in which social conditions are necessary in order for social institutions to fulfill their function (according to their own logic of practice); in this case, schools' essential 'truth' is misrecognized precisely because it is embedded in a culture that is 'arbitrary'. Arbitrariness is therefore not itself arbitrary as such, but a necessary condition for a social function to be performed.

In fact, any one of the 80+ propositions in *La Reproduction* offers ample material for discussion and verification. What emerges is a principled model of education and schooling. In briefest terms, the theory presented throughout this book goes as follows.

'Pedagogic action' is inherently 'symbolic violence' and 'arbitrary' in content and form (including a certain relation to knowledge). The outcome of its action is to 'reproduce' the power relations which are at the basis of its function. The 'imposition' of arbitrary knowledge is possible because it is 'misrecognized' in 'pedagogic communication' – it 'imposes' legitimately. 'Pedagogic authority' implies social sanctions, although this principle is concealed. The 'legitimacy' of such authority is however implicitly recognized, albeit differentially, in terms of the degree to which specific social groups are disposed to recognize the force of sanctions held against them. 'Pedagogic action' entails 'pedagogic work': a process by which durable schemes of action and thought are be inculcated as the internalization of generative structures – *habitus*. Such a *habitus* needs to continue long after the work which produced it in the first place, as it needs to be transposable in order to maintain the original cultural arbitrary. This character of 'pedagogic work' is also concealed and goes 'misrecognized'.

Any pedagogy which did not meet the needs of the dominant class would not be sanctioned by them (implicitly and explicitly). All 'pedagogic action' and consequent 'pedagogic work' by definition therefore serves their interests. It follows that educational reform which violates this principle runs counter to the logic of the 'logic of practice' of the system, and is therefore unlikely to succeed in substantially altering the 'social power relations' which it serves and indeed which established it in the first place. 'Educational systems' must be constituted around characteristics of 'structure and function', the conditions of which ensure the 'reproduction' of the 'cultural arbitrary', and which contribute to the continuation of relations between social groups and classes. 'Self reproduction of the system', 'cultural reproduction' (arbitrary) and 'social reproduction' (classes and social groups) must be symbiotic.

It is important to set this principled model in context. Bourdieu and Passeron were not arguing that schools replicate class structures, that all pedagogic communication is reducible to power relations. What occurs is predisposed rather than being determined. Education *contributes* to the *reproduction* of social classes, which are themselves always in a state of flux. There is a dynamic tension between a view of schools as simply working for social class replication and a naïve view of seeing them in terms of a functional meritocracy.

Book II of *La Reproduction* adds further exemplification to the model. It begins by addressing 'Cultural Capital and Pedagogic Communication'. Here, Bourdieu and Passeron discuss the effect of what they call 'linguistic capital', not simply as a means of communication but as a provider of a 'system of categories'; that is, ways to think with (p. 73). They note that the 'educational mortality rate' (drop-out rate) increases as one moves away from social groups whose inherent language already matches the style and culture of scholarly language. They observe that the function of education is to select, or rather 'to select out', the children from working class backgrounds. Consequently, if the proportion of these were in fact increased in higher education, then the degree to which their selection 'offset' their linguistic handicap would decrease. There would then be inflation in qualifications. Here, the same certificates would buy less and less in the job market and in society as a whole. This conclusion quite accurately fits what occurred in the decades to follow.

Such effects are not uniform. Bourdieu and Passeron noted the morphological changes which had taken place in the French higher education system after the Second World War. Although the numbers actually going to university had increased between 1961 and 1966, which was seen as a result of the 'democratization' of education, the shape of the distribution across social classes remained the same. The actual percentages per class, although generally rising, stayed the same in terms of relative proportions across social groups. This rise in numbers also affected various disciplines differentially. In their earlier work, Bourdieu and Passeron targeted a certain form of 'learned' culture, suggesting it was representative of the dominant social culture. However, in post-war France, many students now gravitated towards 'softer', more fashionable subjects like sociology. Arts faculties and the literary culture were also 'losing out', as the sons and daughters of the new bourgeois classes chose studies in medicine, law and administration. Each of these changes should be understood in terms of differential structures in language, thought and behaviour. The *field* of higher education was multivalent, not homogeneous. However, the mechanism of its internal dynamic obeyed the kind of universal principles developed in Book I, and indeed elsewhere in Bourdieu's work. Briefly, central to this thesis was the idea that forms of thought are developed not simply in terms of the content of knowledge but through a whole relationship to language, which itself was acquired *ipso facto* in the process of gaining linguistic mastery. In France, this amounted to an emphasis of form over content, a style which could be traced from the Renaissance onwards and all the way back to the Jesuits. The implication of this conclusion was that the form and content of education which predominated in France was no longer relevant and suitable for that time, but in one sense, this might not matter when the social *function* of education was still being upheld. This function was one of 'social conservation' of particular social groupings in the overall structure of society. Such conservation operated through the form of examinations and the systems of selection. Bourdieu and Passeron pointed out that the established French practice of open competitive examinations – the *concours* – had all the appeal of being 'scientific' and 'neutral' – values which themselves squared with the Jacobin tradition of equality and fair play. However, as noted earlier, when the culture, the language, the knowledge, the style, and the very relationship to all these is incarnate in the exam, there is a kind of cultural affinity set up between it and those whose background is similarly charged.

Underlying such analyses is the notion that it is the structure of class society which is being played out here – albeit it in a semi-autonomous realm. The operating principles of the educational system unite external and internal functions in the structural homologies existing between them, which are themselves played out in the multiplicity of individual encounters between *habitus* and *field*. It is to the affinities, the convergences, the correspondences, the divergences, the coincidences, the ideological alliances, and the coincidences that one must look in order to see social reproduction in practice; through educational knowledge and the *cultural capital* it implies as a base currency for its medium of the operation. In this way, Bourdieu and Passeron conclude:

> Unable to invoke the right of blood – which his class historically denied the aristocracy – nor the rights of nature – a weapon once used against the distinctions of nobility but liable to backfire against bourgeois 'distinction' – nor the ascetic virtues which enabled the first-generation entrepreneurs to justify their success by their merit, the inheritor of bourgeois privileges must today appeal to the academic certification which attests to both his gifts and his merits.
>
> (p. 210)

Because the idea of 'culture by birth' is 'unnatural', those who gain or lose by it are blind to its function. As a result, school has the distinct advantage of allowing the privileged not to see themselves as such; while the disinherited are convinced that their lack of scholastic success and social destiny is due to their lack of gifts and talents. The authors conclude: 'in matters of culture absolute dispossession excludes awareness of being dispossessed' (*ibid.*).

It is only possible to give a flavor of this book (some 250 pages), which includes many nuanced discussions of the main points above. It is important to emphasize that the book must be set in the context of its times. The sort of hopes and aspirations for education, and the role it would play in the construction of the New World cannot be overestimated. However, as we have seen in Bourdieu's own work, this optimism was increasingly tempered by a creeping realism of what was and was not possible. The 1960s were times of personal liberation and individual expression, evidenced by the explosion of the youth culture, the opening up of the world through travel and media communications, and the protest movements. *La Reproduction* was published just two years after the near revolutionary state which gripped France (see Chapter 11), when a student-led general strike almost brought the government and country to its knees. The influence of Sartre and existentialism – with its message of personal freedom – was still rife. Contemporary society burst out from the principles of the past, which, in terms borrowed from Lévi-Strauss, were seen as 'mythological' and therefore illusory. The title of a book by Herbert Marcuse seemed to say it all: *One-Dimensional Man*. The drugs culture offered an alternative in the form of a 'higher reality' or consciousness. Politically, Marxism continued as a major world philosophy. The Soviet and Chinese regimes apparently offered alternative systems of living. Marxist philosophers were still among the leading political thinkers of the day. It is necessary to see *La Reproduction* as partly a response to these discourses; indeed, it even borrows some of their language. For example, the Marxist philosopher Louis Althusser (1969/1965, 1975/1968) had argued that ideology should be understood as the mechanism by which the capitalist relations of production are *reproduced*. The bourgeoisie ensured that its own dominance was reproduced by creating the systems which emitted an ideological base to 'interpellate' or 'hail' individuals to their position in the social system as a whole. Such 'ideological state apparatuses' – schools, churches, political parties, the media, the legal system – acted in a semi-autonomous way, in the interests of the bourgeoisie but not directly as their representatives.

Similarly, a key condition of 'pedagogic action' for Bourdieu and Passeron was the 'autonomy' of the agency (institution) commissioned to exercise it. They acknowledged the link this theme had with the sociological tradition established by Emile Durkheim (p. 196). For example, in *L'Évolution pédagogique en France*, Durkheim had noted that the relative autonomy of the educational system allowed it to respond to its own internal interests at the same time as meeting the external needs that society had for its function. In short, this amounted to producing its own teaching force and therefore serving its own continuation. Such is one reason why a certain type of education – one which was essentially Jesuit and emphasized form over content – had been allowed to continue to dominate educational principles, which at that time proved out of step with society's needs as a whole. Bourdieu and Passeron went further than Durkheim, arguing that as the essential social *raison d'être* of education was to 'reproduce' class structures, the existence of an educational hegemony was a perfect manifestation of its own logic of practice (p. 149). Schools were able to perform such a role of selection and exclusion all while disguising this function. The legitimate and consecrated culture inherent in schools only had *to be* what it was in order *to do* what it was set up to do in the first place; the precise character of which was accountable in terms of the specific 'objective social conditions' of the time.

Much of Bourdieu and Passerson's discussion took place without recourse to the traditional terms of Marxist philosophy. There is little or nothing about 'class struggle', 'the means of production', and 'communist revolution' in this book. This approach itself ran counter to many contemporary radical theorists. For example, besides Althusser, writers such as Alain Touraine – in *Le Movement de mai ou le communisme utopique* (1968) – were keen to interpret the events of 1968 in classic Marxist terms; of the rise of a new unified revolutionary force in the face of the 'contradictions' inherent in the structures of French society – essentially, the clash between the old and the new economic demands put on workers and the systems they inhabited (see

Chapter 10). Just as he had done so in the case of Algeria, Bourdieu was arguing that the empirical facts did not support this thesis. Rather, a much more complex ethnography must be grasped in terms of changes in the underlying social morphology in order to understand what was occurring. This stance was a further example of the way Bourdieu refused to be led by an overarching theory (but used his own immersion in the empirical facts to elucidate and develop principles, theoretical, explanations). For many Marxist theorists – for example, Baudelot and Establet (1971) – Bourdieu was simply too functionalist since his explanations seemed to offer a picture of static reproduction rather than to see schooling and education as the sites of 'contradiction' and 'class antagonisms' inherent in the subjection of one class of society to the service of another – a defining characteristic of Capitalism. In this sense, the Marxist position is certainly more optimistic than Bourdieu's. For the would-be Marxist, there is the belief that such a state of class struggle may at least be overcome. Indeed, education might even be one way of 'informing' those involved as a means of liberation from its pernicious influence. Bourdieu suggested that it was in the inherent nature of education to function as this form of social reproduction. Like Althusser, he had argued that what was at stake was not simply knowledge but a relationship to knowledge. In earlier work, he had concluded that 'rational pedagogy' and a 'sociology of inequalities' were needed in order to oppose the socially harmful effects of schooling. However, in *La Reproduction*, no such option seems possible since such a 'pedagogy' would logically be unable to survive because it would run counter to the logic of practice of education and schooling. Bourdieu wrote of the 'democratization of education through the rationalization of pedagogy' as 'utopian' (even though he had apparently done so himself!). In his terms, the dominant form of 'pedagogic authority' would logically prevent (even if implicitly) a form of 'pedagogic work' which did not accord with its own logic of practice: 'In short, only a school system serving another system of external functions and, correlatively, another state of the balance of power between classes, could make such pedagogic action possible' (p. 127). It is possible to imagine an 'explicit pedagogy' which reduces the gap between the 'linguistic competences of the transmitter and receiver (and) also knowledge of the social conditions of the production and reproduction of that gap'. However: 'such practice can be expected only from teachers objectively constrained to satisfy a specifically and exclusively pedagogic demand . . . to put it another way, it would require a pedagogic action directed towards the inculcation of a different relation to language and culture' (*ibid.*). This orientation towards teachers and their action was of course the natural conclusion of such analyses. It is such a focus which formed the basis of the 'new' sociology of education.

Most educational research that was undertaken up until the early 1960s came from the discipline of psychology. Investigations were often experimentally based and focused on the processes of learning; behaviorism and Piaget were still highly influential in guiding pedagogy. Educational theory was seen much in the same way as theory in the physical, normative sciences, with its expectation of predictability and testing hypotheses (see O'Connor, 1957). However, in the 1960s, a major shift took place. This shift was led by the British philosopher Paul Hirst, who argued against theory in terms of an 'applied science' model of education. Until that point the *raison d'être* of educational research was seen as developing theories of learning that could then be applied to educational practice. In other words, science could indicate what to do in education. Hirst's seminal work showed that 'educational theory' was intrinsically distinct from 'scientific theory', since education did not behave in the same way as the physical sciences. For Hirst, educational theory provided 'the essential background to rational educational practice' (1966: 38). It offered the knowledge which could be used to determine the practical activity of education. Where was that knowledge to come from? Hirst concluded: 'It could be argued that just as physics uses mathematics but results in distinctive, validated scientific statements, so educational theory uses philosophy, psychology, sociology, etc. and issues in distinctive, validated educational practice' (*ibid.*: 49). For Hirst, the 'foundations' of educational theory were sociology, history, psychology and philosophy, which subsequently were known as the 'foundational subjects', since they provided a rationale for educational practice. Their principles and discoveries offered direction for what to do in schooling. Noticeably, sociology was one of these foundations and, as noted, there was a long and established tradition of the sociology of education. However, recent works by sociologists of education in the UK and USA seemed too content to establish the differential outcome of education and schooling across the social classes rather than examine the reasons why. The 'new' sociology of education took a different tact.

The one book which announced this fresh direction was *Knowledge and Control: New Directions for the Sociology of Education* (edited by Michael Young, 1971). Bourdieu's contributions to the book were the two articles mentioned at the beginning of this chapter: 'Intellectual field and creative project' and 'Systems of education and systems of thought'. The guiding principles of this new direction in sociology were perhaps best demonstrated by the titles of the book's section headings: Curricula, Teaching and Learning as the Organization of Knowledge; Social Definitions of Knowledge; and Cognitive Styles in Comparative Perspective. These titles are indicative of the focus given here to the 'construction of knowledge'. Indeed, 'social constructivism' was very much the *zeitgeist*. Another highly influential book at the time on the broader sociological stage was *The Social Construction of Reality* by Berger and Luckmann, which was first published in 1967 (1971). Its title says it all, with its thesis on the social dialectics in the 'internalization of externality' and the 'externalization of internality' – language that Bourdieu himself used at the time (see 1971a). Both books can be seen as a post-war renaissance of the work of the founding fathers of sociology – Marx, Durkheim and Weber – but this time in an integrated rather than derivative form. In the Preface to *Knowledge and Control*, Young makes the point that the idea for the book first arose in discussion with Bourdieu and his Anglo-saxon equivalent (at the time) Basil Bernstein at a conference in Durham in 1970. In the Introduction, as noted, Young further writes that the book was offered as an alternative to the objects of enquiry current in the sociology of education, namely, the malfunctioning of certain key features of education. Instead, the articles included all addressed the 'problem' of the 'organization of knowledge' in the curriculum. Such organization, of course, can be conceptualized in different ways. For example, in the article by Basil Bernstein, school knowledge is subject to 'classification' and 'farming'. By 'classification' he meant the way disciplines were organized, set apart and existed in relation to each other. He also meant the degree of distinctiveness, or fusion, between them: 'the degree of boundary maintenance between contents' (p. 49). He conceived of academic subjects as having degrees of boundary permeability; some content boundaries are strong, others are weak. 'Framing' on the other hand referred to the strength of the boundary between what might be transmitted and what might not, in the pedagogical relationship. It is the control the teacher and the taught have over what is transmitted and received in its organization, selection and pace. Bernstein had already written about the relationship between 'language' and 'knowledge'. Specifically, he had posited that individual pupils from different social backgrounds – working class or middle class – developed language which might be understood in terms of 'codes'. 'Elaborates codes' had greater affinity with scholastic knowledge to the extent that those possessing these as a result of their upbringing would tend to benefit more directly in the processes of schooling. The opposite was also true: the 'restricted codes' of the 'working class' disadvantaged them. This thesis seemed to share, or at least was congruent with, many aspects of Bourdieu's own; especially, its focus on the 'style' of cultural knowledge and the relationship between this and thought and language.

In another chapter, Nell Keddie examined 'Classroom Knowledge' and the way that subject and pupil orientation were dependent on the perceived abilities of pupils. This thesis is not dissimilar to the way Bourdieu saw 'symbolic violence' in the judgement or verdict implicit in educational discourses, for the way it 'positioned' individuals within a valued hierarchy of performance based only on a misrecognized form of cultural arbitrariness. As noted above, the two articles which Bourdieu contributed to *Knowledge and Control* had both been previously published in French. With hindsight, it is possible to see that what divided the various contributors to this volume was probably greater than what united them, at least in detailed content. Keddie, for example, was interested in the exact point of transaction between pupils and teachers, and had little to say about the form and status of any knowledge (to be) transmitted. Young himself makes the point that there were issues of emphasis in 'agency' and 'content' between Keddie and Bourdieu. These issues were shared by many sociologists of the day. However, Bourdieu, as we have seen, was already developing an epistemology which sought to integrate 'agency' and 'content', structuring and structured structures, subjectivity and objectivity, in short, *habitus* and *field* into a single theory of practice.

Knowledge and Control quickly became a sociological classic, having an influence in a wide range of educational contexts. Again, it is important to set the book in its times. We cannot say that it was the principal motor force in developments in education, educational research and the sociology of education. But, it was a book which perfectly captured the mood of the times and, as a result, the orientation it was arguing for quickly spread throughout the educational establishment. During the rest of the 1970s, culture became a prime focus for education and educational research. Neo-Marxist views had been revitalized. The ideas of the Italian Marxist, Antonio Gramsci were also taken up by many. His *Selections from the Prison Notebooks* was published in 1971. Gramsci discussed ideology and the notion of a 'cultural hegemony'. On education, he concluded, in language reminiscent of Bourdieu, that: 'In a whole series of families, especially in the intellectual strata, the children find in their family life a preparation, a prolongation and a completion of school life; they "breathe in", as the expression goes, a whole quantity of notions and attitudes which facilitate the education process properly speaking' (1971: 31).

Cultural Studies came into vogue. In England at least, such academic institutions as the Centre for Contemporary Cultural Studies at Birmingham University were instrumental in developing a research agenda which was at once culturally orientated, critical and empirically based. One seminal work on education emerging from the Centre dealt with the way working-class boys end up with working-class jobs. The thesis – by Paul Willis – is set up with the question: 'the difficult thing to explain about how middle class kids get middle class jobs is why others let them' (1977: 1). To answer it, the book is divided into two principal parts: in Part 1, a quantity of detailed empirical analyses are presented on 'the lads' – a group of disaffected working-class boys and their exploits both in and out of school; in Part 2, this ethnographical material is theorized in neo-Marxist terms. The sociology of education itself took the same 'ethnographic turn'. For example, a collection edited by Barton and Meighan (1978) both supplied and called for more classroom ethnographies in order to theorize the relationship between what was called the 'micro' and 'macro'. In a sense, this was a time of theoretical and methodological diversity. Bourdieu was just one element in a movement which increasingly analyzed the relationship between language and education in terms of culture and representational ethnography. In 1962, *Thought and Language* had been published, which was the first English translation of the Soviet psychologist Lev Vygotsky, who would become extremely influential in research on language and pedagogic discourses. The second volume of his work, *Mind in Society: the Development of Higher Educational Processes* was published in 1978. Although these books had yet to make the impact they eventually would, it was indicative of the 'social constructivist' orientation that much social and educational research was now taking that they appeared at this time. Vygotsky's thesis – that nothing appeared in the individual psychology without first appearing in the social group – had a perfect resonance with a theory of knowledge, which had been explicitly stated by Berger and Luckmann; one that drew on a theoretical synthesis of Marx, Weber and Durkheim, and formed a tradition in the vanguard of which Bourdieu himself was member. The publication of *La Reproduction* in 1977 may therefore be seen as either fortuitous or as social destiny.

I have already emphasized that Bourdieu's own work on education must be understood in terms of a much broader project; one which is as much philosophical as sociological, and methodological as much as political. Nevertheless, many aspects of the 'new' sociology were inherently radical, and implicitly (and explicitly!) critical. If schools were complicit in reproducing the inequalities of society, then they needed reform. A policy of 'deschooling' emerged; one where the harmful effects were by-passed, or at least compensated for. This was a time of cultural celebration. If, in effect, schools were promulgating a certain kind of culture, which excluded the masses and privileged the sons and daughters of the middle and upper classes, there were three alternatives. Either resistance could be mounted – if the dominant culture was alienating and pacifying, it should be opposed. This approach amounted to a 'blowing the whistle' on what was going on and unmasking the causes of social inequalities. Or, 'alternative' cultures could be celebrated – indeed, partly as a form of resistance; in this case, the 'non-hegemonic' culture was held up for its rich diversity and alternative way of seeing the world. Or, 'compensatory' measures might be undertaken so that those who were 'culturally deficient' could be 'topped up' with the requisite cultural attributes. Here, even 'positive discrimination' was seen as one possible tactic to ensure that those who had hitherto been deprived of contact with the necessary culture – in form and content – were now given the opportunity to acquire it in the form of academic knowledge, which would enable them to enter the social world on an equal cultural footing with their contemporaries.

It would be true to say that at one time or another Bourdieu flirted with both of these alternatives. There is support for each in some parts of his writings. However, as noted, his earlier optimism – present in his calls for a 'rational pedagogy' and a 'sociology of inequalities' to redress the balance in scholastic achievement derived from social origin – was eclipsed by what now surrounded him. The logic of the theory of practice he was developing suggested that if the fundamental function of education and schooling was to reproduce the structures of society, then they were unlikely to be easily shifted by explicit policies aimed at changing the situation. In other words, it was the logic of the practice as the essential function of education that had to be fulfilled. If the form of its operation was changed, it would only reconstitute itself according to its own logic to redefine the way this logic could be operationalized. In other words, according to the theory of *field* and *habitus* which he had himself produced, changing one element in the *field* changed its whole configuration. Its essential function, however, would have to be reasserted in a different form in a continuing attempt to honor its generative purpose. There is a fundamental issue about policy and practice here. One of the reasons for the popularity of the 'foundational disciplines', and indeed the 'sociology of education', was their practical orientation. Throughout the 1970s and much of the 1980s, teacher training programs, both pre-service and in-service, were indeed organized around the disciplines of sociology, psychology, philosophy and history. These were often taught separately in a non-integrated manner. It was therefore assumed that the necessary integration between these diverse fields would be made by the teachers or by individual trainees themselves. Moreover, that somehow, by knowing what was going on, teachers could act to counter its effects. However, as Bourdieu and Passeron concluded:

> It is impossible to imagine a teacher able to maintain with his own discourse, his pupils' discourse and his pupils' relation to his own discourse, a relation stripped of all indulgences and freed from all the traditional complicities, without at the same time crediting him with the capacity to subordinate his whole pedagogic practice to the imperatives of a perfectly explicit pedagogy which could actually implement the principles logically implied in affirmation of the autonomy of the specifically scholastic mode of acquisition.
>
> (1977a/1970: 126)

It was clearly too much to expect that an individual teacher, or even a small group, could somehow effect radical change in pedagogy simply by understanding the way that classroom knowledge was produced and the effect it had on individual pupils' academic achievement. Yet, in many ways, that is exactly what the 'new' sociology of education was doing by the way it formed a part of teacher education programs. Bourdieu was aware of this assumption at an early stage of his work on education.

In conclusion, the influence of *La Reproduction* within sociology and the 'new' sociology of education must be re-emphasized. It made a major contribution to a trend which had far-reaching consequences but, finally, floundered when faced with the socio-political reality of teachers' everyday lives and, indeed, parental fears and expectations for the future of their children's academic achievement. When confronted by anxieties about scholastic performance – and what this buys in terms of social trajectory – talk of resistance, celebration and compensation fits uneasily with individual aspirations for a large proportion of the parents. But, what is the alternative in Bourdieusian terms?

The development of Bourdieu's thinking on educational policy and practice is followed up later in the book. However, first, it is necessary at this point to take a step back to consider Bourdieu's response to the events of May 1968.

Chapter 10

The Academic Field

Previous chapters in this part of the book have shown how Bourdieu's early work on and concern with education developed throughout the 1960s. The last chapter considered how Bourdieu established himself as a sociologist of education as part of the 'new wave' of that discipline which emerged in the 1970s. Yet, there is a question to ask as to whether Bourdieu can really be called a 'sociologist of education' at all. Above, I suggested that his preoccupations seem almost incidental to education, and that his concerns might more accurately be understood as a focus on the mechanisms of class reproduction, the nature and effects of 'symbolic violence', and indeed a theory of knowledge that can be operationalized in practice. In the 1960s, he seemed as much concerned with culture as education, and subsequent publications moved into many other fields, including economics, politics, language, the media and art. Both the early and later studies – on education and in other areas – drew on Bourdieu's own ethnographic training to produce what we might call 'morphologies' of his fields of study. In the Béarn, Algeria, and finally education, he showed how changes in the structural morphology of these *fields* and subfields should to be analyzed in order to explain what was occurring in them and to understand these changes. In another way, Bourdieu's project can be seen as 'methodological' as much as substantive to the topic of his study. Chapter 4 described Bourdieu's ideal French *Homo academicus*. This title was subsequently reused for his next major book on education, published in 1984 (Bourdieu, 1988/1984). Before *La Reproduction*, much of Bourdieu's published work on education dealt almost exclusively with the student body. The new book now turned its attention to the teaching corps of higher education. At its core is an account of the events of May 1968. Bourdieu had been collecting data, fortuitously perhaps, when a national strike, started by students but soon snowballing to involve a large percentage of the workforce, almost brought France to its knees. Bourdieu used this data throughout *Homo Academicus*; indeed, at one point he described it as 'an ascetic book with regard to the use of data' (1992a: 64), meaning that he had never handled so much data. Certainly, the text is copiously illustrated with a number of tables, figures and statistics. Perhaps this is why it took another 16 years for the book to be published, and even then, Bourdieu claims, he was reluctant to do so. This reluctance might also be connected with his own acknowledgement of how controversial its content would appear to those who shared the academic *field* with him. The first chapter is entitled, 'A Book for Burning?' and he heads it with a epigraph from the Catholic socialist Charles Péguy, to the effect that 'historians do not want to be counted amongst historical order'. Although they historicize, they do not want to be the subject of historical analysis themselves. Bourdieu goes on to show the necessity of choosing to study the social world which he, as well as other academics including sociologists, inhabited as a necessary part of establishing 'scientific knowledge' in the social sciences. He argues that sociological analysis is generally prone to 'self-centered' subjective readings, both in the 'construction of the object of study' and in its interpretation. Thus, he announces his ambition to define a methodology which escapes from this academic tendency without falling into the trap of adopting 'common criteria and classifications'. Bourdieu asserts that many institutionalized representations and practices can only be understood as 'collective defense mechanisms'. He also draws an important distinction between the 'empirical individual' and the 'epistemic individual' (p. 21) (which I have elsewhere referred to as 'empirical' and 'scientific' respectively). The 'empirical' individual is like everyman, he responds naïvely to what surrounds him. The 'epistemic individual', on the other hand' is the product of scientific training and experience (cf. Bourdieu and Grenfell, 1995b: 29). Consequently, they have at their disposal the necessary epistemological tools to approach the social world as an object of enquiry that renders the resultant knowledge scientific. Being able to 'objectify their objectifying stance' is an essential part of this method (see also Chapter 7). He describes this process as, 'the work on himself that the researcher must accomplish to try to objectify everything that links him to his subject' (p. 32). This chapter is about the nature of scholastic knowledge implied in this Introduction to *Homo Academicus*. However, first it addresses the actual events of May 1968, which are central to his theoretical argument.

May 1968

The need to place Bourdieu's work within its own times continues to be a defining principle in our discussion. Such a 'remembering' is not to relativize it, but to draw attention to the 'practical' conditions to which Bourdieu was responding and which inevitably shaped what he produced. In the 1950s and early 1960s, Bourdieu's work was produced very much in response to the social, political and theoretical agendas of the day. The last chapter referred to the special character of the 1960s, with its student protests, liberation movements and culture of free expression. May 1968 represents for France the apogee of this era. It has entered into the history books as perhaps the last 'revolution' of contemporary France. The photographs, slogans and art of the period now hold iconic status. What happened?

The global context was important: communications were opening the frontiers of hitherto closed cultures; the youth of the day were unsullied by the experience of war; there was a new confidence in the air about the possibility of sweeping away the past and building a new world. France was, however, a particular case. As a consequence of the trauma of repeated war over the previous 100 years, the development of modern France had remained sluggish. To recap, up until the Second World War, most industry was heavy and located in northern regions. A large proportion of the population remained rural and traditional in outlook. With the experience of collaboration and a division in the country behind it, the Fourth Republic had been politically weak. The sense of urgency for economic and social renewal was acute. In the Fourth Republic and later in the Fifth, the key to regeneration was an economic and social policy, which was centrist and interventionist. New industry was sited around key cities in France – *Métropoles d'équilibre* – and a whole raft of economic objectives were set out in line with a series of Five Year Plans.

These plans were drafted in consultation with all participant organizations in the French economy, their aim being to ensure concerted planning and implementation of economic policies. By almost any indicator, the plans were successful in delivering social renewal and subsequent economic growth. Presided over by the Second World War veteran-cum-President, Charles de Gaulle, France at last entered the twentieth century with a dynamism which was impressive to an international audience. Of course, such economic changes also had social implications. New towns were planned and built. A large number of cheap modern apartments were also constructed around each of the major towns and cities in order to accommodate the workers who moved from the country to the towns, often at short notice, in order to take up jobs in the new sector industries – so-called HLMs (*Habitations à loyers modérés*). Universities were also built or expanded to train and educate a new generation of students.

In one sense, as in the Béarn and Algeria, this was a situation where the old and the new world were juxtaposed, and the impact these changes had on individual lives and experiences should not be underestimated. However, such changes might also be interpreted in Marxist terms: as the growth of Capitalism, with all that it entailed in terms of worker exploitation, alienation and domestic hardship, the priorities of the economy took precedence over personal lives. When France was gripped by strikes and protests in May 1968, and a united alliance seemingly formed between students, public sector and industrial workers, it is tempting to explain the situation in classic Marxist terms of a 'crisis in capitalism'. Indeed, much of the language of the protesters was Marxist, if not Anarchist, in tone in its opposition to the social and economic systems which 'oppressed' them. It is therefore not surprising to find writers such as Alain Touraine (for example, 1968) analyzing the events in terms of the traditional Marxist paradigm of class struggle for 'liberation'. As is often the case with Bourdieu, his own position was somewhat ambiguous. He went around and spoke at all the Faculties. In fact, he also quarreled with Raymond Aron, who had sponsored his appointment to the Centre de Sociologie Européenne, over his support for the protesters. However, as mentioned above, for Bourdieu, adopting the Marxist interpretation of what was occurring was again to substitute the empirical facts with a theoretical fiction. In actual fact, the student protests were sparked off by an issue as mundane as access to dormitories between male and female students. Nevertheless, the ensuing protests involved all sections of French society: a crisis which went to the very heart not only of the Fifth Republic but the very character and direction of contemporary France itself. *Homo Academicus* was Bourdieu's analysis of the situation in terms of the causes and consequences to be found in the academic field. It would however, be, another decade and a half before it finally appeared.

Bourdieu's studies of education followed a methodological approach developed in Béarn and Algeria; namely, to construct a social taxonomy of the *field*. This principle represents an important methodological procedure. Rather than take a *sample* of individual students and analyze their traits in order to construct generalities, Bourdieu was interested in the structural morphological changes in the *total* population. His approach to the French *Homo Academicus* was consequently to study academia as a *field* first and foremost, and only then consider how individuals' dispositions – *habitus* – could be viewed both as a procedural part and product of this 'social space'. Chapter 7 described the way that Bourdieu suggested a '3-level' approach for analyzing *fields*: the position of the *field* within the field of *power*; the structure of the *field* itself; and then individual *habitus*. *Homo Academicus* was probably his first explicit application of such a procedure. Bourdieu explains his approach, thus:

> (to) evoke the structure of the field of power and the relation that the university field taken as a whole maintains with it, analyse – as far as the empirical data permit – the structure of the university field and the position which the different faculties occupy within it, and, finally, analyse the structure of each faculty and the position that the different disciplines occupy within it.
>
> (1988/1984: 32)

This analysis is 'topped and tailed' in the book: first by a discussion on the need to 'objectify the researcher' according to their links with the subject of their study, and their position within the different spaces they occupy (perhaps, the major issue at stake here); and second an understanding of the actual events of May themselves. Therefore, the book offers, first, an analysis of the 'social space' of faculties as part of the *field* of power in the way that their individual characteristics reflect different manifestations of it; and, second, the 'foundations and forms of power' in the arts and social science faculties on the eve of 1968. So, the structure of the university *field* as a whole is sketched out, together with that of the arts and social science faculties in order to identify what were the 'determinants and object of certain transformations' (*ibid.*). It is only after a structural analysis of the academic field at various levels that one can begin to explain what Bourdieu called 'the critical moment' – the crisis itself. Two determining factors emerge as of paramount importance in understanding the events of May from an academic point of view: first growth in the student population together with the resultant changing *field* structures; and second the way that academic disciplines had developed in relation to each other since the Second World War. Both determinants, for Bourdieu, needed to be understood in terms of *field* and *habitus*, objectivity and subjectivity, morphological and ideational structures (and the complicit homologies between them); in brief, the content and form of the social, economic and cultural capital that existed between these levels of social reality and mediated between them in the unfolding nature of the contemporary world.

The Academic Space

The background to Bourdieu's analysis of the academic *field* was the enormous rise in the size of the student population following the Second World War. The student body had almost quadrupled between 1949 and 1967. Many of these students orientated themselves to the new, 'popular', arts and humanities courses and came from the middle managerial classes (57% of children with parents from the top managerial and liberal professions went on to university in 1967; while only 3.4% did so from the working classes (see Hanley *et al.*, 1979: 36)). This increase in the size of the student population resulted in a need for more teachers.

Bourdieu saw the structure of the university *field* as a homologous reflection of the structure of the *field* of power. The Imperial University had existed since 1808 when it had been established by Napoleon to train a social elite. Its dominant disciplines were Law and Medicine, which were created in order to provide doctors and lawyers. Its systems were authoritarian, and highly hierarchical and centralized. These disciplines, together with Theology, represented the 'higher faculties', to use Kantian terminology. They existed in a paradigm which explained 'underlying causes', and were, because of their relationship to the establishment that formed them, particularly prone to implicit political influence. They were dependent on the continuation of a certain way of doing things. The 'lower faculties', on the other hand, – Language, History, Geography – were more independent and able to produce knowledge 'free' from conventional content. Bourdieu used 'correspondence analysis' to offer a pictorial representation of the 'space of faculties'. Two forms of knowledge were defined in terms of 'scientific competence' and 'social competence'. These cut across the disciplines and were not exclusive to particular disciplines. For example, within the medical faculty, the opposition between clinical practitioners and biologists could be explained in terms analogous (and homologous) to that between the science and art faculties; that is, knowledge guided by 'experience' versus that gained by pursuit of 'underlying causes' (p. 59). These oppositions were even noticeable in the patterns of political practice of those involved; for example, 30 per cent of arts lecturers were members of trade unions, compared to only 6 per cent in medicine.

Bourdieu looked at the character, derivation and mode of operation of various forms of power – represented by types of *capital* – within the academic *field*. Thus, he constructed the 'space of faculties' according to two poles: the 'society' pole (law and medicine) and the 'scientific pole'. The former was characterized by power accumulated by holding positions of control over other positions; while the latter was founded on investment in the activity of research alone. However, this opposition did not operate purely in terms of different faculties. On the contrary, the arts and social science faculties had a homologous structure within them: an opposition between those who were mostly orientated towards research and the intellectual *field*, and those who were more orientated towards 'the reproduction of the cultural order'. One thinks of the choice that a higher education academic has to make these days between pursuing a career path in their discipline or in HE management. Moreover, this opposition operated both between individuals and institutions: between older, established and newer, younger figures; and between those basing their power on the relative status of their academic discipline – for example, the Collège de France as compared with the École des Hautes Études. Just as he had done with students, Bourdieu describes an idealized *Homo Academicus* and the way they construct their academic power: X is a graduate of the School of Athens; he gives up archaeology for the history of literature; he is on all the university councils; elected to the CNRS; he is well known but produces very little; he gets into the École Normale 'at his first shot', even though he has nothing to say; he is well published, works quickly because he never stops to 'take thought' (p. 84). What Bourdieu is describing is the way academic power is accrued by a combination of *social* and *cultural capital* within the *field*. It helps to be close to the established bourgeoisie whose positional power allows for influence. Such positioning takes time to acquire and Bourdieu talks about the 'sacrifice of time' that is needed in order to attend all the right committees, etc. Academic power presupposes time commitment. It takes time to write a thesis, to publish a book, etc. – and the rewards are commensurate with this sacrifice. Bourdieu saw another opposition homologous to the two poles of the university *field* in the management of time economy. On the one side are those who invest in their work and accumulate academic *capital* (lectures, books, etc.); on the other side are those who invest in the representation of their work and the 'accumulation of a symbolic capital of external renown' (p. 98). Bourdieu has in mind what he calls the academic 'export-import trade' – colloquia, symposia, conferences, etc. – as well as the 'media intellectual'. A similar opposition existed between professors who were mostly involved in research and those who taught; which itself was analogous to the structural opposition found in society between writers and professors – in brief, 'between the freedom and audacity of the artist's life and the strict somewhat circumscribed rigor of *homo academicus*' (*ibid.*).

Such hierarchical oppositions were found everywhere in Bourdieu's analysis and marked the academic *field* in France at a particular point in time: homologously, the Collège de France was to the École des Hautes Etudes what the Sorbonne was to Nanterre University, with scientific or intellectual *capital* on the one side and institutional academic *capital* on the other. The position of disciplines within this space was changing. Bourdieu quotes the case of 'Philology', which he points out has been relegated to museum status by linguists. The point to recall is that because academic boundaries between disciplines are arbitrary, the promotion and relegation of disciplines occurs really because of the functional needs of groups – in this case academic ones – to define a medium for their reproduction. Bourdieu makes the point that such positioning – in this case of the philologists – is out of space and time, and is really analogous to the aristocrats and bourgeois at the time of the French Revolution. Bourdieu writes that the resultant *hysteresis* is similar to that found in the Béarn, with the misalliance in the matrimonial market at a time of social crisis (1988/1984: 127). Graduates of the ENS and the aggregation also found themselves 'out of place' in the academic market when, due to the inflation of qualifications because more students were gaining particular degrees, they discovered that their certificates did not buy them the anticipated jobs – a phenomenon that continues into the twenty-first century.

The point is that the internal state of the academic *field* depends on its power structure, and yet at the same time is also determined by its position in the overall *field of fields*. There is therefore a multi-layered analysis to be undertaken in unpicking the various levels of operation and their relations both inside and outside of the *field*. Bourdieu looked at the relative position of different disciplines: the size of the teaching ratios; the number of tenured professors; the percentage of young and female staff; and appointment procedures. For him, large numbers of students meant that more teaching staff had to be employed. Often, they were less qualified. Those without the *agrégation* (a highly selective national examination guaranteeing a prestigious teaching position) tended to be against it. The 'newcomers', Bourdieu argued, were too young to have internalized the 'logic of practice' of the *field*. The career they obtained was not the one to which they aspired, as the tenured professors drew on the newcomers – the 'mass reserve' – to cover their teaching. Student-lecturer ratios also increased. The crisis in the academic *field* – a conflict of generations rather than of age – could therefore be expressed in terms of time differentials. Academic success depended predominantly on 'deferred gratification', where present work was an investment for the future. However, the future payback became more and more distant; this was true as much for the lecturers as the students:

> If the crisis of the university hierarchy has crystallised around the opposition between professors and lecturers, it is because the latter (more than assistant and senior lecturers) were condemned to feel in all its intensity the contradiction between promises written into their appointment and the future which was ensured by the unchanged career procedures.
>
> (*ibid.*: 152)

In short, along with individual dispositions and recruitment, the balance between academic expectations and probable trajectories had been upset. The 'natural order' of succession had been broken. Bourdieu refers to the way new entrants came in and would supposedly 'leap-frog' over career paths by offering a different form of 'production', more suited to the new 'scientificity' (more empirical and less theoretical). At the same time, they represented a 'collective challenge' against the university authorities on the career paths of both young and old lecturers. In effect, this amounted to universities being laid open to the 'combined effects' of 'the old career law and transgression of that law' (*ibid.*). As was the case with students, Bourdieu concluded that the possibility of a 'rational' alternative – 'where recruitment and promotion depend on the sole criteria of pedagogical or scientific productivity and efficiency' (p. 158) – is scarcely believable and probably illusory.

The Critical Moment

When Bourdieu finally comes to the 'critical moment' – the events of May 1968 themselves – he begins by once again emphasizing the methodological issues at stake. The crisis, he argued, in fact leads to a break with the relations which produced it. His approach was to 'reconstruct' the conditions whereby several partly autonomous events intersected. This reconstruction is multilayered and requires subtle analyses; above all, Bourdieu argued, we must avoid simply hanging tailor-made hypotheses onto what occurred. Here, he is again targeting all those who start with a theory which they then apply to events. What he is proposing as an alternative is a kind of socio-historical, structural analysis of the academic *field* in a way which shows up its homologies with other *fields* involved in the crisis. What were the ingredients of this crisis in academia?

First, there is the aforementioned increase in size of the student population. However, to note the resultant tensions and the strains in the system as a result was not enough. The main point for Bourdieu was that the increase in population was a function of the position it held in the social and academic hierarchies of establishments. So, for example, the *Grandes écoles* were less affected than universities; and, in their turn, the law and medicine faculties were less affected than the arts faculties. Of the latter, the traditional disciplines were much less affected than the new – for example, Sociology and Psychology. It is in the new and less traditional areas of the academic world that the new influx tended to be located, providing a place for individuals who would not traditionally go on to higher education.

The second factor in provoking the crisis in the academic system concerned qualifications. The whole of Bourdieu's 'sociology of education' is predicated on the relationship between *habitus* and *field*: the way the two interrelate in education through configurations of *capital* – especially *cultural capital* – and how their 'complicity' functions to provide a system of reproduction within the social class hierarchy. In this context, Bourdieu employed the word *conatus* to describe the psychological aspects of *habitus*; as the form of 'ideological production' implied by a combination of disposition and interests associated with a particular place in the social space. Indeed, one's whole 'identity' is based on an assumption of standing in the *field*. For Bourdieu, academic qualifications carry with them an implied valuation of social position. As a result of more students gaining qualifications, they now 'bought' less social esteem and expectations were thwarted. However, even here, crude overgeneralizations should be avoided. The details of the mismatch between objective and subjective valuations of position and potential had to be analyzed in terms of particular cases. Once this analysis has been done, the phenomenon, and its apparent opposite, are seen as an example of the same thing. For example, some students (and lecturers) found themselves in jobs that they would not normally gain because of the increased need for these posts. The way this was experienced was as a kind of 'dual conscious-ness' between how they valued themselves according to internalized objective schemes of perception (based on the post) and the way they were valued in the *field* (based on new emerging structures). In this case, some members of the academic corps might 'over-value' themselves according to their position, all while suffering the conse-quences of both heavier teaching loads, etc. than was the norm for professors, and of being weakly integrated into the academic system.

A third factor which cuts across the crisis in the *field* is 'time'. Indi-vidual relations to time manifest themselves in distinct contexts. For example, Bourdieu argued that some members of the dominant class, especially those with less academic *capital*, orientated themselves to the 'new' disciplines like Sociology. Such disciplines offered only a 'vague' future in terms of employment, which was congruent with an 'indeterminacy of social identity'. In this case, these disciplines attract 'agents with maladjusted expectations and provide them with conditions for encouraging the perpetuation of the maladjustment' (p. 168). This is a case where a distance is created between the reality and the representation of the self and social future. The structural condition had to be understood as being homologous across stu-dents and lecturers and, indeed, with *fields* outside the academic *field*. Bourdieu concluded that a process of 'synchronization' ensued as coincidences of dispositions were set up, local and general crises res-onated, and 'conjunctural alliances' formed. An 'objective break' in the circle of expectation then occurs:

> ... an important faction of the less subordinate among the subordi-nate ... leave the race, the competitive struggle implying acceptance of the rules of the game laid down ... and (to) take up a struggle which we may call revolutionary ...
>
> (p. 172)

If there were alliances between students and workers in 1968, it was because they both shared homologous positions in their respective *fields*; the match between their position (involving *cona-tus* and 'lived experience') in their *fields* of power and the social *field* as a whole. However, Bourdieu commented that such alliances were illusory in that, although students and workers shared homologous positions in their *fields*, and thus expressed the same positional tensions, the substance of their 'hysteresis' or 'dual consciousness' was distinct. Therefore, their alliances were likely to be all the more powerful the more they were kept apart. This was indeed the case in 1968; apart from sharing a spirit of protest, workers and students had very little in common once they met to discuss policy reforms. However, there was a moment, before the revolutionary verve became routine, and concrete proposals had to be formulated, when emotion took over in a timeless realm of communal empathy. Bourdieu writes (p. 185) that time in *fields*, with its multiple time scales and substance, is replaced by one common time, the content of which is empty or vague, as everyone shares in a festive temporality where ordinary existence is inverted, and where the actual effects of the crisis are materialized. For a while, the world is turned 'upside down': professors have to listen to students; Sartre interviews Cohn-Bendit (the student leader). Bourdieu (p. 183) again drew a link between these occurrences and what he observed in Algeria, where the old Kabyle peasants could only respond with stupefaction when faced with the modern farming methods used by the young – the *incredible*.

There are many, many more analytical nuances to be found in *Homo Academicus*. What are we to conclude from it as an example of Bourdieu's method? As an exercise in reflexivity? Or, as a straightforward sociological analysis of academia and the crisis which erupted in it in 1968? Or, maybe all three of these – and more! Bourdieu later claimed that in analyzing May 1968 he was, in a sense, putting forth some of the elements of all crises (1992a: 89). Two crises, internal to the university system, were provoked by autonomous evolutions: the rapid swelling in numbers of the university teaching force, which led to tensions between dominant and subordinate categories; and the 'overproduction' of graduates, with the resultant effect on credentials. The crises spread to other *fields* where there was an 'incipient' conflict between 'the established holders of the legitimacy of discourse and new contenders' (*ibid.*).

The outcome of 1968 indeed led to a number of reforms, many of which might seem to be responding precisely to Bourdieu's earlier called for 'democratization' in education. To an extent, the 1968 spirit which argued for *autogestion* (self-management) and *participation* was honored by emergency measures to satisfy the protesters. But, looking back in 1983, Bourdieu concluded:

> What has remained of this great shaking of the symbolic order? In the political field, frankly almost nothing: the logic of the apparatus and the parties that the liberal critique did not spare, is better constituted to express the virtuous rationalisation of corporate interests than the anti-institutional sentiment which will remain for me the truth in the laughter of May.
>
> (2002b: 62)

As this passage shows, there was, and always has to be, an emotional response to May 1968, as well an understanding both of its actual and symbolic significance. However, in a lengthy preface to the English version of *Homo Academicus*, it is the element of 'reflexivity' which Bourdieu stresses in his reconsideration of the text. It is with this aspect of the book that I will conclude the current chapter.

Scholastic Reason

Bourdieu at one point refers to *Homo Academicus* as a work with which he was able to use 'instruments of reflexivity' and reflexivity 'to produce more science, not less' (1992a: 194). The book is 'an attempt to test the outer boundaries of reflexivity in social science and an enterprise in self-knowledge'. How so?

The Preface to *Homo Academicus* opens by returning to the issue of reflexivity in terms of the writer, in this case the sociologist, objectifying his position in the *field*:

> One cannot avoid having to objectify the objectifying subject. It is by turning to study the conditions of his own production, rather than by some form or other of transcendental reflection, that the scientific subject can gain a theoretical control over his own structures and inclinations as well as over the determinants whose products they are, and can thereby gain the concrete means of reinforcing his capacity for objectification.
>
> (p. xii)

By applying his theory of practice to his own *field*, Bourdieu argued that he was undertaking an example of 'structural constructivism', or 'constructive structuralism' in the sense outlined in Chapter 7: that is, a phenomenological apprehension of the social world through a dialectical relationship with its objective structures. If the sociologist does this to their own field, they are able to see the position of it and their own homologous position within it. Such an objectification was indeed Bourdieu's project and one he believed himself to have undertaken. Detail is added. He refers to the fashionable group of post-modernist philosophers – Althusser, Barthes, Deleuze, Derrida and Foucault – remarking ironically that they in fact existed only on the margins of the university *field*, so much so that they were not permitted to direct research. His structural analysis of the social space allows us, so to speak, 'to put ourselves in their place'. Bourdieu called this process an exercise in 'participant objectification' (p. xviii), which entails reconstructing the point of view, the social conditions, from which their intellectual project was mounted. He remarks that these philosophers needed to be understood as distinct from the classical university professors of philosophy, to be found at the Sorbonne, for example. The latter had institutional (temporal) power gained from their position in the academic hierarchy; while the post-modernists had no such position and therefore no such power. Therefore, they gained their status through strong connections with the outside intellectual world; for example, through publications in leading reviews, journalism and creating a media profile. This positioning was just one aspect of the contemporary academic *field*. Bourdieu remarked that the first post-war intellectual confrontation was between Sartre and Lévi-Strauss (subjectivism and objectivism, structuralism and existentialism), which itself can be seen as a struggle between their two academic disciplines, two ways of seeing the world. However, a further confrontation in terms of *field* structures took place between philosophy (the established tradition) and the social sciences (the new science). Such struggles occurred at the level of institutional structures and the resultant power positions, but they were also transposed into intellectual forms – ideas themselves. He argued that writers such as Althusser and Foucault rejected what might be called the 'philosophy of the subject' and 'humanism', the most obvious example of which was existentialism, for an epistemology of the history of science as represented by such figures as Bachelard, Canguilhem and Koyré, by whom Bourdieu himself had been influenced, as noted in Part 1. But, then their engagement with this tradition allied itself to a 'subjectless philosophy' through associations with notions of the unconscious found in the work of Freud, Saussure and Durkheim; in other words, society transcended the man.

> Thus through a strange ruse of intellectual reason it happened that the Durkheimian philosophy of man became rehabilitated, with the more acceptable face of an anthroplogy legitimated by linguistics, in opposition to the 'philosophy of the subject' that an earlier generation of *normaliens*, that of Sartre, Aron and Nizan, had set up in the thirties in opposition to the 'totalitarian' philosophy of the Durkheimians, among others.
>
> (p. xxiii)

The implication of this line of argument is that philosophers, whether classical or post-modernist, do not undertake such an analysis of their own thinking, and therefore do not know the limit of their own thinking. This reasoning was taken up by Bourdieu some 13 years later when he published *Méditations pascaliennes* (2000a/1997), which is the book that most directly extends the thesis in *Homo Academicus*. If the latter dealt with the structure of the academic *field*, then *Pascalian Meditations* analyzed its products: science, knowledge and truth. The theme is announced in the first chapter, which, in an echo of the eighteenth-century idealist philosopher Immanual Kant, is entitled a 'Critique of Scholastic Reason'. The other chapter titles indicate the direction of Bourdieu's argument: 'The Three Forms of Scholastic Fantasy'; 'The Historicity of Reason'; 'Bodily Knowledge'; 'Symbolic Violence and Political Struggles'; and 'Social Being, Time and the Sense of Existence'. What is at stake is the status of scholastic knowledge – 'truth' itself. Bourdieu opens the book by suggesting that if he had resolved to ask some questions of philosophy, he would have preferred it that these had been posed by philosophers themselves (p.1). The implication is that they have a vested interest in not asking them, since to do so would reveal the limits of their thinking and thus undermine its recognized value. Bourdieu then returns to the principle of 'objectifying the subject of objectification'. He writes that by this he means dispossessing the 'knowing subject' (in this case philosophers) of the privilege it grants itself: the privilege of making 'objective' statements which, for Bourdieu, is only possible by ignoring the 'presuppositions' included in the object of knowledge, but not *recognized*. For Bourdieu, these presuppositions are of three 'orders':

> To start with the most superficial, there are those associated with occupation of a position in social space, and the particular trajectory that has led to it, and with gender . . . Then there are those that are constitutive of the *doxa* specific to each of the different fields (religious, artistic, philosophical, sociological, etc.) and, more precisely, those that each particular thinker owes to his position in the field. Finally, there are the presuppositions constituting the *doxa* generically associated with the *skholè*, leisure, which is the condition of existence of all scholarly fields.
>
> (p. 10)

How to perform this act of reflexivity is, of course, a moot question, and one to return to later in this book. Indeed, it is possibly this philosophical aspect of Bourdieu's theory of practice which has the most profound methodological implications in his work and continues to have the most lasting relevance to contemporary debates. In a way, Bourdieu clearly believed that in *Homo Academicus* he had indeed undertaken an exercise which would divest his work of the presuppositions inherent in its production. On one level, the book is an exercise in positioning both itself and the object of its study in terms of the *field* which has produced it and the *doxa* to be found therein. In the third presupposition – the *skholè* – Bourdieu is offering a radical critique of the *free time* scholars have at their disposal in order to undertake scholarly work at all. Such work already presupposes a distance from empirical, everyday experiences and is an objectification which assumes a different form of relationship with it. That such a positioning necessarily includes *interests* specific to those who hold it, which are undisclosed, offers a corrosive view of the form and status of the resultant knowledge and the ends to which it is put. To acknowledge such in one's own academic own work itself is a difficult thing to do as it suggests a relativizing of what has been *done* and, consequently, what is *known*. In this respect, it cannot be undertaken without a biographical reflection on personal identity and practice. In another sense, consequently, *Homo Academicus* needs to be seen as a biographical statement; although Bourdieu was also to refer to it as an 'anti-biography' (1992a: 213). Rather than give a personal, auto-biographical account, it seeks to undertake 'self-analysis by proxy' (1988/1984: xxvi). The necessity to do this, Bourdieu stated, was encouraged by his own move from philosophy to the social sciences and his need to gain 'rational control' over the disappointment he experienced with the 'annihilation of the truths and values to which he was destined and dedicated' (*ibid.*) – itself the only alternative to feelings of self-destructive resentment when he applied the logic of the theory of practice to his own practice.

The question then is, to what extent the study is unique and valid to France and Bourdieu, and to what extent it has applicability to and implications for any academic *field*? These themes are explored in the next chapter and Parts 3 and 4 of this book.

Chapter 11

Educational 'Nobility' (Higher Education)

Bourdieu published three major works on education. The first was *La Reproduction* (1970), which was the culmination of his studies of the student population. The focus here was academic discourse – *cultural capital* – and the nature of the systems which produced it. The second was *Homo Academicus* (1988/1984) in which he analyzed his own academic – intellectual – field and the cause and effects of May 1968. The third appeared in 1989 and was entitled *La Noblesse d'État* (1996b/89).

Bourdieu had often drawn an analogy between the way many sectors of the French State and establishment currently behaved and those of the *Ancien Régime*. In *Homo Academicus*, he had referred to the 'official oblates of the higher-educational clergy' (p. 112), and to himself also as an 'oblate', albeit a somewhat bewildered one. The implication, drawn out increasingly in explicit terms, is that sections of French society perform the same functional role as those of pre-revolutionary France: in other words, the surface structural appearance had changed, but the underlying process – in this case reproducing class hierarchies – remained the same. It is therefore more than ironic that *La Noblesse d'État* should be published in 1989 – the bicentennial anniversary of the Great Revolution of 1789. The English translation did not appear until 1996. It went under the title 'State Nobility', with the subtitle, 'elite schools in the field of power'. The French subtitle was *Grandes écoles et esprit de corps*, which refers more explicitly to the French system of elite training schools established 'above' the universities, to which the sons and daughters of the most well-off members of the French bourgeoisie were sent; and the consequential moral cement that linked them as they took their position in the upper echelons of the French establishment – ministerial *cabinets*, the media, politics, the Civil Service and industry.

Bourdieu's main thesis can be summed up as follows. In earlier times, the French aristocracy based their socially privileged position on birth. *Noblesse de robe* was a God-given right gained through noble birth, or conferred upon you by the sovereignty of the monarch. In a pre-contemporary world, where legitimation was established through the power of God and the King, this system – a combination of the spiritual and the temporal – functioned as a means to maintain a stable ruling caste in society. However, the world had changed. The Church and King had been swept away, in France at least. Bourdieu argued that similar functions were now being performed by education. Unable to evoke the rights of birth or hereditary, the modern ruling elites have had recourse to other means in order to assert and maintain their positions; in particular, education had become the modern medium of legitimation, and the State its vehicle of domination. Bourdieu saw two correlative 'inventions': first the State itself and the bureaucratic machinery which served it; and second the new educational academies, colleges and boarding schools. These two were (and still are!) complementary and self-serving. They establish a hierarchy of privilege, which entitles those who occupy positions in it to sanction their place on the basis of educational qualifications and merits the acknowledged and recognized social value that accrues from possessing them. Thus:

> We see that, contrary to what has sometimes been claimed, through error equivalent in its principle to the one made by the proponents of the 'liberating school' regarding the relationship between noble titles and academic titles, 'the world of the Parliament was not built through the elimination of the nobility', but that on the contrary, it annexed the most fundamental aspect of the former nobility and integrated a significant proportion of its members.
>
> (1996b/1989: 379)

The modern *noblesse de robe* had to build the State – with all its related connotations of 'public service' and the political philosophies which surround it – in order to create and reproduce itself. Service to the King is replaced by 'service to the state and public'. Indeed, Bourdieu shows how this move from aristocratic to State patronage was going on in France even before the King was deposed. Education became increasingly important from the sixteenth century as academies were established for noblemen. From 1760, there was a large expansion in the number of boarding schools available for the children of state profession members. Later, universities were founded. This new infrastructure was instrumental in creating an 'esprit de corps' among those who now shared affinities based on a common education.

La Noblesse d'État is, therefore, more than simply an historical account of the development of higher education in France. The titles of its main sections again describe the journey on which Bourdieu takes us: 'Academic Forms of Classification'; 'The Ordination'; 'The Field of the *Grandes écoles* and its Transformation'; 'The Field of Power and its Transformations'; 'State Power and Power over the State'.

The Field of Higher Education and Academic Thought

The main body of *La Noblesse d'État* (1996b/1989) is preceded by a Prologue in which Bourdieu returns to the idea that social structures and mental structures are homologous. He reiterates that his mission is to uncover the deep structures buried in the social world; by which he means the relationship between cognitive structures and (institutional) objective structures. It is only ever possible to talk about one side of this relationship at a time, but it must continually be borne in mind that the two are always co-terminus. In *La Noblesse d'État*, although Bourdieu is concerned with educational institutions, which he refers to as 'immense cognitive machines', he begins with an analysis of the individual cognitive structures that lecturers and students use in constructing the social reality of their actions and representations. Clearly, those with a vested *interest* in the academic game have something to gain by the continuation of the *illusio*; in this case, of the principle of 'school as liberating force' – the guarantor of 'achievement over ascription', 'what is conquered over what is received', 'work over birth', 'merit over talent', and 'heredity over nepotism' (p. 5). Bourdieu consequently recognized that the process in which we are engaged is likely to cause some suffering on the part of those whose very schemes of thought, mental constructions, perceptions, visions, actions and beliefs – in short, mental structures – are literally 'embodied' as incarnate *cultural capital* formed by a particular social universe. One should therefore possibly anticipate violent reactions from *field* participants as the true nature of academic schooling is 'unveiled': namely, 'as one of the foundations of domination and of the legitimation of domination' (*ibid.*). For Bourdieu, 'scientific' objectivity of these implicit functions of educational institutions is perceived as an attack because they break with the enchantment of the 'natural attitude'. Indeed, arguments in academic matters, for example the very *raison d'être* of education, resemble religious wars because what is at stake is a defense of 'natural assets' (*cultural capital*), and is therefore experienced as akin to the questioning of one's own 'mental integrity'.

In describing the style and content of the academic *field*, Bourdieu is pointing to the way a certain class – in this case, those destined for the elite positions in the *field* of power – is reproduced. What is valued, and considered virtuous, is indicative of a whole lifestyle. Correlations and oppositions are everywhere. Recalling, perhaps, the epigraph to *Les Héritiers* (1979b/1964), Bourdieu writes that not everyone has academic talent, and it is educational institutions which 'decide' who are and are not 'the talented'. There is a 'privilege of ease' where precocity is seen as a 'gift'. To make an effort betrays one's origins. To be erudite is not enough – it is necessary to have style. Bourdieu sees this process of classification in something as simple as the language used to assess students and their work: 'brilliant/dull; effortless/laborious; distinguished/vulgar; cultured/scholastic; inspired/banal; original/common; lively/flat; fine/crude; noteworthy/significant; quick/slow; nimble/heavy; elegant/awkward' (p. 17). It is in this sense that the educational institutions are a 'cognitive machine'. It is almost as if they hold up a structural mirror to the minds of those who pass through them. There are consequent affinities, convergences and divergences, the basis of which is the match/mismatch between one form of *cultural capital* (constituted by and through *habitus*) and another. The school does not have to do anything for 'natural selection' to take place.

Much of this process is played out in the minds of teachers and the consequent relations they have with their students. It is not, of course, a case of crude determinism. Attitudes, beliefs and postures are nuanced. For example, the teachers from a petty bourgeois background position themselves between an intellectual avant-garde and the canonical conservatives, a position which is itself homologous to its own social provenance, situated as it is between the 'proleteroids' and the dominant members in the *field* of power. Such teachers' petty bourgeois background can lead to a 'petty', 'middle of the road' conservatism in academic matters; in particular, a predilection for a bureaucratic, administrative orientation to their professional careers. At its root are systems of classification, which are actively produced by students and teachers, and their practical knowledge to put the principles into practice in a way that is not open to explicit representation.

Bourdieu's target in this case is the *Grandes écoles*; for example the École Normale Supérieure. He notes: 'every *normalien*, to varying degrees, partakes of that universe of possible virtues to which all *normaliens* quite naturally apply the adjective *normalien*' (p. 49). Their position is defined intellectually, morally, and, hence, socially. Because their like attracts like, and shares their likeness, a veritable 'esprit de corps' is set up. Such a process begins long before a student enters a *Grande école*; for example, *cultural capital* is already being bestowed on them in their home environment. The khâgnes (preparatory classes), competitive exams and training schools all operate to enhance its 'purchasing power'. Further mixing with the offspring of certain social groups itself offers return on time spent establishing a network of well-placed associates. Bourdieu quotes Pascal: 'To be of noble birth is a great advantage ... at the age of 18 it places a man within the select circle, known and respected, as another would have merited it at 50. It is a gain of 30 years without trouble' (p. 373). Attending a *Grande école* is therefore a kind of social guarantee for those already well endowed with the prerequisite *cultural capital*. It consecrates that which already exists. Bourdieu again uses semi-religious language to refer to the elite as a 'sacred group', one whose 'monopoly is converted into nobility' as a 'magical shareholding in symbolic capital' (p. 79). Content is arbitrary. In France, such nobility is defined in terms of individual academic achievement (itself a defining principle of a Republican system that defines all as equal).

The opposite is true in English public schools, where the cult of the team sport and a predominant form of anti-intellectualism originates in Imperial values, and the need to submit to group interests and loyalty to the King.

It must be emphasized that Bourdieu is not simply arguing that a dominant form of educational knowledge is being recreated across generations to reflect the style of a certain dominant sector of the French social system. On the contrary, the *field* is constantly in flux. We can see that the preparatory school is developing and instilling an entire style of education and intellectual work by what it includes and excludes from its curriculum, and the way it is organized and delivered. In the case of the French preparatory school, Bourdieu describes them as 'the subordination of learning to the imperative of urgency' (p. 85). Newcomers are inducted into a system which emphasizes the need to 'confront' critical situations – only the best survive. There is twice as much drilling as lecturing, and the guiding principle is 'intensive use of time' – a precondition to survival. However, very distinct subcultures open up. In France, the elites traditionally went to one of the key *Grandes écoles*: the École Polytechnique (EP) (for positions in the military and political world), the École Normale Supérieure (for teaching and education), the École des Hautes Études Commerciales (HEC) and the Écoles des Mines (EM) (for commerce and industry). However, following the Second World War a new *Grande école* had opened; namely, the École Nationale d'Administration (ENA). This new training school was established specifically to supply a new breed of State technocrat, destined to drive the French economy and political machinery as it strove to modernize its structures. There are distinctions to be made between these various schools and the type of education they offered, and to what end. For example, Bourdieu recognized two types of knowledge – general and specialized – which distinguish themselves according to 'opposing' dominant principles: general and technical; conception and execution; theory and empiricism; and synthesis and analysis. For Bourdieu, there was a hotly contested boundary in these divisions; namely, the distinction between the 'specialists of the general' and the 'specialists' proper, which itself is the same as that between the upper-level managers (*polytechniciens*) and the middle managers

(*cadres*). The graduates of the ENA (the *énarques*), in particular, Bourdieu saw as exhibiting a precocity, which predisposed them to take
up positions that early on constituted a 'cadre' for the nation – giving
them a sense of superiority and self-legitimation – all while waiting
for more lucrative jobs in the private sector once they had established
their position and their particular sphere of operations.

There are two perspectives on this work – *habitus* and *field* (as ever!)
– or, the individual and the space they occupy.

Culture again features as a medium for definition and legitimation.
It is through culture that the elite are 'crowned'. In culture, the
select are separated from the masses, the sacred from the profane.
Internalized culture becomes an expression of being: 'I am master
over myself and over the universe' (p. 110). Style is all and wins out
over content: 'They taught us nothing at Eton ... that may be so,
but I think they taught it very well' (*ibid.*). These images conjure up
the picture of earnestness of the autodidact: they know everything,
but have no style. Bourdieu comments somewhat ironically that it is
through education and culture that 'real men' are created as distinct
from 'ordinary men' but, in the process, the young man with his
'passions, desires and nature' must die. These images take us back to
the founding images of Bourdieu's anthropology seen earlier in his
work in Algeria and the Béarn. However, they also relate to Bourdieu's
own personal experience of what it was like to become 'educated'.

This account is more than simple personal biography. Indeed, at
one point Bourdieu insists that, 'if we want to get back to things in
themselves' – the Husserlian, phenomenological aspiration – then,
we have to look at the structure of the social space and the strategies
by which they develop. Bourdieu saw such structures in the higher
education field. There is a kind of double structural homology. On
the one side, there are the children of the Upper Bourgeoisie who
go to the *Grandes écoles* – the *Grande Porte*, which supplies the top-level
executives. On the other side are the children of Petite Bourgeoisie
who go to the *Petites écoles* – the *Petite Porte*, which supplies workers in
middle management. Even among the highest *Grandes écoles*, social
provenance and educational destiny are inexplicably linked. The sons
and daughters of teachers go to the ENS; those of the Higher Civil
Servants go to the ENA; and the offspring of commercial executives

go to the HEC. The point, as ever with Bourdieu, is that this mechanism is not operating in a socially deterministic way. Rather, there
is perfect autonomy for parents and children to do what they want
and go where they want. However, the nature of the system ensures
that because of the structural homologies between *habitus* and *field* –
and the 'elective affinities' operating a multitude of individual contexts and decisions – the social structure of society is predisposed to
reproduce itself, all while it transforms itself in a dynamic of socio-
economic historical evolution. Bourdieu is taking us through levels
of analysis: the ways of the thinking of those concerned; the culture
they express and its place in education; the structure of the higher
education field; the place of higher education in the economy and
in the *field* of power as a whole. Thus, at the first level, to go to one
or another *Grande école* – or university for that matter – is not simply
a question of professional orientation. Rather, it involves developing
an entire 'matrix of preferences' for the way one structures one's life.
Ultimately, these preferences are defined in terms of individual dispositions along continua of opposing attitudes – involved/disinterested,
gratuitous/useful, etc. – not to mention life activities, like which newspapers are read, interest in sport, theatre, music, etc. However, the
root of these differences can be found in what Bourdieu calls the 'chi-
asmatic' structure of the space of the *Grande écoles* (p. 152). Oppositions are everywhere: between the private and the public; size of fees;
length of courses; management and engineering; art and research.
Moreover, there is academic activity which is 'intellectual' in that it
pursues knowledge for its own sake, and there is activity which is
more orientated to work in public and private sectors. For Bourdieu,
this constitutes a fundamental opposition between two 'poles': one
'intellectual', the other 'temporal'. Of course, this contrast is similar
to the one found at the heart of the higher education system itself, as
discussed in the previous chapter.

La Noblesse d'Etat (1996b/1989) is full of empirical exemplification of the way the social elite in France is preserved. For example,
Valéry Giscard d'Estaing, the former President of France, represents
an 'entire evolution of the bourgeoisie in a personal trajectory leading from the most traditional fractions, close to Pétainism, to the
new Bourgeoisie' (p. 275). The morphology of the ruling classes was

changing. However, its operation in social reproduction still worked to maintain what might be called 'the organic solidarity in the division of labor of domination' (p. 187).

The Structure of Higher Education and the Field of Power

In *La Noblesse d'État*, Bourdieu attempted a 'structural history' of the higher education *field* between 1967 and 1987. The fundamental shift which had taken place was the way that *economic capital* had been displaced by *cultural capital* as the currency to buy position in the ruling elite. This was symptomatic of the way French society was changing and, with it, the centers of its socio-economic power. It is not a coincidence that the HEC was set up in 1881, while the ENA was established in 1945. In these two opposing 'palaces' we see the way that commerce in some ways confronted public sector management as the motor force driving French society at two points in time. Indeed, the creation and rise of the ENA was one of two major developments in the *field* in the post-war period. The other was the development of new institutions of management, marketing, advertising, journalism and communications – the new service industries. Bourdieu makes the point that many of the children of the business bourgeoisie enter these professions as a way of circumventing the rise in power of *cultural* (academic) *capital* over traditional *economic capital*. Faced with the rise of a new, powerful middle-class elite, basing their legitimacy on education, it was necessary for the monied classes to find their own legitimate position within the structure of the French elite. As previously noted, student populations increased in size between 1950 and 1972, especially in the humanities and law faculties. Engineering schools also grew. In 1966, the new *Instituts Universitaires de Technologie* (IUTs) were created in order to give higher-education status to studies with a vocational, technical focus. The fact that each of these attracted their own student market demonstrates the way that shifts were occurring within the French population with respect to higher education. Yet, at the same time, overall structure and outcome remained the same. In fact, Bourdieu noted, the top *Grandes écoles* received an even higher percentage of pupils from the dominant classes, all while maintaining levels of recruitment. One could therefore argue that the distance between the mass of the student population and the elite schools in higher education actually grew. The ENA had won out over the HEC, while the Normaliens began to lose their previous prestigious position as the value of knowledge for itself was eclipsed by a new social pragmatism.

As always, one must read these changes in the *field* two ways: first, back to the *habitus* and the individual *habitus* which produces it; and second, forward, to its relationship to the overall structure of the *field* of power.

As noted, Bourdieu saw a direct structural homology in the relationship between the worlds of 1789 and 1989. In both cases, certain factions of society – the 'lesser' aristocracy from the provinces in the former case, the academics dependent on the competitive exam in the latter – ended up compensating for their social regression by a 'conservatism born of despair' (p. 278). This resulted in either an assertion of old ways of doing things – a *doxa* that becomes an orthodoxy – or supporting forms of reconversion strategies leading to transformations in the *field* by legitimizing them in terms of the 'old' – two sides of the same coin. At base, in Bourdieu's eyes, is the reconversion and reconfiguring of forms of *capital*, itself implying different forms of reproduction. As noted above, the base contrast is between economic and academic *capital*, but the latter is also differentiated into subforms constituted by the *academic field* as it was evolving.

> Yet we still see within the same economic space the coexistence of the family-controlled transfer of hereditary right to property, as with the heads of family businesses, and the transfer of a power limited to a lifetime (founded on the academic title) more or less completely guaranteed and controlled by the school (and the state) – which, unlike property titles or titles of nobility, cannot be passed down along hereditary lines.
>
> (*ibid.*)

Even so, Bourdieu notes, the propensity to work to accumulate educational/academic (cultural) *capital* increased as the strength (ties, influence, impact) with business weakened. There is also a distinction between Paris and the Provinces. In the latter case, the business bourgeoisie sent their children to private schools, while in Paris, the bourgeoisie *de robe* (those dominant in both technically controlled and State-controlled companies) made use of the top *lycées* in Paris in the fashionable neighborhoods, leading especially to the ENA. Even at the level of the family, such differences manifested themselves in the way that individuals related to each other. In contrast to economic heritage, which can be disputed among those likely to inherit, those with large amounts of *cultural capital* have an interest in supporting each other – they have everything to gain by the symbolic power of association, not to mention social networks, etc. The nature of social solidarity itself is therefore transformed in the new order – as *social capital*.

There is also the distinction between private bosses in the regions who wield power more or less only within the economic *field*, and the State bosses, many of whom have been in the Civil Service, have worked in ministerial cabinets, nationalized industry and, indeed, may even hold important positions in the elite schools (ENA, Sciences-Po and Polytechnique). In this way, the public and private are opposed, but in a way in which both positions in the social space are utilized in the individual and collective transformations that take place within society as a whole and for the individuals who have lived out these changes. Thus, for example, the power of banks increased in opposition to private, accumulated wealth. At the same time, Capitalism had 'socialized' itself. Bourdieu saw the tendency of large-scale enterprises to socialize themselves, through a 'democratization of capital', as homologous with the so-called democratization of schools. One offshoot of this change is that men could no longer appeal to their accumulated wealth as heirs to fortune. To legitimize their privilege, they must present themselves as 'self-made men'. There are, however, many principles of legitimation: '... interpenetration of the public and the private sectors, and the coexistence of the family mode of reproduction and school-mediated mode ... combine to make the historic combination, thus realized a highly euphemized and sublimated form of power' (p. 335).

Bourdieu concluded *La Noblesse d'État* with a consideration of the relationship between the power of the State training schools and the power of the State. Of course, for Bourdieu, the term 'State' is itself a rather mythologized concept. In effect, the State, as he sees it, is not well-defined and clearly bounded – a unitary entity – which stands in relation to other things: 'In fact, what we encounter, concretely, is an ensemble of administrative or bureaucratic fields (they often take the empirical form of commissions, bureaux and boards) within which agents and categories of agents, governmental and non-governmental, struggle over this peculiar form of authority consisting of the power to *rule* via legislation, regulations, administrative measures (subsidies, authorizations, restrictions, etc.)' (1992a: 111). In short, although the State is 'all-powerful', it partly derives its power from its pervasiveness and amorphousness. It is the sum total of 'the ensemble of fields that are the sites of struggle'. What is at stake here is the monopoly of legitimated *symbolic power* – the power to define what is and is not valued, and thus what may and may not exist. This legitimation is a consecration, thus, a near 'sacred' act. No wonder that Bourdieu often refers to the 'magic' of the State.

As noted, Bourdieu saw a similarity between two periods of history, both of which, as the *noblesse de robe*, defined themselves in terms of the ruling authority – the King during the *Ancien Régime*, and the modern State in contemporary times. The point is that the dominant class created itself by creating the State and, in so doing, established itself. The only functional difference between the two times is that, formerly, allegiance to the King came with birth into nobility, while in modern times, commitment to 'public service' and the State was much more of a choice and a vocation (cf. p. 379). However, the change from one to the other operated through a 'collective conversion' of minds – ways of thinking – which went *misrecognized* as such, and which can only be restored to men through the type of sociohistorical analysis being offered by Bourdieu's method – so distinct as it is from conventional forms of history. For Bourdieu, academic titles were invented by the State, or at least those who created it and benefited from its existence in order to bestow privilege in the same way that royal favors were granted by nobility during the *Ancien Régime*. However, qualifications cannot be passed down in the traditional way from father to son – and daughter! Rather, they have to be regained each time on the basis of technical competence. Following Bourdieu's entire thesis on the social function of education, schools were thus invented to ensure this mechanism of social reproduction (albeit in a dynamic, ever-changing sense). The democratization of schools, the 'liberating' school, is therefore a 'myth', since its legitimizing principle runs contrary to its structural (generative) logic. Bourdieu emphasizes that it is necessary for both privileged parents and their children to 'not see' this true function of schools: 'How could they have thought of the new academic "elite" as a nobility . . . (they would have to break with) an entire universe of more or less unconscious representations' (p. 373). But, the analysis is impersonal. Bourdieu is not being critical of any particular type of individual. Rather, he sees the changes that have taken place in the academic field – in this case, the elite training schools – as simply symptomatic of changes in society as a whole; in this case, the advance of modern, capitalist economy, which requires a certain class of men to drive it forward. He returns to conceptual tools offered by Durkheim, in particular, the contrast between *mechanical* and *organic solidarity*. If the former was represented by a simple form of division of labor and an 'undifferentiated' political structure which relied ultimately on the power of one man – the King – the contemporary world had developed a complex structure of fields, subfields and networks – all of which were both distinct and dependent on each other. As a result of this change, power itself has become almost 'invisible', anonymous even, and is less focused on one individual. Rather, it is expressed through forms of *capital* and the social reproduction they mediate. Indeed, Bourdieu defined 'progress' in terms of the 'symbolic efficacy' that correlates with 'circuits of legitimation' (p. 387) in the *field*, and which are only offset by the potential for subversion. The mechanisms of educational institutions are an example *par excellence* of systems where legitimation and subversion can challenge one another. Bourdieu is not value-neutral, however, since what is described here does of course imply not only the intrusion of one *field* of power – political – into another – education – but also the imposition of ways which benefit one group of society over another. Nevertheless, the fact that what occurred was not simply a struggle between dominant and dominated factions of society, but between sectors of the dominant classes, meant that in such struggles a little bit is added to what is 'universal': reason, disinterestedness, civic-mindedness. Bourdieu refers to the system of 'symbolic universalization of particular interests' (p. 389) which is implied in the struggles between dominant factions of society, and which inevitably does lead to the advancement of the universal.

Coda

There is an irony perhaps that in a book which in many ways can be read as a damning indictment of modern French society in general, and its education systems in particular, Bourdieu ends it on this seemingly optimistic note. In some ways, it is perhaps a stylistic device, to offer a vision of a renaissance of the 'enlightenment' and how it might come about, for Bourdieu, through an application of his own 'scientific' sociological method. There are two related issues in the present context. First, the role of the intellectual in this project. Second, the question of the extent to which the social mechanisms Bourdieu describes are particular to France, and how far they are applicable elsewhere.

Essentially, what Bourdieu analyses in *La Noblesse d'État* is the structure and state of the academic training field. He sets out to show how the major elite schools set up in post-Revolution France reproduce the social function of forming the ruling groups in society in ways analogous to the rights of hereditary in the Ancient Regime. However, he offers a detailed study of the way different factions of the French social elite had evolved and changed over the subsequent 200 years. A primary claim is that such changes were in many ways symptomatic of socio-economic shifts in the development of modern France. A second claim is that the elite schools themselves changed, expanded and contracted, and were supplemented by further academic institutions designed to provide a functional fit between the needs of the ruling establishment and the formation of those to provide leadership within it.

In the course of such developments, the nature and role of intellectuals themselves had changed. As noted in Part 1, the word 'intellectual' itself was not really used in France until Zola mobilized writers, artists and journalists of the day when he published his open letter to the French President – *J'accuse* – at the time of the Dreyfus Affair. After this, French intellectuals took on a variety of roles, including that of conscience to the nation during the 1930s and 1940s. Traditionally, Bourdieu argued, there was a kind of tacit agreement between conservative and radical intellectuals in a shared form of activity, most clearly expressed in the tension between, 'production for the sake of production and production directed to an outside demand' (p. 338). Here, we again see the division between 'temporal' and 'scientific' power. Formerly, there was an implied agreement on the values of intellectual activity, which different (politically opposed) factions of the intellectual class shared in the very common weapons they used to attack each other. In other words, the old-style intellectual refused to compromise with the economic world. However, Bourdieu finds that a new antagonism had become apparent in the contemporary world, which characterized itself by two types of intellectual who refused to recognize each other. In the face of intellectuals who simply assert the value of their ideas, there had arisen the 'managerial intellectuals', or 'intellectual managers', who, as holders of forms of *cultural capital* recognized in the *economic field*, accepted the status of bourgeois employee, and were ready to satisfy a demand for a new kind of intellectual service. So, an intellectual agency such as INSEE (*Institut National de la Statistique et des Études Économiques*) situates itself between government and the scientific *field*, claiming legitimation from both. Thus, the intellectual, the economic and political are brought into close proximity to each other, albeit in a site which claims its own 'autonomy'. Indeed, referring back to Tocqueville's 'enlightened egotism', Bourdieu argues that autonomy is a necessary condition of (in effect) subservience. The ruler(s) only get effective symbolic service out of their intellectual class insofar as they are given the capacity to legislate on their own terms (see p. 385):

> The choice is clear indeed, although rarely distinguished: either accept one of the two social functions imparted by the new social definition to cultural producers, that of expert, charged with assisting the dominants in the management of 'social problems', or that of professor, locked away in erudite debate on academic questions'.
>
> (p. 339)

The second issue raised in this coda is the extent to which what Bourdieu describes is applicable outside of France. In a sense, this question – of the contemporary relevance and applicability of Bourdieu's approach – will be dealt with more extensively in Part 4 of this book. However, it is worth asserting here that both *Homo Academicus* (1988/1984) and *La Noblesse d'État* (1996b/1989) need to be read as an implicit invitation for others, in other national contexts, to perform similar analyses on their own academic *field*. In the Foreword to *La Noblesse d'État*, Bourdieu's long-time American collaborator, Loïc Wacquant, touches on this issue. He notes the 'sharp horizontal dualism' in France between the *Grandes écoles* and the universities, and within the *field* of the *Grandes écoles* themselves, between the major and minor schools. He also notes how each of these service different parts of the French class structure, as well as fractions within specific groups. Such a dualistic system does not exist in the USA. However, a structural analysis of the two *fields* merely reveals a different morphology with a similar function. So, in America, there are a series of oppositions – private and public sectors, community colleges and four-year universities, mass tertiary education and the elite institutions of the 'Ivy League' – which perform the same role of separating out education for the elite and for the masses:

> Due to the deep-rooted historic preponderancy of economic over cultural capital, the opposition between the two poles of power, and between the corresponding factions of the American dominant class, does not materialize itself in the form of rival tracks or schools. It is projected instead *within* each (elite) university in the adversative and tensionful relations between graduate division of arts and sciences, on the one side, and professional schools (especially law, medicine and business) on the other, as well as in the antipodean relations these entertain with the powers-that-be and in the contracted images of knowledge they appeal to (research versus service, critique versus expertise, creativity versus utility, etc.).
>
> (p. xiv)

But, what can be done about this situation? Again in his Foreword, Wacquant echoes Bourdieu: that it is beholden on intellectuals, elite as they are, to bear the 'corporatism of the universal', whereby a by-product of their production, in its very elitism, is to add to the universal unfolding of reason. The more that reason is evoked by the dominant in order to legitimize their rule, the more it is possible for the dominated to acquire the same instruments. Wacquant concludes: 'Such is the political meaning of *The State Nobility*: to contribute to this rational knowledge of domination which. . .remains our best weapon against the rationalization of domination' (p. xix)

In fact, in the summing up of the alternatives of intellectual activity given here – 'social service' or 'locked-away professor' – Bourdieu adds a third choice: 'to efficiently (that is, using the weapons of science) assume the function that was for a long time fulfilled by the intellectual, that is, enter the political arena in the name of the values and truths acquired in and through autonomy' (p. 339). In effect, this is exactly what Bourdieu did: by using the position and relative autonomy granted to him as a result of his position as Professor at the Collège de France, he engaged in a number of political activities – both direct and indirect – which targeted educational reform. This question of the possibility of reform, in this case of the curriculum and education system, is now the subject of the final chapter of Part 2.

Chapter 12

Policy and Curriculum

So far, in this part of the book, it might be concluded that what Bourdieu offers is quite a fatalistic, even pessimistic, view of education. Certainly, his analyses suggest that schools, colleges and universities are
at best the unknowing perpetrators of processes set in place to ensure
the continuation of a certain bourgeois culture and society, albeit in
its unfolding nature. At worst, those operating educational systems
know of and deliberately ignore the inequalities existent in education; for fear that addressing them will threaten their own position
within it. At best, they are simply ignorant of, or misrecognize, them.

In a sense, the last three chapters of this part of the book have been
quite theoretical. In books such as *Reproduction*, *Homo Academicus* and
State Nobility, Bourdieu offers a structural anthropology of various
sectors in the education *field* in terms of his theory of practice. His
analyses include rich complexities of analysis and exemplification to
support his world view. Reading through these texts – both lengthy
and dense – it is easy to forget that Bourdieu's preoccupations were
in fact practical. Earlier, I suggested that Bourdieu's entire work output could be understood as responding to practical situations and
contexts, often found in a single image. With education, Bourdieu's
initial impetus was simply to understand the social phenomenon of
'student' – who they were and what produced them – in order to add
some clarity to an area which, he felt, was little understood in France.
Yet, in *Les Héritiers*, Bourdieu had concluded by arguing for a 'rational
pedagogy' to guide educational practice, and for a sociology of social
inequalities. In this chapter, I want to return to these practical issues;
in particular, of policy and curriculum. This shift in focus first neces-
sitates a step back to the early 1960s to re-establish the principles of
Bourdieu's concerns with schools and education. Next, I shall look
at his political response to 1968 and the measures he argued for at

the time. There is discussion of the reforms which were put in place by the new socialist government of the 1980s and the part Bourdieu played as adviser to it. The chapter then concludes with the picture offered of education by Bourdieu and his team in *La Misère du monde* (1999a/1993). This is the point where Bourdieu completed his own writing on education. Issues then arising from the discussion of Bourdieu's theory and practice of education will be taken up and extended in Parts 3 and 4 of the book, where the implications of Bourdieu's view of education and its continuing relevance to policy and practice are considered.

In this chapter, three issues should be kept in mind throughout. First, again the need to be aware of the particular context – social, economic and political – which generated Bourdieu's writing on policy and curriculum; in other words, the pressing social events and the public climate of the day. Second, an acknowledgement that Bourdieu was operating in two overlapping spheres: academic and social/public. In the first, his duty was to establish, as rigorously as possible, a science of educational processes. The fact that what he did offer seemed to be particularly lacking in optimism for reform should therefore be set against the calls on him for practical solutions. The ways in which he responded to these calls, and indeed the pragmatic proposals for change he put forward, should not be seen as implicitly undermining conclusions of his empirical studies. Third, and connected to the last point, is again the issue of the place or role of the intellectual in society and politics. This question had been addressed by Bourdieu from the very outset of his career. It should be recalled that Bourdieu, as an intellectual, apparently became much more politically engaged as his career developed. The *field* of education was a principal site in which Bourdieu would work to define what it was to be intellectually active and effective in a practical context. But, such an involvement was not without its consequences.

The Democratic School

Previous chapters referred to the 'myth' of the 'democratic school'. The same description applies to universities and training institutions.

When talking about these, Bourdieu insisted that it was important to be clear about which institutional reality one was referring to: the one that actually existed, or the potential that it might be. Again, here is a recurrent theme in Bourdieu's work: the distinction between illusion and reality. This issue also poses the question of what conditions need to be established in order to realize the potential for change from one state to another? By looking at the events of 1968, there presents an opportunity to define these conditions and show the principles on which they should be based for Bourdieu. An archive from 1968, logged with the Collège de France (see 2002b: 63), is a petition signed by over 70 individuals, including Bourdieu. It gives a good indication of the interpretation of events at the time by a representative sample of academic intellectuals (i.e., those working at the Sorbonne, HEC, EPHE, ENS, CNRS). The document stresses the need for a 'democratic transformation of the French university' but argues that a 'coherent and explicit program of reform' can only emerge by looking at the 'function', both technical and social, that the university fulfills. In other words, what was needed was a fundamental consideration of the founding principles of the university, not just a piecemeal list of reforms. The document then draws attention to two important issues: first, that the biggest victims of the present system were in fact outside it – those who had already been eliminated by it; second, that it was necessary to acknowledge the way the current system in fact perpetuated the established social order. Academic access was an issue. In 1968, the students had 'declared' all teaching sessions open to outsiders, workers, etc. – a symbolic act of acknowledging the shared needs of different groups in society. The petition then argues the need to look at the training of teachers, claiming that it was not just at university level that reform was necessary. Real change would only come about if the French could counteract the scholastic mechanisms of 'elimination and relegation', and minimize the effect of social class heritage. Scholastic certificates themselves, it was argued, should be downgraded as the sole expression of competence. In the education system itself, democratization had to be seen in terms of a reform of the examination system, not just teaching styles. More exams should be criterion-, rather than norm-, referenced, and teachers needed a more progressive training in pedagogy. However, such developments also had to be accompanied by a reform of the very structures themselves – of disciplines, certificates and the curriculum – in order to remove terminology and ways of assessing, many of which were out-of-date if not 'ancient'. The document ends on a further democratic note: that developing this program of change would only work if all social groups involved in its eventual implementation participated in its formulation.

There is a range of questions which arise from such a document, the most significant of which might be: first, how many of these proposals are still relevant, today?; and, second, the question of the extent to which they were responded to at the time and were met in subsequent reforms? Answering each question would involve an analysis of the French education system over the past 30 years or more, which is clearly beyond the scope of this part of the book. A brief response, however, would note that a number of reforms were indeed introduced and concessions made in the name of 'democratization', 'equity', 'autogestion (self-management)' and 'participation' – reforms which matched those in society and the world of work as a whole. The final conclusion, nevertheless, would be that there was subsequently very little real change in the French educational system in terms of the fundamental reassessment called for in this document. In fact, what did change amounted to little more than piecemeal concessions to pacify the 1968 protesters, and these were soon frittered away when ongoing leadership and support was not offered to back up their implementation.

A further document from 1968, this time from the Centre de Sociologie Européenne (see Bourdieu 2002b: 69), reads almost as a manifesto for a policy of democratization in education. It sets out principles on which the mechanisms for democratic change should be based:

1. Attention needs to be given to the differences in linguistic expression between everyday and scholastic language; in particular, between pupils from different social backgrounds. Children need to be taught verbalization and expression, and the way to manipulate technical structures.
2. As from nursery school, efforts should be made to give all children the same experiences as those from the most well-off families.

3. Extra efforts need to be made to counteract the drop-out of pupils from the least well-off sections of society; especially during the secondary phase of education. In particular, training needs to be given to teachers in the way 'orders of merit' are actualized within and between institutions. And, grants should be made available to support secondary education.

4. A systematic effort should be made to reduce inequalities between schools by reducing differences of quality between establishments.

5. Extra support be provided for boarders so that evening classes, for example, are not so much after-school sessions but, instead, genuine lessons.

6. Complementary and compensatory education is organized both in term time and vacations, so that children from the less well-off families, who might be falling behind with their studies, are able to catch up, particularly in key curriculum areas.

7. A 'core core' curriculum should be established for secondary education which avoids premature specialization towards 'science' *or* 'humanities'.

8. The traditional teaching of humanities is replaced by a true cultural education, which gives an anthropological and historical understanding of Hebrew, Greek and Roman cultures.

9. Everything needs to be done to bridge the gap between school and adult education.

10. There should be in place a 'systematic and diversified' policy of allowances and student grants to support families in the participation of their children in education.

In a sense, this is a wish-list, and now in the twenty-first century it might read as idealistic, if not naïve. Curiously, however, the list does contain a range of issues that have contemporary relevance. Indeed, the principles are reminiscent of recent UK policy. What was Bourdieu seeking to achieve? This question returns us to the work he was undertaking at the same time as these documents were being drafted – namely, *Les Héritiers* and *La Reproduction*. It also again raises the question of the relationship between the academic, the researcher, or intellectual, and the world that surrounds them. How much influence can, or even should, they have on actual policy?

Reproduction Revisited and the Intellectual

In 1989, Bourdieu had occasion to return to his work in *Les Héritiers* and *La Reproduction* (see 2002b: 73). Here, he again refers to his address given to *La Semaine de la Pensée Marxiste* (1966) some 20 years earlier (see page 92). It is not necessary, in the present context, to reiterate in detail the message he gave, which essentially was that the students who have come through and succeeded in the school systems are those who by circumstance have most faith in the 'liberating school'. Of course, prominent in this group were French intellectuals, in particular, those on the Left of the political spectrum. Bourdieu believed that many misunderstood his message, which was not just the common one that schools eliminated children from the working class. Rather, he claimed that a principal message of these early books was to 'explain why' this was the case and what 'responsibility' or 'contribution' schools held in the reproduction of social divisions. To ascribe a liberating potential to schools was a theoretical idea, in much the same way that students were described as a homogeneous whole by neo-Marxist intellectuals looking to extend 'class struggle' theory to relations between teachers and their students. For Bourdieu, this was a theoretical reification of reality: students were in fact highly differentiated, and schools' essential functions undermined their potential to be instrumental in social liberation.

Bourdieu refers to the reception of these works. He states that the very word 'reproduction' itself became 'catastrophic' since it was used – particularly as a paradigmatic metaphor in the USA – so much that it affected intellectuals' interest in the book. Those who did read it were keen to interpret it according to their own world view: 'Bourdieu says that the school system reproduces classes ... he says that this is good, so he is a conservative' (p. 76); 'Bourdieu says that the school reproduces social classes and it is bad' (*ibid.*). In the first case, the speaker is reading normatively; in the second, radically. Another pushed Bourdieu's thesis to an extreme: 'schools preserve, it is therefore necessary to suppress them' (*ibid.*). Bourdieu argued that this was (and still is!) a common strategy for dealing with issues which cause difficulties. The idea is extended to such extreme lengths that its original message is rendered absurd. Bourdieu states that this is not even 'utopic' but a form of 'stupid nihilism'. Controversy was rife. Bourdieu himself states that he was one of the intellectuals most criticized by the communist party in France; which was rather ironic since he was also often accused of being a neo-Marxist. Bourdieu describes how his work was almost 'put in quarantine', that is, a line was drawn around it as a way of excluding it. It is not so much that his work was prophetic, he claims, but just as with prophesy, it overturned mental structures. Previously, schools were seen as places where one went to learn progressive, universal knowledge. To show that in fact school had conservative effects was in some ways a heresy. It was therefore necessary to 'neutralize' the message – no one thanks you for pointing out misrecognitions! Another response to his conclusions, Bourdieu stated, was to accept the thesis but to argue that nothing could be done about it. However, he insisted: 'it is because one knows the laws of reproduction that one can have a small chance of minimizing the reproductive action of the scholastic institution' (p. 77). How? – through intellectual action.

Bourdieu presented himself as a certain sort of intellectual and his work as a certain kind of intellectual work. As previously noted, the character of intellectuals in France had changed and with it the sphere and means of their operations. This change was presented in terms of an opposition between the 'temporal' and the 'scientific'; in effect, the new willingness of intellectuals to become involved with the establishment in all its manifestations. As early as 1972, he had spoken about the 'Doxosophes': intellectuals of training who go on to assert a certain political *doxa* through an economic and social philosophy of the State. The training schools written about in the last chapter were the sites for such intellectual nurturing. Yet for Bourdieu, 'Science-Po' – in effect, political science (a highly prestigious training in France) – amounted to a kind of 'de-politization' since not only did it deradicalize the traditional role of the intellectual in French society, but also it was a phenomenon created specifically to propagate a particular view of the world: in this case, *techniciste* and *dirigiste*, with economic achievement as its principal success criteria.

Schools like the École Nationale d'Administration, as we have seen, gave birth to an entirely new group within the ruling classes. However, intellectuals were also differentiated in other ways.

Michel Foucault, who had sponsored Bourdieu in his election to the Collège de France, had written about the difference between intellectuals as 'spokesmen of the universal' and the 'specific intellectual'. The latter had become more common in France and performed a certain functional role as 'expert' voice. Their natural habitat was the media where they were called upon to provide a 'technical voice' on specific topics. The problem was, however, that increasingly such intellectuals subordinated their opinions to the needs of the establishment; in particular, they framed what they thought and said in terms of the expectations of the media in which they were appearing. Bourdieu was against these so-called 'media intellectuals'. At the same time, he argued against the notion of the 'total' intellectual – someone who spoke of universals, as spokesman for the working class. Clearly, he had Sartre in mind. But, Bourdieu was not a 'conscientious objector' in the war of words that was being fought among intellectuals and between intellectuals and the political establishment. His response to the invasion of Poland by the communist regime in 1981 is one example. When the Soviet troops arrived in order to suppress the Solidarity trade union Bourdieu made contact with Michel Foucault. Petitions were signed among the intellectual class denouncing the invasion. However, Bourdieu and Foucault also set out to establish a relationship with the leading French trade union CFDT, not to set themselves up as 'party intellectuals', but as a partnership between workers and their own intellectual activity. Bourdieu made the point that there is a world of difference between 'the intellectual *and* the CFDT and the intellectuals *of* the CFDT' (1985b: 93). What he was intending was to define a new site for intellectual activity: one which was distinct from both the traditional model of intellectual and the new 'media' intellectual. Bourdieu asserted that intellectuals were not the spokesmen of universals. They did, however, 'have an interest in the universal' (p. 94). What this position amounted to was offering a clear voice and the conceptual analyses that would give insights based on scientific analyses to contemporary issues. Bourdieu pursued this philosophy with a personal involvement in a number of social movements concerned with equal rights – gay, feminist, immigrant – as well as establishing an *Internationale of Intellectuals* (1992c), bringing together writers, artists and playwrights from across Europe in an association which opposed a 'politics of purity' to State rationality. However, it was in the field of education that Bourdieu's political involvement as an intellectual was most extensive, and it is to the area of educational reform that I wish to turn.

Educational Reform

When France voted for first a socialist President and then government in 1981– the first of the Fifth Republic – there was a general mood of optimism and a spirit of reform in the air. It is impossible to believe that Bourdieu did not share in this mood of change, almost in spite of the logical conclusions of his work. Direct involvement in the socialist mission came soon. In February 1984, President Mitterand called on the 'Professors' of the Collège de France to produce a report on the future of education in which they would 'reflect on the fundamental principles of education ... integrating literary and artistic culture with the most recent knowledge and methods in science' (see 2002b: 199). The final report included nine 'principles' which should guide future reform. The following is a synopsis of these:

1. *The Coherence of Science and the Plurality of Cultures*
   Here, what is recognized is that lifestyles, knowledge and cultural sensibilities are diverse. It is therefore necessary to have an education which reconciles the 'universalism' of the physical sciences with the relativism of the social sciences.
2. *Diversification in Forms of Excellence*
   Education should recognize forms of excellence other than 'intelligence' defined in a narrow sense, and avoid the 'hierarchies' of achievement.
3. *Multiplication of Opportunities*
   Here, it is important to reduce the consequences of 'scholastic judgement'; especially in the way they 'condemn' those who 'fail'. More needs to be done to open up links between disciplines and lessen irreversible closures in academic routes.

4. *Coherence In and Through Pluralism*
   Liberalism and 'étatisme' must be reconciled. The less well-endowed institutions should be protected against open competition between schools and colleges, creating conditions of emulation between independent and diversified institutions.
5. *The Periodic Revision of Subjects Taught*
   This principle states that content should be revised periodically so that lesser and marginal subjects are pruned from the curriculum in favor of the latest knowledge bases.
6. *Unification of Knowledge Taught*
   Each scholastic establishment should set out a knowledge base that is necessary at each level, defined in terms of historic cohesion.
7. *An Education that is Uninterrupted and Alternate*
   Education should continue throughout life. Also, everything should be done to reduce the abruptness of passage from compulsory education and entry into the active life of work.
8. *Use of Modern Techniques of Education*
   The action of initiation, orientation and support by the State must occur through a methodical and intensive use of modern techniques in the diffusion of culture; notably, television and state-of-the-art audio-visual techniques.
9. *Openness In and Through Independence*
   Scholastic establishments must develop themselves as 'learning communities', coordinating their discussions and their activities with other institutions, including cultural centers, in order to create a real center for civic education. In parallel, the independence of the teaching body needs to be reinforced by re-evaluating the role of teacher and by enhancing the competence of teachers.

In a sense, many of the themes listed are familiar, by implication at least, to anyone who had read *Les Héritiers* and *La Reproduction*. Yet, they must also be read with some sense of paradox when set alongside the other work that Bourdieu was publishing, or preparing to publish, at the time – in *Homo Academicus* and *La Noblesse d'État* – since many of the conclusions from these publications would seem to suggest that such principles were impossible in actual contexts as they challenged the innate logic of the education *field*. This is perhaps an example of the 'scientific Bourdieu' as opposed to the 'public Bourdieu'; in the latter, we have 'public' Bourdieu, the man, proposing (along with the other professors of the Collège de France) the principles for progressive reform within education. In support of the report, Bourdieu undertook a series of interviews (1985a, 1986c). He was aware that the report was an intellectual act and the fact that it came from the Collège de France, with all that signified in terms of *cultural capital*, gave added status and impetus to the report.

Bourdieu had called for a 'rational pedagogy', all while insisting that any attempt to introduce it would fail if it defined itself simply in terms of establishing equal opportunities of access to education; in other words, not addressing the conditions of inequality – *social*, *economic* and (especially) *cultural* – would ensure that 'the democratization of education' would not have real effects. In an interview given at the time of publication of the Collège de France report (see 2002b: 203), Bourdieu singled out two principles which he felt were central to the 'reproductive' role of the scholastic system: first, the effect of the 'verdict' (3. above), which he saw as enshrining and justifying social effects as 'essential' – naturally determined; and, second, the effect of scholastic 'hierarchization' (2. above), or rank ordering, as the idealization of a 'linear order' of competence, which only functions if one accepts a 'perfect knowledge' so that we all exist in effect in various forms of failure. Bourdieu argued that the scholastic system is analogous to *The Trial* by Kafka, the story where a man stands accused of a crime, yet he never discovers what this crime is! Bourdieu states that what he was attempting in his work – which in turn could be found in the Collège report – was to reintroduce a historical dimension as a fundamental aspect of our understanding of education, and a socio- (if not sociological) historical aspect at that. In this way, he claims that it was possible to 'de-dogmatize' education, to uncover its social function and, in so doing, offer the means to 're-appropriate the structures of our own thought' (*ibid.*: 206). What is suggested here is more than a 'leveling' of opportunity and access. Rather, it is a way of thinking and seeing education that radically critiques its traditional role, as well as providing possibilities of thinking about the system differently. The significance of culture in producing, or not, the *homo academicus* is an example of this thinking and its consequences; for example, in the way that those who are deprived become unaware of their deprivation.

For Bourdieu, education was caught in a 'double bind': it had, through incontrovertible evidence, accepted its role in maintaining social inequalities, and yet the immediate response to this only resulted in the inequalities being re-expressed in different forms. Furthermore, 'dumbing down' education to the lowest common denominator was, for him, just one way of accommodating the resentment felt by many of those excluded from it. What Bourdieu argued for instead was 'diversification' and 'multiplication'; education where differences were valued and celebrated. Bourdieu noted that people would defend to the 'nth degree' their differences when they felt under attack (*ibid.*: 209). Therefore, he called for groups to have a sufficient number of titles and guarantees for them to be freed from the limiting effects of such titles and guarantees. This was the way groups would have to be formed and constituted in order for them to operate in the terms of the report. Bourdieu insisted that such change did not come about simply through introducing reform but by creating conditions which were necessary for its implementation.

What are the chances of such changes in the 'real world'? Bourdieu was aware of the possible charges of 'idealism' that he would be attracting as a result of what he was proposing. After having gained power, the socialist government undertook an extensive and expansive program of policy reform, much of it radical. However, a mounting economic crisis forced them to backtrack and, in effect, adopt neoliberal politics in all matters – social and economic – similar to the policies of Margaret Thatcher in the UK and Ronald Reagan in the USA. Many of the educational reforms proposed by Bourdieu and his fellow collegians were either watered down or passed over. Bourdieu notes the irony (1986c: 4) of a 'socialist government' in power, 'forced' now to abandon the 'illusions' which brought it to power in the first place. He recalled an old Kabyle proverb – 'he put the East in the West for me' (*ibid.*) – to describe the way that the new 'technocrats' and the politicians they served, had placed the 'Left' in the 'Right' of politics. The traditional socialists were now busy appropriating and re-expressing exactly the same socio-economic philosophy as those of the traditional conservative politicians they had replaced.

The worst result of this, for Bourdieu, was not so much a betrayal of political vision, as the loss of people's confidence in all politics, which was sure to guarantee the collapse of the alternative the socialists had once offered. Bourdieu described the new philosophy which had gripped education as 'the struggle of all against all', 'enterprise and competition', which was directly analogous to the direction of 'liberal economics' – the search for maximum profit in effect was replaced in education for the need, 'without mercy', to obtain the top grades. Behind education, therefore, there exists not simply a wish to maximize achievement, but a fundamental issue about the type of individual that was being developed by educational institutions (*ibid.*).

Rather than further reforms, still less a kind of idealistic utopia, what Bourdieu was arguing for was a true 'educational project' that would be undertaken as a social collective. It was not enough to 'abandon selection'. This would only lead to negative effects. What was needed in its place was to develop measures which would ensure that when there was competition, it occurred on equal footing, and, that support was present to ensure that social inequalities were compensated for. Bourdieu argued that such an approach required social commitment to find ways in which those who were in the school system would exist in a greater state of interdependence and collective responsibility with those around them.

These claims from 1986 were made soon after the report of the Collège de France was published. Bourdieu himself was balancing the rather pessimistic conclusion of his sociological analyses with the exigencies of social responsibility; the need for political acumen with the need to stay loyal to the implications of his work; and the rigor of his theoretical perspective with the practical requirements of making a difference. Behind this debate was, of course, the issue of the interface between the worlds of politics and academic science. It may be felt that Bourdieu was poorly equipped to navigate a path through the ferocity of late twentieth-century political structures. Nevertheless, Bourdieu did have one further attempt to engage with the official systems of reform when he presided over a commission set up to establish, 'Principles for reflecting on the curriculum' (1992b/1989). The committee was initiated by the then Minster of Education and co-chaired by Bourdieu and François Gros, and included other notable French intellectuals such as Jacques Bouveresse and Jacques Derrida. The final report addressed the 'restructuring' of the division of knowledge, the transmission of knowledge, the elimination of out-moded forms of knowledge and the introduction of new knowledge coming from research. Proposals were listed under seven principles, here set out in synopsis form:

1. Course content must regularly be reviewed so that new knowledge demanded by scientific progress and changes in society (European unification being a prime example) can be introduced. Any addition of knowledge must be compensated for by a reduction elsewhere in the program.
2. Education must give priority to all the areas which can lead to a way of thinking which is endowed with a validity and applicability of a general nature as opposed to areas where knowledge could be acquired just as efficiently (and sometime more pleasantly) through other means. It is important to ensure that education does not leave unacceptable gaps which could endanger the success of pedagogic objectives. Most notably, attention should be given to fundamental ways of thinking or knowledge that are expected to be taught by everyone and yet may never be taught by anyone.
3. Open, flexible and changeable programs are a framework not a prison. There should be fewer and fewer constraints the further one travels up the hierarchy of the educational system. Teachers need to collaborate in order to define and implement programs. There must be progression – vertical connections and coherence – and horizontal connections within specialist areas and, equally, at the whole program level (for each class and year group).
4. A critical review of the compulsory curriculum must always reconcile two variables, compulsoriness and transmittability. On the one hand, the acquisition of an area of knowledge or of a thought process is more or less indispensable for scientific or social reasons at certain levels; on the other hand, its transmission is more or less difficult depending on the ability that the children have to assimilate it and the quality of the training of the teachers involved.

5. In order to improve the effectiveness of the knowledge transmission through a diversification of teaching methods (while at
   the same time taking account of the real rather than theoretical
   knowledge that has to be assimilated) it will be necessary to distinguish between specialisms, as well as within specialisms, what
   is compulsory and what is optional. Teachers responsible for different specialisms would come together to develop collective and
   group learning through, for example, field work and field-work
   approaches.

6. Concern to reinforce the coherence of teaching should lead to
   the enhancement of team teaching that brings together teachers
   from different disciplines. It should lead to a rethinking of the
   divisions within disciplines and a re-examination of certain historical regroupings. It might succeed, although always gradually, in
   bringing closer together different areas created in the evolution
   of science.

7. The search for coherence should be accomplished by a search for
   balance and integration between the different specialisms and, as
   a consequence, between different forms of excellence. It would be
   especially important to reconcile the universalism which is inherent in scientific thought and the relativism taught through the
   historical sciences, and this should reflect the plurality of lifestyles
   and cultural traditions.

These 'principles' speak for themselves. In some ways they do not
represent anything 'revolutionary' and some of them, or dimensions
of them, can certainly be found in various progressive reforms of
pedagogy, education and policy. Some have been tried and failed in
certain contexts; others exist in various forms. They were not especially original at the time either. Rather, they represented a 'collective'
summative statement at one point in time. They continue to offer a
framework to be used as principles of reflection on theories of curriculum design and policy implementation. However, this Part concludes
by returning to the actuality of education in France in the 1990s, as a
way of measuring the extent of change, the results of change, and the
effects of change in education – changes in circumstance, policy and
practice – against which we might compare other national contexts.

The 'Misery' of Education? – Return to Opposition

The discussion has shown how Bourdieu's work moved from highly developed sociological analyses of education to direct involvement in political systems in order to bring about reform, without one taking precedence over the other. His engagement in the processes of reform in the 1980s was undertaken during a time when the new socialist government was experiencing the first flushes of enthusiasm for change, and optimism for what might be achieved was at its height. This gradually gave way to disappointment at the apparent abandonment of cardinal Left-wing principles by socialist politicians when faced with the practical reality of power. Reforms, including those of educational structure and policy, were either abandoned or did not deliver their intended outcomes.

What became of education in France in the 1990s? In 1993, Bourdieu published *La Misère du monde* (*The Weight of the World*, 1999a/1993). The book was assembled by Bourdieu and a team of collaborators and is offered as a series of 'témoinages': personal accounts of daily lives and experiences. Each is an individual slice through French society but, as a whole, they build up a picture of what it was to live in France in the last decade of the twentieth century. A number of sector experiences are covered; for example, industrial relations, farming, politics, urban housing, youth and old-age pensioners. If they have one thing in common, it is the 'social suffering' of which all of these groups are victims. Why suffering? The reasons are many, some social, others more personal. In some cases, individuals are caught in situations where they suffer the consequences of government policy; in others, it is the effects of modern living. Some are caught 'out of time', just as the Algerian peasant, in a condition of 'hysteresis' where the modern world has passed them by. Or, they are caught in a 'double bind': situated in a structural context with contradictory demands. Aspects of each of these issues apply to those involved in education – both students and teachers. Why?

In a sense, Bourdieu's case studies dealing with teachers and students in education can be read as ethnographic accounts of the consequences of previous decades of educational reform in France. If the guiding principles of such reforms had been 'vocationalization and democratization', their effects seem to be far from being uniformly positive. In fact, their outcomes include many unanticipated side effects, which often seem worse than the malady they set out to cure. For example, it is all very well insisting that more students stay on at school and go to university – France had a policy that at least 80 per cent of the post-16 age group should undertake further education. However, the unintended effect of this policy was that many schools were now full of disaffected youth who did not want to be there. Or, they gained qualifications which seem to have little value in the outside world. In effect, Bourdieu's own theory predicted such a process and outcome, where the elite find other means to ensure their entry into the upper echelons of education on their way to the best jobs, while the rest work at gaining certificates that have been severely hit by 'qualification inflation'. Many new qualifications seem to buy little in terms of real jobs. Such qualifications are 'simulacra', illusory in character. In a sense, disaffection is assured when students are caught in the 'double bind' of an education with no end, on the one hand, as training routes proliferate, and with outcomes of unreliable value, on the other.

Another side effect of the 80 per cent policy was that the weaker students were 'sifted out' earlier, so that the necessary stay-on percentage was achieved by reducing the total number of students in post-16 education. All that had happened, Bourdieu argued, in an age which had insisted on equal access and opportunities, was that competition had intensified. Parents were forced to keep their eyes on all the changes happening in education and to respond immediately to them in order to maximize the chances for their children's success. At a time when selection came earlier, children had to get ahead as early as possible; the least delay, or failure, accumulated consequences as the child's scholastic career proceeded. Absurdities also existed in the curriculum itself. The 'royal road' was (and still is!) science. This is the route for the most academically able. At baccalauréat level (university-entrance level), even if a student is intending to study 'arts' subjects, it is still better to follow a 'scientific' track in order to maximize one's opportunities in terms of university/course choice. The overwhelming conclusion is that French education still exists in two principal forms: one for the 'best' (the elite) and another for the rest (the 'masses'). Life for teachers is described in *La Misère du monde* as often being 'intolerable'. They are forced to work with pupils who 'should not be there'. Little wonder, therefore, that pupils' behavior is appalling. Work is 'relentless' as they have to implement one reform after another – '*reformettes*' – in work conditions that leave much to be desired and barely cover the essentials in terms of resources. Educational 'black-spots' exist, often in centers of severe urban deprivation. Here, State aid is high, as is unemployment. All this has an effect on educational achievement. There is, then, clearly a wide gap between a political rhetoric of 'diversification and individualization' and a reality of social and economic penury.

In this large survey of the poverty of experience in contemporary France, Bourdieu and his team were keen to link the present state of education with the economic philosophy which directed policy. So, liberal economics, with its doctrine of free-market competition, when applied to public institutions such as schools, simply resulted in a withdrawal of State, and thus public, support for them. In a situation where competition between schools is deliberately opened up, the result is to create a 'scholastic exodus', as parents and pupils abandon one school in favor of another. A further effect of such a policy is to define failure as the school's fault, not the social conditions, still less the political policy, which had formed them. It is important to read these statements not simply as popular rhetoric, since they were based on extensive empirical data. They need also to be understood in terms of the *structural* changes (brought about by policy) to which education had been subjected. Such structural changes were managerial and organizational, but they all had real consequences in terms of finance and, ultimately, scholastic outcomes. Similarly, on different occasions, Bourdieu makes the point that these unexpected and unwelcome consequences of changes in education policy are the results of political short-termism – changes brought in to tackle immediate problems rather than taking time to consider fundamental rethinking and reshaping of education and its institutions. He writes that 'real revolution' would be something 'modest ... more intelligent ... with familiarity with the realities, attention to small things and "small people"' (1984b: 90). Such changes, though, would take 'at least three or four generations' to implement (Bourdieu and Grenfell, 1995b: 24).

As noted earlier, the decade of the 1990s represented a period of increased political activism for Bourdieu himself, albeit not in a politically partisan way. In 1992, he formed part of a group of educational researchers whose aim it was to offer a 'reflection' on higher education by means of bringing together documents, analyses and texts with a view to providing a sort of urgent 'diagnostic and remedy' for a 'university in peril' (see 2002b: 293). This group, named ARESER – *l'Association de réflexion sur les enseignements supérieurs et la recherche* – undertook a number of activities aimed at counteracting the application of liberal economic philosophy to education: the division of academic and vocational education, human resource policy, financial strictures, enforced managerial independence, and the restructuring of the workforce. In 1997 ARESER published an article (see 2002b: 301) in the leading French newspaper – *Le Monde* – in which it showed up the 'true' nature of the Bayrou reform of the time (it dealt with issues of grants, the balance of teaching and research, and quality assurance). The group claimed that the reform was an 'illusory' epithet because it listed actions which were already in place or simply moved financial burdens from one area to another; for example, on the upkeep of buildings – from the State to the individual institution. Their case was that instead of evaluating what had gone before, ministers were creating the illusion of change by proposing what was already happening or tinkering at its edges, while the main thrust of policy remained the same. But, the sociological theory and analysis which can be used to illuminate the generative structures of such practical policy arguments should never be forgotten; namely, that these reforms were explicable in terms of the guiding principles of the *fields* and the neoliberal economic theories which now acted as their logic of practice. In short, the language of the reform discourse itself had been captured by this self-defining and self-justifying logic, one which had a substantive aim other than the one through which it presented itself.

This example returns us to the issue of language and the way social reality is represented through it. In 1990, Bourdieu responded to a letter from a group of sixth-form students asking for support by pointing out the way that language was being used to reify them as a group, offering a media-driven image of who they were rather than presenting the complexity of their make-up (2002b: 226). A later text from ARESER appeared in *Le Monde* in 1994 (see 2002b: 297), in which they drew attention to the language of a questionnaire sent out to all young people aged between 15 and 25, and the way it misrepresented them through its language of inclusion and exclusion. In effect, it therefore presented a view of a world for its own political ends. For Bourdieu, concepts such as 'youth' became more real – especially in a media age – than the thing they represented. This occult nature of social (mis-)representations was a fundamental danger of the modern age, and apparently rife in the education *field*.

Conclusion

This chapter has addressed issues of curriculum and policy across the decades of Bourdieu's involvement in education. In many respects, this involvement was always political in terms of the implications of his response to education as an object of sociological study. The early works arose both from and addressed a policy agenda. Similarly, publications from his middle-career period were not without their political dimension in the type of reform they suggested. Bourdieu became directly involved in political committees during the 1980s and co-authored various reports for government with a view to educational reform. This discussion highlights issues surrounding the relationship between the worlds of academia and politics, as well as the place of the intellectual at the interface. Finally, Bourdieu somewhat abandoned this 'insider' position for a more direct form of opposition to what he saw as the pervasive influence of liberal economic philosophy and the effects of its application to education at all levels and to all involved within it.

Part 3

Reception and Influence of Bourdieu's work

Introduction

An important strand throughout this book has been the importance of adopting a 'socio-genetic' view to Bourdieu and his work. Consequently, the socio-cultural context into which Bourdieu was born and grew up has been discussed, both in terms of his personal and intellectual trajectory. Early influence in schools shaped much of his thinking, and experiences in Algeria resulted in him abandoning philosophical study for sociology, a subject discipline which had little status when he was beginning his career. Socio-economic developments in the 1960s had led to profound changes in the make-up of French society, and Bourdieu analyzed these and their consequences as part of the development of his particular theory of practice. Students were among his first topics of study. At the same time, he was developing analyses of culture in studies of museums and photography. Both areas of work reflected how Bourdieu saw education and culture functioning in Algeria, his home village, and French society as a whole. Bourdieu wrote at a time of major expansion in global consciousness, as frontiers broadened as a result of the explosion in mass communications. His career certainly benefited from the opportunities, both financial and institutional, which existed in a world rejuvenated after the trauma of world war. Bourdieu's theoretical perspective developed in a particular academic and intellectual climate, both national and international, where ideas competed for salience. It is, therefore, important to understand the reception and influence of Bourdieu's work in terms of the academic and intellectual discourses of the day. Part 3 of this book does this. It takes Bourdieu's work in a chronological order to reinforce the synthetic development of his theory over the course of five decades. The aim here is to enhance and understand the intellectual space in which this development took place. In following this tack, the reception and critique of Bourdieu's work will itself provide a deeper understanding of the issues, both theoretical and practical, which were and are still at issue.

Bourdieu was, of course, a highly prolific writer. Education was only one part of his work (albeit a prominent one). It is therefore important to keep in mind the many other topics of his analyses and writing – media, culture, history, economic, politics, philosophy, language, biography – which are only possible to refer to *en passant*. The core of Bourdieu's work in many ways is synonymous with the development of the sociology of education, and this Part of the book begins at the point of the emergence of the so-called *new* sociology of education. The sociological issues at stake are set out, together with the reception of Bourdieu's account of them in general. Alternative perspectives are used to exemplify the debates of the day. This Part then considers reactions to *Homo Academicus* (1988/1984) and *The State Nobility* (1996b/1989). Both practical and theoretical issues are addressed. The book then concludes (Part 4) with discussion of the way aspects of the new sociology of education developed in the latter part of the twentieth century. Bourdieu's own output amounted to several hundred publications. That figure could be multiplied again when counting the many references to his work, leading to both incidental and comprehensive discussion of it. The arrival of the new millennium offers a convenient cut-off point. Part 4 will consider some of the more recent discussions of Bourdieu's work and the applications to which it has been put. I shall also add my personal views about of the scope and potential of using Bourdieu's ideas in educational research.

Chapter 13

The New Sociology of Education

In Part 2, Chapter 11, the social climate of the 1960s and the events of May 1968 were discussed. It was notable how these events, and accounts of them, were highly infused with the spirit of the times, one of individual liberty and self-expression. It was stated that any writers at the time were keen to apply a neo-Marxist account to what occurred. Alain Touraine, in his *Le Movement de mai ou le communisme utopique* (1968) was not alone in seeing the unfolding contemporary events in classical Marxist terms of 'class struggle', 'alienation' and 'exploitation'. The work of the writer Jean-Paul Sartre gave a philosophical twist to this version of the New World, with its sentiments of 'existential bad faith'. Structuralism had also had its effects, so that a Marxist such as Louis Althusser argued that social change was essentially economic but 'mediated' through ideological apparatuses (1976/1970): political, educational, etc. In a sense, this was an extension of Marxist terminology, shared by such writers as Poulanzas and Gramsci. 'Schools' were one such apparatus and were implicated in the 'reproduction' of social classes. Baudelot and Establet (1971) adopted similar terminology in their *L'École capitaliste en France*. This book in fact appeared after *La Reproduction* (Bourdieu, 1977a/1970). They attributed the latter with putting school in its 'rightful' position as the 'number one ideological apparatus' (p. 314). They also compliment Bourdieu and Passeron for establishing the link between culture and education in explaining the social differential outcome of schooling. Although they state that students will find much in *Les Héritiers* (Bourdieu, 1979b/1964) and *La Reproduction* to explain their experiences before and during May 1968, they find the authors 'wide of the mark' in terms of theory and politics. In place of a cultural 'inheritance' they seek to re-establish a language of 'exploitation', 'oppression' and 'dominance' so essential to

a Marxist view of the reproduction of social class struggle. For Baudelot and Establet, Bourdieu and Passeron were confusing 'causes' with
'effects'. They also criticized them for adopting an 'ambiguous' position with regard to 'culture'. They argue that everything Bourdieu and
Passeron were saying seemed to be attributable to the transmission
of culture. This view might appear congruent with Marxist concepts.
However, what was missing, for them, was a recognition of 'ideological
struggle' in which the dominated were imposed upon by the dominant, and a working-class culture is repressed. School, for Baudelot
and Establet, is the place where contradictions are expressed in the
struggle for ideological domination. These struggles are not acknowledged by Bourdieu and Passeron, rather they see schools as simply the
context in which cultural deficiencies have material consequences. As
such, for Baudelot and Establet, Bourdieu and Passeron are simply
too 'functionalist': everything is thought of in terms of structure and
function – in a Durkheimian and Weberian way – rather than as seeing essential economic forces at play in a Marxist sense. For them, it
is not enough to acknowledge the inequality in schools and the way
that society is reproduced as a result: there needs to be an acceptance
of 'class struggle' as being at the heart of the capitalist system. Yet,
clearly, Bourdieu and Passeron were not thinking in these classical
Marxist terms: they focused more on the empirical individual and
what gets misrecognized in social processes, rather than an idealized
collective and a grand theory of socio-economic conflict.

Of course, it might also be argued that 'class struggle' was indeed
at the heart of the thesis of Bourdieu and Passeron, in the way that
different cultural aspects, and their logics of practice, are in constant
conflict for legitimation, symbolic power in the *field*. However, for
Bourdieu and Passeron, social processes cannot be reduced to bipo-
lar oppositions. For example, a type of cultural competition can exist
as much within the bourgeoisie as between them and the working
class. However, Baudelot and Establet do not acknowledge this possibility and charge Bourdieu and Passeron with a theory which is based
on 'automatic functionalism', 'school as a cog in the wheel', and thus
a 'sociological fatalism' leading finally to political defeatism (p. 316).
This latter point is also made by Antoine Prost in a review article
entitled 'Une sociologie stérile: La Reproduction' (1970) in *Esprit*,

the publication founded by the Catholic intellectual and personalist Emmanuel Mounier. The way such a review as *Esprit* responded to *La Reproduction* is significant. The team behind this periodical came from a personalist tradition, in which education played a crucial role as a means of developing the personality – if not soul – of the individual. As we have seen, education and culture were central pillars to social policy in France in the decades immediately following the Second World War. In Bourdieu's description of their underlying function, operations and outcomes ran directly against this view of them as the deliverer of social objectives. Prost first describes the thesis of Bourdieu and Passeron; in particular, stressing the claimed relative autonomy of the education system, the nature of pedagogic authority, and the role that culture – and its arbitrary nature – played in education. The 'symbolic violence' of education is also commented upon, as well as the way it is expressed in academic language. He concludes that what they present is 'fair' (p. 856). However, he goes on to argue that, in effect, what Bourdieu and Passeron are offering is a sort of 'nihilism'. Taken to its logical conclusion, according to their thesis, the content of pedagogy and schooling would become increasing empty, as education developed more or less simply to perform its social reproductive function. Differences in pedagogy are of relative, if not incidental, importance.

Prost also castigates Bourdieu and Passeron for their 'structuralist' tendencies, which he sees as sacrificing any comparative or historical analysis to the need to define structural coherence in terms of a rigid essentialism. He also takes exception to their call for a 'rational pedagogy' as the sole possible solution, which he finds 'utopian' and out of touch with the need to find actual policies in the real world. Finally, he concludes that what we have here is really the expression of a crisis among the intellectual class rather than a practically relevant analysis: a 'dissertation from ex prep-school pupils for ex prep-school pupils' (p. 859). As such, he finds that their language is often 'esoteric', and they engage in 'self-destructive' word games. In sum, *La Reproduction* is the 'end-game' of the Parisian mandarins.

This review illustrates two of the common reactions to the conclusions to be drawn from *La Reproduction* and *Les Héritiers*: first, an acceptance, grudging or enthusiastic, that much of the empirical analysis is correct; second, a sense of outrage or fatalism, or even denial, in the face of the logical realization that there is little that can be done to change the situation, either rapidly or dramatically. How any one individual responded to this new perspective on education really depended on where they placed themselves with respect to these issues.

Part 2, Chapter 10 set out how the 'new' sociology of education developed in Britain and the part that Bourdieu's work played in it. In a sense, the 1970s were Bourdieu's decade as a 'sociologist of education', as it was at this time that key texts began to appear in English. In general, they were received with enthusiasm or denial, again depending on the extent of the individual's sympathy with Bourdieu's case. This range of responses was also cut across by another issue – that of the accuracy of interpretation of Bourdieu's arguments, whether for or against. English translations of articles by Bourdieu were published in the 1960s. However, an article including his empirical analyses did not first appear in English until 1974. By then, *Knowledge and Control* (Young, 1971) had already had an impact. The mood was radical rather than reformist; Marxist in spirit, if not in politics. Key concepts were 'dialectical relations' in theory, and Marxist notions of infrastructure and superstructure were being replaced by such writers as Berger and Luckmann with their *The Social Construction of Reality* (1971/1967) and 'the internalisation of externality and the externalisation of internality'. Phenomenology was also in the air and, with it, a focus on individual subjectivities and micro-analyses of 'ideology'. For *Knowledge and Control*, this meant classroom knowledge, the way it is constructed between teacher and pupils, and the resultant outcomes. Some of the titles of books from that period now make for heady reading: *Power and Ideology in Education* (1977), *Identity and Structure* (Gleeson, 1977), *Ideology Culture* (1981), *Theory and Resistance in Education: A Pedagogy for the Opposition* (Giroux, 1983a), *Education Under Siege* (Aronowitz and Giroux, 1986). The talk was often of 'deschooling', as if one could be inoculated against the dangerous effect of education. Cultures other than those most obviously expressed in state education were celebrated, including counter-cultures.

Initial commentaries on Bourdieu took up a range of these issues as part of presenting his work to an English-speaking world. An early account (Kennett, 1973), for example, sets out 'the main postulates' and the 'theory of culture', claiming that 'Of course, Bourdieu is a Marxist' (p. 238). Richard Nice, Bourdieu's chief translator, also asks the question as to whether his enterprise is a Marxist one, before concluding that essentially it is (1978: 29). However, both Kennett and Nice were really claiming Bourdieu to be a Marxist by implication; the former in terms of the resonances with a Marxist theory of the ideological function of culture, the latter in the sense that Bourdieu's theory is 'orientated by reference to the ultimate determinacy of the relations of production' (*ibid.*). But, this is 'Marxism' by proxy since there is no direct link in Bourdieu's work between the 'means of production' in the economy and the structure of the ideological field – education. In fact, both Kennett and Nice also acknowledge the influence of Durkheim in Bourdieu's thesis, albeit blanched of its moral positivism. Bourdieu's epistemology certainly shares features of Marxist theory: for example, its dialectical theory in the relation between subjectivity and objectivity, the illusory nature of the social world, the practical logic of the capitalist economy and, mostly, its critical radicalism. It is also based on a theory of knowledge that is akin to Marxist theory. Culture is the central tenet of this theory. It is important to recall that Bourdieu had written that there were two traditions in the study of culture: the structuralist tradition – which sees culture as an instrument of communication and knowledge – and the functionalist tradition, which sees culture as an ideological force (1968). The first tradition (structured structure) was clearly that of Lévi-Strauss who saw culture in terms of signs and symbols based on a shared consensus of the world. The second tradition (structuring structure) was that of the relations between material conditions – material and ideological – and the way they develop a moral force. However, this second tradition had two traditions within itself: the positivist – of Durkheim and Parsons – which sought to show what made for a healthily functioning social system; and the radical/critical – of Marx – which saw it in terms of the imposition of an ideological force for the benefit of the few against the many.

It is easy to interpret Bourdieu in terms of one of these traditions, while ignoring the way his theoretical perspective is in fact co-terminus with all three. For example, in another early, largely positive response, David Swartz (1977) wrote that Bourdieu's work on education was concerned with exploring, 'the relationship between the higher-education system and social-class structure', and that 'the system of higher education functions to transmit privilege, allocate status, and instill respect for the existing social order' (p. 545). Up to a point, such an interpretation is true. However, it overly asserts the functional aspect of Bourdieu's work and points to a determinism which Bourdieu constantly fought against. For Bourdieu, the social class structure is a dynamic entity; higher education itself is constantly in flux; and the structure and content of such notions as 'status' and 'respect' are constantly changing according to *field* conditions, which themselves are symptomatic of a particular socio-economic state of society. In other words, it is possible to make Bourdieu's approach far too narrow, static and rigid. His concepts only have meaning if they are considered alongside his epistemology as set out in such books as *An Outline of a Theory of Practice* (1977b/1972), *The Logic of Practice* (1990c/1980) and *The Craft of Sociology* (1991b/1968).

Issues of method also arose in an article by Bredo and Feinberg (1979). In what is called a 'Review Essay', they begin by presenting the two parts of *La Reproduction* and the main thesis of Bourdieu and Passeron. In what Robbins later called the 'philosophy of science misconception' (1998: 35) they then focus on the 'problems' they see in the book. Issues of 'functionalism' immediately appear. They assume Bourdieu and Passeron adopted 'a normative standpoint', which allows them to see things in one way rather than another. For Bredo and Feinberg, functional analyses always run into the problem of seeing processes as multiple functions in one respect and dysfunctional in another (p. 323). In other words, it is possible to argue the data both ways; for example, the analyses of participation in higher education by working-class students could be read as a positive phenomenon where more disadvantaged children have the opportunity to extend their studies than was the norm previously. They swipe at Bourdieu and Passeron for their 'conflict functionality' and for presenting the discovered outcomes of education as 'inevitable' (p. 325). In fact, what they do like about *La Reproduction* is more concerned with the symbolic aspects of education. For example, they accept the analyses of the 'aesthetics of student evaluation' and the way style is connected with background cultures of home and school. However, they find Bourdieu and Passeron to be overly eager in asserting that these effects always occur. Bredo and Feinberg ask for more ethnographic detail to show under exactly what conditions they exist. It is clear that their objections are methodological. They are particularly unconvinced by the proliferation of 'key concepts' in *La Reproduction*, which are seen as disguising scientific evidence. 'Symbolic violence' is taken as a case in point. If this term is an 'imposition of a culture arbitrary', what do Bourdieu and Passeron mean by 'imposition'? They see theoretical ambiguity in the way the concept is handled: at one time, as if 'imposition' is against someone's will; at another time, a simple inculcation. They find such differences of interpretation to be important as such a concept can take on an ideological force precisely because it 'exploits' ambiguities; for example, the way that pedagogic action is seen in terms of symbolic violence both in schools and in the family can lead to damaging conclusions (p. 326). They conclude their essay by again criticizing Bourdieu and Passeron for not coming up with a 'moral framework', which will offer an alternative approach and change the relations of dominance: 'their own analysis, for example, says little about the way in which material conditions structure educational possibilities nor does it address the question of the kinds of norms which are appropriate for carrying out an educative enterprise' (p. 331). In sum, they find that the 'science' that Bourdieu and Passeron are offering is questionable. It does not conform to conventional research approaches and denies having any ideological perspective. It does not make use of the full potential of such techniques as multivariable analysis. And, it is based on a series of prefabricated concepts, which are overly used in an imprecise way. In effect, this critique is to set their own positivist approach against the method of Bourdieu's 'theory of practice', with all that entailed in terms of procedure; indeed, it is almost to ignore that the latter exists.

Similar themes arose in a review article by Paul DiMaggio (1979). Right from the outset, DiMaggio links Bourdieu's work in *La Reproduction* with the *Outline of a Theory of Practice* (1977b/1972) and with his work in Algeria. From *Outline*, he draws attention to gaining 'praxeological knowledge' as the goal of his work; namely, the interaction between individuals and the objective structures which surround them. He points out that it would be misleading to 'misrecognize' Bourdieu as a Marxist thinker; although he 'sounds' very Marxist – especially when he speaks about class struggle. He concludes that he is a materialist, if not a Marxian materialist, and is essentially gloomy about a picture of the world as one without revolution, or even social change, but rather of endless transformations based around the same logic of social class hierarchization. Generally, DiMaggio is positive about Bourdieu and draws attention to the ways his work could be useful to American sociologists. However, the tension between an American and a French way of viewing the world is at the heart of his criticisms of Bourdieu. The crudest way of expressing this tension would probably be between the empirical and literary traditions. At base here is the issue of what is 'science'. So, for DiMaggio, Bourdieu is more of an 'artist' than a scientist, and his work is finally 'inchoate'. He comments that Bourdieu's prose is complex with long sentences including several subclauses. He accepts that Bourdieu has much of value to say about 'empirical insensitivity' and the way it deals with the nature of the objective social structure. He also recognizes that Bourdieu is, in his use of statistics, more empirical than most French writers. However, Bourdieu is, he argues, more prone to go for systematic explanation than correlational analysis; as such, his method is better at generating hypotheses than confirming them. DiMaggio claims that Bourdieu's explanations are based on a conceptual apparatus that is circular, ambiguous and imprecise. DiMaggio is arguing for much more empirical evidence. For example, it is not enough to assert that differences in social-class background produce a different *habitus*; it has to be shown with empirical proof. He also asks for evidence to demonstrate the determinants of 'relative autonomy' of *fields*, not just assertions that they do in fact exist according to their internal logics. In a word, Bourdieu's conceptual thinking tools are seen to be at once inflated and imprecise. These criticisms seem to turn on methodological choices. However, it would be truer to see them in terms of epistemology. Bourdieu replies to criticism that his concepts are too 'open-ended' by stating that this approach is a way of rejecting positivism:

Concepts have no definition other than systemic ones, and are designed to be *put to work empirically in systemic fashion*. Such notions as habitus, field, and capital can be defined, but only within the theoretical system they constitute, not in isolation.

(1992a: 96: Emphasis in the original)

In fact, Bourdieu eschewed 'laws of the middle range' – grounded theory of micro-contexts – which he saw simply as 'satisfying positivistic expectation' or 'positivistic gratification'. He argued that concepts are like people: they only make sense in terms of the relations they hold with those around them. This is why the concept of *fields*, and the technique of 'correspondence analysis' which he used to analyze them, are so important, since they 'think' in terms of *relation*. What is at stake, therefore, is the distinction (outlined in Part 2) between two forms of knowledge: one substantialist, coming down from an Aristotelian tradition, and the other relational: 'I could twist Hegel's famous formula and say that *the real is relational*: what exist in the social world are relations – not interactions between agents or intersubjective ties between individuals, but objective relations which exist "independently of individual consciousness and will", as Marx said' (1992a: 97).

Here, issues are philosophical as well as methodological and procedural. Both of these were central to responses to Bourdieu and the 'new sociology of education' generation. Because of their radical perspective, political consequences and possible action must be considered as another key question for both Bourdieu and other writers in this movement and their critics. Bates (1980) concluded that the 'new sociology of education' was developing four principal strands, which were all important in contemporary educational policy:

'a coherent epistemology related to the ideas of critical theory whose justification is by appeal to criterion of human betterment; systematic analysis of social, economic, cultural, epistemological hierarchies and their interpenetration; a conception of political theory which depends upon the application of critical social theory and the analysis of procedures of hierarchy and control in the actual practice of teachers in their concrete social, educational and political situation; and a conception of political action which rejects large-scale utopian visions but concentrates instead on the improvement of practice in particular situations through the processes of critical reflection and innovation' (p. 77).

Clearly, a hybrid of phenomenology and Marxism was seen as a way of developing a perspective which was both philosophically robust and practically relevant in an age when human rationality, indeed the whole modernist project, began to be questioned. What was sought was a way of knowing beyond the technical, a form of theory that was validated in practice, and which led to an improvement in human conditions. However, the attacks on the new sociology of knowledge came from two sides. One side saw the whole 'Marxist-phenomenology' marriage as a form of theoretical sloganizing: a heady brew of cognitive and linguistic behaviorism, ethnomethodology and antipathy to commodity society (see Davies, 1977: 190), leading to the fatalistic conclusion that education cannot 'through mass transmission of differentiated knowledge produce a less-exploitable pluralistic society' (*ibid.*: 201). The other side worried that the work of such writers as Bourdieu and Bernstein tended to 'reduce culture, ideology, and consciousness to "mere" functions of capital, wherein the "logic" of capital subsumes not only labor but all areas of human life, be these cultural, ideological, or institutional, such as the school' (Gorder, 1980: 343, referring to Aronowitz, 1978). The point that Aronowitz makes is that such an assumption is only a tendency, and that one must not exclude the contradictory practices of oppressed groups, such as minorities, women and others. This point brings us to the question of the scope for resistance in Bourdieu's work.

Resistance

Above, the fatalism, if not pessimism, implied by Bourdieu's theoretical account arising from his empirical analyses was noted. Educational policy reform hardly changed the situation and, despite morphological changes, the logic of practice underlying educational systems continues its social reproductive function. What then of resistance?

Henry Giroux took up the issue in an article in 1983b. He had noted that Marx himself used the notion of 'reproduction' in *Capital*:

'every social process of production is, at the same time, a process of reproduction ... Capitalist production, therefore, ... produces not only commodities, not only surplus value, but it also produces and reproduces the capitalist relation, on the one side the capitalist, on the other the wage-labourer' (p. 257). He also notes that this concept was used by 'radical educators' in their critique of liberal views of schooling. His main thesis is that by downplaying the importance of human agency and the possibility of resistance, reproduction theories seem to offer little hope for challenging the undesirable consequences of schooling. Bourdieu's work is taken as an example. He sets out Bourdieu's case: especially the centrality of culture as mediating between school and society, and the relative autonomy of scholastic institutions; neither independent of external forces, as in the idealist position, nor mirroring the economic system, as in the radical position. He takes up the notion of *habitus* as 'embodied history', which will include emotional, sensory and physical disposition, as well as the intellectual, concluding that it is in the relations between personal histories and the knowledge systems that surround them that social control is exerted. In other words, it is not in a process of imposition of ideology that reproduction occurs; rather, it is almost automatic given the essential logic of differentiation in the constitution of, and between, *habitus* and *field*. All this is in agreement with Bourdieu. However, he concludes that Bourdieu's work is seriously 'flawed'. It is flawed, he argues, mostly because of 'mechanistic notions of power and domination and the overly determined view of human agency. Giroux quotes a paper Bourdieu had written on language and linguistics – 'The economics of linguistic exchanges' (1977c) – as evidence of determinism: 'the choices constituting a certain relation to the world are internalized in the form of durable patternings not accessible to consciousness nor even, in part, amenable to will'. Giroux further argues that where the possibility of resistance does appear in Bourdieu's work, this does not rest on critical reflection and subsequent action but occurs in the mismatch between an individual *habitus* and the structural *field* position one occupies – presumably, what was earlier referred to as *hysteresis*. Resistance for Bourdieu is, therefore, an epiphenomenon of conflict rather than the result of, 'the power of reflexive thought and historical agency' (p. 271) which, Giroux claims, are relegated to minor detail. He goes on to argue that Bourdieu sees working-class culture as homogeneous and as 'merely a pale reflection of dominant cultural capital' (*ibid.*) And: 'Working-class cultural production and its relation to cultural reproduction through the complex dynamics of resistance, incorporation, and accommodation are not acknowledged by Bourdieu' (*ibid.*). In short, the potential for culture to transform the individual through another, different structuring process is missed by Bourdieu.

Giroux criticizes Bourdieu for offering a 'one-sided' treatment of ideology. Here, he takes exception to the fact that Bourdieu did not acknowledge the imposition of ideology on students in education and, consequently, the way that opposition and resistance is already apparent in the way parents, teachers and students react to it. He claims that Bourdieu fails to develop ideology as something that is dialectically created, resisted and accommodated, and therefore excludes the 'active nature' of domination and resistance (*ibid.*). *En passant*, one might note that this latter 'criticism' is especially surprising, as this 'active' aspect is presumably exactly what lies at the heart of Bourdieu's theory of practice. Finally, Giroux objects to the way Bourdieu apparently passed over material conditions as the foundation of ideology; in other words, the link between domination and economic forces. Bourdieu's notions of capital and class, he finds, are 'static'; while what is needed is something much more dynamic and oppositional. He concludes on Bourdieu's work: 'What we are left with is a theory of reproduction that displays little faith in subordinate classes and groups and little hope in their ability or willingness to reconstruct the conditions by which they live, work and learn. Giroux asserts that: 'A theory of resistance is central to the development of a radical pedagogy ... [and] It helps bring into focus social practices in schools whose ultimate aim is the control of both the learning process and the capacity for critical thought and action' (p. 292).

> Finally, Giroux argues, the new radical pedagogy must come from 'a theoretically sophisticated understanding of power, resistance, and human agency ... [and] Schools will not change society, but can create in them pockets of resistance that provide pedagogical models for new forms of learning and social relations – forms which can be used in other spheres more directly involved in the struggle for a new morality and view of social justice' (p. 293).

It is again important to set publications in their socio-historical contexts. This is true for Bourdieu's work and it is no lesser the case for others. Giroux's writing therefore has to be seen in terms of its own time: 1983. This was before many of the practical implications – in theory and practice – of Bourdieu's work had been grasped. It was also before Bourdieu himself had undertaken an explicit series of 'acts of resistance', and had shown what this meant for him. Giroux himself later acknowledged that in this article he had not been doing justice to the full sophistication of Bourdieu's perspective. Nevertheless, it is important to note the characteristics of the wider sociological tradition that originated in the 1970s, and to which Bourdieu made a significant, even central, contribution. That discipline field, 'new' sociology of education, was critical and radical. For example, the section titles of a book such as *Power and Ideology in Education* by Karabel and Halsey (1977) give a fair indication of the direction those involved in the movement were taking: 'Education and Social Structure', 'Education and Social Selection', 'Education, "Human Capital" and the Labor Market', 'The Politics of Education', 'Cultural Reproduction and the Transmission of Knowledge', 'Social Transformation and Educational Change'. Giroux too continued his radical critique of schooling – for example 1983a, 1983b and 1986 – in terms of resistance, or a pedagogy of opposition, to an education system which was seen as being 'under siege' from conservative and liberal ideas. It has to be said that Bourdieu saw the potential for resistance coming from a difference source.

Other Responses to *La Reproduction*

The 'new' sociology of education, and Bourdieu's work in particular, had a large impact on education in the 1970s and 1980s, and could be characterized as radical, critical and essentially phenomenological. It drew attention to the construction of pedagogic knowledge. The underlying assumption in this work was often that it was possible to 'sensitize' teachers to issues in children's development and education in a way which allowed them to avoid the mistakes in the past. A further question then arises concerning how such sociological findings and principles – for example, in the case of Bourdieu, the way that home background affected subject take-up of pupils – might be acted on in the context of actual classrooms. It was assumed that knowing about these issues was necessarily a good thing. At the very least, teachers might be able to respond to what confronted them in ways which were more appropriate than had been the norm up until that point. More ambitiously, it might be possible to radicalize teachers in such a way that they would become the agents of change, the engineers of a new society. This was a tall order and, as we shall see, the way that Bourdieu's theory might indeed affect classroom practice is both more subtle and more profound than a simple raising of awareness. Nevertheless, the 'radical' strand of sociology of education continued well into the 1980s and 1990s (see for example, Popkewitz, 1987), and indeed continues to this day, albeit that it is now largely infused with post-modernism. In terms of educational policy, the challenge that the radical wing of the sociology of education laid down has been met in many countries by government reform of teacher education systems, including more centrally directed system of curriculum planning, enforced by State-sponsored sanctions and inspection, and an attack on educational research, its value and worth (see Grenfell and James, 2005).

The way the 'new' sociology of education was articulated to teachers in training came through the reception of books such as *Knowledge and Control* and *La Reproduction* and in the publication of collected articles such as *Identity and Structure* (Gleeson, 1977) and *Sociological Interpretations of Schooling and Classrooms* (Barton and Meighan, 1978). The bibliographies of the latter books are peppered with references to the former key texts, as well as other radical sociologists and cultural theorists: Apple, Bowles and Gintis, Althusser, Cutler, Bernstein, Giddens, Gramsci, etc. However, the first article dedicated to Bourdieu in the *British Journal of the Sociology of Education* appeared in 1984. In it, a sociologist of education from New Zealand (Harker) argued that the potential of Bourdieu's work was yet to be realized; that hitherto, his theories had been 'bolted on' to empirical investigations rather than employed from the outset; and that a greater acknowledgement needed to be made of Bourdieu's complete work, of which his studies of education were only a part, in order to address the 'higher levels' (Harker, 1984: 125) of reproduction in society.

Issues of 'theory' and 'practice' were however finely poised, and it was clear that with a slight slip of the pen or misinterpretation and the entire project was lost. For example, in an otherwise positive account of Bourdieu's theory, Bidet (1979) commits 'the error' of employing the word 'determinism' to describe the relationship between structure and *habitus*: 'structures produce habitus which *determine* practices, which reproduce structures' (my emphasis, p. 203), which eventually leads to the conclusion that for 'reproduction' we need to read 'perpetuation' and, 'The disregard for structural contradictions (e.g. within the relations of production) which define practices as adequate to the modification of structures leads us to think of structural efficiency as that which reproduces the identical, and to view the relationship between history and sociology as a purely external one' (p. 207). Bourdieu's later collaborator, Loïc Wacquant, makes a similar accusation that the theory underestimates material determinations and historical transformation (1987). However, as Bourdieu later argued, 'Circular and mechanical models of this kind are precisely what the notion of habitus is designed to destroy' (1992a: 135). In place, he sought to put a dynamic theory which attributes social position to the interaction between the social and the biographical, and the way dispositions and the logic of practice of particular contexts co-respond.

Another critique, from Margaret Archer (1983), takes a similar direction. In an article entitled 'Process without system' she compares the work of Bourdieu and the English sociologist of education, Basil Bernstein. She objects to the way Bourdieu and Passeron apparently 'universalize' educational processes on the basis of the particular French case. Her target is the theoretical statements set out in Book 1 of *La Reproduction*, the so-called 'Foundations of a Theory of Symbolic Violence'. For example, she selects a part of the second section in which Bourdieu and Passeron state that the unification of symbolic markets for educational goods is one means by which bourgeois society has multiplied the ways in which it is able to submit the educational outcomes of those dominated by its dominant bourgeois 'pedagogic action' to the 'evaluation criteria of the legitimate culture' – thus, confirming its domination. Archer accuses Bourdieu and Passeron of 'ethnocentric bias' (p. 132), making the point that 'strong unification' only works in highly centralized systems; for example, France with its national competitive exams, State training of elites, and the Napoleonic university tradition of education as servicing the State. She goes on to state that, 'Bourdieu categorically asserts that every educational system necessarily monopolizes teacher training and imposes standardized methods, texts and syllabuses to safeguard orthodoxy' (*ibid.*). If this is a mark of 'institutionalization', she argues, other 'decentralized' systems should be considered 'less institutional', which clearly they are not. She concludes that an unfortunate consequence of what she calls 'their neglect' of the educational system itself is that 'general theories of cultural transmission and cultural reproduction are severed from historical and comparative sociology of education' (p. 137), while what is needed is 'the development of a more comprehensive theory capable of unifying processes of structuration and enculturation in education' (*ibid.*). Such a theory would consider the 'historical antecedents' of 'knowledge codes' and the 'cultural arbitrary' in order to show the 'action-chains' and conditioning whose consequences have produced the present state of educational affairs in a country. She ends by stating that the authors: 'cut their theories off from comparative sociology because their homogenization of educational systems precludes the cross-cultural examination of systematic structuration' (*ibid.*).

In response to this critique, one might make the point that in a book with a series of over 80 'theoretical foundations', it is clearly the case that some may be more or less 'true' or universal. Moreover, it is in fact the case that since Archer wrote these words many national systems have become more centralized, and thus institutionalized, in exactly in the way that Bourdieu and Passeron describe. It could also be added that what Archer is urging them to do is exactly what others are criticizing them for doing: namely, comimg up with a deterministic theory that links historical cause with inevitable present effects. The issue at stake is once again fundamentally methodological. Bourdieu and Passeron were not attempting to produce a general theory of educational practice, even though the way that *La Reproduction* was presented might have suggested they were. What they were offering were 'foundations' for a 'theory of symbolic violence', which was an example of and an extension of the 'theory of practice' that Bourdieu was developing. This undertaking had a different type of 'theory' as its goal, one which would give rise to praxeological knowledge. What Bourdieu's approach is offering in *La Reproduction* is not a type of deterministic knowledge to describe all education systems – a set of universals exemplified with empirical evidence – but a set of axioms and thinking tools which could be used to illuminate other national systems. By immersing himself in practical data, his aim was not to develop a general systems theory, or even to link culture with event, but to highlight strong and weak connections and correspondences in a way which would give rise to meta-theoretical statements, which, to coin a phrase of his, are visible to the extent of the results that they yield – it is not to build theory. Passeron (1986) himself warned that: 'one must beware of taking a model of social reproduction as a comprehensive model of society, as a law or trend which appears to regulate the order of historical evolution' (p. 629). He goes on to argue that reproduction models are approximate models, 'constructed on a pattern of extremes', of hypotheses which would be the case if they existed in 'systematic perfection': 'society is not a system, and that is why it is the task of history to create a form of description of the dependencies and continuities which the use of models and typologies can never replace' (*ibid.*). In this respect, we might charge the critics of Bourdieu and his mid-career work on education with theoretical zealousness, or at least over-ambition. Bourdieu says as much himself when he addressed the range of attacks he sustained, as mentioned above:

In addition to the title of my second book on the education system, *Reproduction*, whose brutal consciousness helped to establish a simplified version of my vision of history, I think that some of the formulas born of the will to break with the ideology of the 'liberating school' can appear to be inspired by what I call the 'functionalism of the worst case'. In fact, I have repeatedly denounced pessimistic functionalism and the dehistoricizing that follows the structuralist standpoint ... Similarly, I do not see how relations of domination, whether material or symbolic, could possibly operate without implying, activating resistance. ... There exist dispositions to resist; and one of the tasks of sociology is precisely to examine under what conditions these dispositions are socially constituted, effectively triggered, and rendered politically efficient.

(1992a: 79–82)

When discussing the socially constituted dispositions, Bourdieu refers to Paul Willis' *Learning to Labour* (1977), previously mentioned as a text which was seminal in showing the way a group of working class 'lads' opposed the school system through horseplay, truancy and delinquency. It is necessary to contextualize these works in terms of the times and place from which they arose. If Bourdieu was mostly responding to what he saw as a conservative view of schooling in the 1960s, Willis was very much of the 'counter-culture' generation. It is sometimes quite paradoxical to realize that Bourdieu's own theoretical perspective would suggest that the 'resistance' of the lad simply locks them into systems in which they will continue to be dominated. Willis was part of the Birmingham Centre for Contemporary Cultural Studies, a group of academics with whom Bourdieu held close associations; for example, Richard Nice, Stuart Hall and Willis himself. The next chapter further addresses the link between education and culture, and critical commentary on Bourdieu's work on it.

Chapter 14

Culture and the *Homo Academicus*

In Part 2, Bourdieu's early work on education and schooling was described as developing hand in hand with his analysis of culture; indeed, that culture was central to the functional practice of educational systems. His three principal publications during the decade of 1979–89 served to underline that link, although increasingly the two strands were treated as distinct. *Distinction* (1984a/1979) should be treated as a 'sociological classic', with its analysis of the social construction of taste; how class runs so deeply in our *habitus* that it touches our deepest aesthetic senses. If his thesis on education trod on the corns of the inheritors of personalism and those who believed education offered the best means to transform society and Man, *Distinction* was always bound also to offend these groups, with its account of the social distribution of style and taste and, more importantly (just as in education) how culture was used as a means of sustaining systems of domination.

Central to Bourdieu's thesis is an analysis of class and the way its taste and aesthetics are expressed differentially across the social spectrum. A number of ethnographic and visual texts are used to analyze aesthetic responses. There is also a large number of statistical tables offered to indicate the result of questionnaires on art and aesthetics, including correspondence analysis. Bourdieu had stated his project elsewhere:

The subjectivist intuition that seeks a meaning in the immediacy of lived experience would not be worth attending to for a moment if it did not serve as an excuse for objectivism, which limits itself to establishing regular relationships and testing their statistical significance without deciphering their meaning, and which remains an abstract and formal nominalism as far as it is not seen as a necessary but only purely temporary moment of the scientific process.

(1990a/1965: 2)

Bourdieu is here using every theoretical means at his disposal – both ethnographic and statistical – to explain the logic of practice of his chosen field of study.

In *Esprit* (the revue founded by the personalist Emmanuel Mounier) Phillipe Raynaud (1980) placed *Distinction* (Bourdieu 1984a/1979) in a line of development which began with *The Inheritors* and continued with *Reproduction*. Familiar objections are raised about the fatalism and the closure of the method Bourdieu employs and its outcomes. The spectre of functionalism is raised and the textual effects and consequences of the ideas expressed: repetition, exhaustive analyses leading to a collapse of meaning, and finally paralysis. If *Reproduction* had led to discouraging teachers, *Distinction* would do little to redress the balance. In effect, it is, Raynaud claims, a thesis leading to political nihilism. Better therefore to pass it off as an intellectual ruse, a game aimed at other intellectuals, than the basis for cultural policy. Thus, Bourdieu's extensive empirical work and the practical methodological approach he was adopting, which gave rise to his conclusions on cultural issues, were yet again 'misrecognized'.

Other English-speaking authors responded to *Distinction* by focusing on its theoretical underpinnings. Ostrow (1981), for example, considered culture as 'a fundamental dimension to human experience', as incarnated in Bourdieu's 'theory' of *habitus*. He traces the line which links Bourdieu to the philosopher of experience, John Dewey, as well as phenomenologists such as Husserl and Merleau-Ponty. In language which echoes Bourdieu, rather than challenging him, Ostrow wants to 'locate the dynamics of habitus within the structure of experience, as not only a pretext for human practice, but a context' (p. 290). This is an attempt to allow for greater innovation and initiation in the substrate of human facticity. Here, there is the tension between objective *field* conditions and subjective reactions to them. Ostrow is looking to allow greater individual potential, so what they do is 'controlled' by the *field* but not 'determined' by it.

Still other writers are more deeply rooted in traditional Marxist theories, and wish to emphasize human subjectivity less – except for the possibility of resistance and freedom – and more socio-historical conditions as the determiner of human action. They also lay claim to stricter definitions of social class in the Marxist sense. For example, Gartman (1991) finds Bourdieu's conception of the working class 'degrading', despite its empirical origins. In particular, Gartman seeks to attribute to human praxis the express trans-historical need for freedom. Gartman consequently draws a distinction between Bourdieu and his structuralist view of culture as 'reproducing structure', and the position of the critical theorists who seek to realize expressed human needs in a conception of culture as praxis. With affiliation to the Gramscian School, critical theorists see the liberating potential of culture. Gartman does not then agree that culture simply performs the function of reproducing class structure, it can also be liberating. Furthermore, he claims that Bourdieu's view is ahistorical, particularly in the way it overlooks a fundamental aspect of the development of Western capitalism – class struggle – which has the potential to 'revolutionize' existing class structures. In other words, Bourdieu is too pessimistic about the extent of mass reification and thus subjugation to dominant class hegemony.

Other cultural theorists did not grasp that Bourdieu was not intent on developing a grand systemized social theory, or a 'general theory of symbolic domination' (see Martin and Szelényi, 1987). Brubaker (1985), for example, attacked Bourdieu for his 'extreme generality' in his conception of class. He objects, quoting *Distinction* (pp. 106 and 112), to the way that the term 'class' is used as a system of 'pertinent properties' by a 'whole set of factors operating in all areas of practice – volume and structure of capital, defined synchronically and diachronically ... sex, age, marital status, place of residence' (Brubaker, 1985: 769). He is arguing, therefore, that Bourdieu is using the term 'class' in a way which is vastly different from the way it was used by Marx and Weber, who employed it to designate a particular mode of social grouping. Brubaker even charges Bourdieu with the intent of constructing a 'systematically unified meta-theory', and goes on to quote Weber that such ambitions are bound to lead to terms which are 'devoid' of content since the more they attempt to include the common elements of the largest number of phenomena, the more abstract and general they become.

Bourdieu's response would again be epistemological and thus methodological. What was not clear to Brubaker was that Bourdieu was not constructing 'theory' to take into the analysis of empirical date. Rather, being immersed in such data, he was describing the correspondences and emergent patterns he was seeing, employing a range of theoretical tools. In other words, theory construction was a secondary by-product of acquiring the praxeological knowledge he was attempting to find in understanding particular practical phenomena. Strictly speaking, Bourdieu had no interest in conforming, denying or extending classical Marxist or Weberian definitions of 'social class'; he was coming from a different direction, and with a different goal. When Bourdieu wrote about aesthetics and taste, he was offering a description of objectified subjectivity, which was itself an internalization of objectivity in the dialectical relations and structural homologies he saw between *habitus* and *field*. Social phenomena, for Bourdieu, must be understood in terms of naïve empirical experience, objective conditions and subjective dispositions at one and the same time; as well as operating so that the researcher and the researcher are subject to the same epistemological processes of objectification:

> ... immediate lived experience, understood through expressions which mask objective meaning as much as they reveal it, refers to the analysis of objective meanings and the social conditions which make those meanings possible, an analysis which requires the construction of the relationship between the agents and the objective meaning of their action.
>
> (1990a/1965: 4)

And that objectification necessarily includes statistical analyses. It is worth considering the following again:

> If it is true that this detour via the establishment of statistical regularities and formalization is the price which must be paid if one wishes to break with naïve familiarity and the illusions of immediate understanding, it is also the case that the properly anthropological

project of re-appropriating reified meanings would be negated by
the reification of the re-appropriated meanings in the opacity of
abstraction.

(*ibid.*: 2)

Bourdieu's mission seemed to offer a different way of doing things
in terms of research methodology, which produced a different way of
knowing things; a way of knowing that was counter to salient trends in
the intellectual sphere and which had his theory of practice at its core.
In *An Invitation to Reflexive Sociology* (1992a: 193), he claimed that he
constructed this approach, specifically that of 'field analysis', as a way
of destroying both 'intellectual narcissism' and forms of objectivity
that either rest on a singular case or place individuals within social
categories which are so broad that they are meaningless. Reflexivity
is central to this project.

We have seen that *Homo Academicus* can be read on several levels,
which are not mutually exclusive. In some respects, it is a *field* analysis
of higher education in France; in others, a sociological account of
socio-historical changes in both the teaching and the student population; yet, at another level, it is simply a sociological analysis of 1968.
And, over and above all this, it is an account of Bourdieu objectifying
his own position within the then academic and intellectual field, an
undertaking he had consistently argued for as part of his method.
In fact, *Homo Academicus* was received in France in part as a kind of
narcissistic exercise in knowing where you stand; for example, deciphering the names of leading intellectuals behind the initials used by
Bourdieu in the first French edition – a kind of intellectual precursor
of the 'top ten' lists that are now so common on popular television.
Collins (1989) noted its very 'French' nature, both in method and
content. It was very easy, therefore, to pass it by as a French intellectual's book for French intellectuals, not as an invitation to undertake the same exercise in other national contexts as a way of understanding the processes and outcomes of particular academic *fields*,
which might indeed have offered an opportunity for cross-cultural
comparisons.

The whole thrust of the Foreword prepared by Loïc Wacquant
for the English edition of the *La Noblesse d'État* was to address this

issue: what he called 'doggedly Francocentric in empirical substance and scope' (1996b/1989: ix). Collins too (*op.cit.*) argued that Bourdieu's approach showed few of the characteristic methods of American sociology, locked as it was (is!) in its frameworks of dependent and independent variables. Yet, as noted in Part 2, Wacquant finally concluded that the analytic tools were just as applicable in a totally different national context. All that was needed was to consider changes in the nature and character of *cultural* (educational) *capital*, and its basic mechanisms then operated in the same way in both France and America. His conclusion elsewhere was similarly that, although *La Noblesse d'État* did not offer solutions to all the problems it posed, it did provide, 'analytical tools and a provisional model for the comparative and historical analysis of the "ruling classes" of different epoch and societies' (1993: 13). He furthermore makes the point that Bourdieu's hope was not so much to contribute to the 'process of dissolution within the ruling class', as Marx would have it in *The Communist Manifesto*, but 'at least to register a note of dissent in the concert of congratulation orchestrated by the new socialist nobility of France enough to "compel the truth of power relations to come into the open if only by forcing them to veil themselves yet further"' (*ibid.*).

It would be wrong to conclude that *Homo Academicus* and *La Noblesse d'État* have not informed studies in higher education (see the discussion in Part 4). For example, Tomusk (2000) argues that one of the salient patterns of the production of a Soviet elite was the systematic destruction of *cultural capital*. With the fall of communism, State assets were privatized. Privileged access to higher education was given to students with backgrounds in collective farms, industry and the military. However, the lack of institutionalized and legitimate forms of *capital* accumulation had given rise to widespread corruption. The new state elite – former second-rank party bureaucrats – sought *capital* accumulation (they need *capital* to mediate their field operations), and therefore sent their children to fee-paying schools, leading to jobs in law and business. He argues that this development has fragmented higher education and led to questions about the role of the State as provider and guarantor of quality.

However, the challenge laid down by Bourdieu has scarcely been taken up in any systematic way. In 1998, Derek Robbins set Bourdieu's sociology within an academic *field* in which the sociology of education and traditional sociology were 'either opposed or, more insidiously, subtly appropriated' (p. 50). He concludes that the process of appropriation through assimilation is a principal means by which the sociology of disclosure that Bourdieu is offering is neutralized. Referring to the 'university league tables' in which all universities are placed in an 'order of merit' according to a series of performance indicators, he states:

> [In an article in *The Times Educational Supplement* in September 1993] I argue that Bourdieu's *La Noblesse d'État* offered a convincing sociological analysis of the hierarchical status of the 84 *Grandes écoles* and that a comparable analysis could be undertaken of the UK with respect to the 100 universities. I suggested that the league table produced by Tom Cannon exploited sociology in that it subsumed the findings of the sociology of education in concocting a 'value-added' institutional rating to be placed alongside other institutional performance indicators. I tried to suggest that the managerialist analysis was accommodating sociological insights so as to neutralize them and construct a non-sociological league table. There was absolutely no comment on my article from any quarter and, of course, the league tables continue to appear, manifesting the same managerial deception.
>
> (Robbins, in Grenfell and James, 1998: 50)

This analysis again leads to a pessimistic conclusion concerning the scope for impact of these ideas on changing policy. The issue is the extent to which economic and political power devalues autonomous and meritocratic achievement in the *field,* so that there should be no inter-generational threat to social class positioning (in its unfolding nature). No wonder, therefore, that a review of *La Noblesse d'État* in France at the time of its publication had the title: *Pierre le Fataliste.*

Bourdieu did address this issue:

> I believe that sociology does exert a disenchanting effect, but this, in my eyes, marks a progress toward a form of scientific and political realism that is the absolute antithesis of naïve utopianism. Scientific knowledge allows us to locate real points of application for

responsible action . . . While it is true that a certain kind of sociology, and perhaps the one I practice, can encourage sociologism as submission to 'inexorable laws' of society . . . I think that Marx's alternative between utopianism and sociologism is somewhat misleading: there is room, between sociologistic resignation and utopian voluntarism, for what I would call a reasoned utopianism, that is a rational and politically conscious use of the limits of freedom afforded by a true knowledge of social laws and especially their *historical* conditions of validity. The political task of social science is to stand up both against irresponsible voluntarism and fatalistic scientism, to help define a rational utopianism by using the knowledge of the probable to make the possible come true. Such a sociological, that is, realistic, utopianism is very unlikely among intellectuals. First because it looks petty bourgeois, it does not look radical enough. Extremes are always more chic, and the aesthetic dimension of political conduct matters a lot to intellectuals.

(1992a: 196f)

His sociology might therefore be considered not only one of disclosure but, through making misrecognitions evident, also offering intellectual weapons of resistance.

Chapter 15

Social Theory

This chapter now returns to social theory per se, both to see how Bourdieu's theory of practice measures up against different versions, and to consider his response to the alternatives to his own.

Social theory is itself, of course, always in a state of flux. This condition of change is true across the decades and centuries. Indeed, disciplines such as philosophy, psychology, anthropology and sociology are continuously evolving, both individually and in relation to each other. Earlier parts of this book have discussed Bourdieu's immediate intellectual background and the possible effects it had on his thinking. The relationship between anthropology and philosophy as they were developing in the 1950s and 1960s was also considered. It is impossible to give even a general overview of the subsequent transformations in philosophy and the social sciences and remain true to the heterogeneous complexities of their various strands. Still, it is possible to say something about principal directions.

Bourdieu's work in sociology and philosophy arose as part of a radical tradition of social criticism. As set out in Part 1, this tradition can be traced back to the eighteenth and nineteenth centuries and the socio-political commentators of the day: Rousseau, Montesquieu, Tocqueville, Comte, etc. These writers can be seen as the intellectual forefathers of the founding fathers of sociology: Marx, Weber and Durkheim. Sociology is, by definition, radical in that it objectifies and holds up for comment, the functions and outcomes of society. Bourdieu's work placed himself in this tradition. Philosophically, the metaphysical school founded by Kant established an interpretative approach to human knowledge. The sociological tradition gave rise to functionalism and Marxism (in some cases, at the same time); the philosophical tradition to phenomenology and hermeneutics.

These traditions coalesced in various combinations in the 1950s and 1960, sometimes joining with different brands of ethnography, to give us existentialism and anthropological structuralism. The whole thrust of human sciences was then brought to a head and eclipsed by post-modernism: a philosophy which turned the philosophy of man into a philosophy of language based on the 'linguistic turn'. The outcome of post-modernism was a form of philosophical relativism which eschewed traditional humanist notions of truth, reason and progress. Thus, post-modernism represented a major evolution in human thought. It is a 'condition' from which we are still recovering. Bourdieu believed that post-modernism was extremely dangerous, since it destroyed hard-won aspects of human progress, such as the notion of the State and how it operated to support its populace. He also predicted that in the vacuum created by the post-modernist meltdown of human values, reactionary forces would regenerate. It is necessary to keep these issues in mind while considering the following three social theoretical approaches and their implications and responses to Bourdieu's own theory.

Economic Sociology and Rational Action Theory

If the 1950s, 1960s and 1970s were a period when State intervention was at its height in terms of 'managing' society and the economy, this slowly gave way to a return, in the 1980s and 1990s, to 'the power of the market' as a mechanism for directing social resources. 'Liberal economics' promoted competition, privatization and the withdrawal of state intervention in management of the economy. This approach to economics went hand in hand with a social philosophy, which downgraded the significance of society – in fact, 'society did not exist' – and re-emphasized the individual. A policy of open competition between individuals and the accentuating of inequalities as a means of stimulating ambition and industriousness went with this. This economic philosophy was predicated on the law of the market, since markets were seen as the best and most efficient means of distributing resources, including information. Social actors then made 'rational choices' and undertook 'rational action' in order to maximize their benefits: 'the best way for the agent to satisfy his desire, given his belief; the belief is the best he could form, given the evidence; the amount of evidence collected is itself optimal, given his desire' (Elster, 1986: 16). Clearly, this is a vastly different world from the neo-Marxist, radical one. Indeed, at one point one of the main advocates of the Rational Action Theory (RAT) approach to social theory, Jon Elster, claimed that Marxist theory and ideologies were in a 'lamentable state' (1990: 88). He also criticized Bourdieu for tending 'to see every minute detail of social action as part of a vast design of oppression' (p. 89). For example, he argued, when Bourdieu accuses intellectuals of playing with language as a means of excluding the petty bourgeois who cannot play language games, he is in fact espousing a conspiracy theory which actually borders on functionalism; that this is all that intellectuals have in mind. Elster argued that people do not acquire 'semi-compulsive tendencies' (dispositions in Bourdieu's terms) but 'preference structures', which determine the choice of a certain action over other options. What is at stake is causality versus intentionality (p. 98). For Elster and RAT theorists, people do have scope for individual choice. They also mobilize 'social capital', but their concept of this vastly different from Bourdieu's. For RAT theorists, people do not simply act alone for their own self-interest, in the classical economic sense, but make use of networks of social interdependence (see Coleman, 1990: 301). However, in RAT, subjectivity is all important: the objective environment can have no influence on people if they do not have rational grounds for believing certain options are not available to them.

For Bourdieu, this view of people is simply another example of the intellectualist/subjectivist tradition, which has dominated Western philosophy up to and including Sartre's view of voluntaristic freedom of choice as a maxim for individual liberation. To see, as RAT does, action in terms of explicitly posed goals, or consciously posited ends, is, for Bourdieu, an illusion. Moreover, 'economic sociology', which relates action directly to economic interest or narrowly defined causes is 'unaware that practices can have other principles than mechanical causes or conscious ends and can obey an economic logic without obeying narrowly economic interest' (1990c/1980: 50). Indeed, such a position is at the core of Bourdieu's entire oeuvre, from the marriage strategies of the Béarnais peasant through to the Algeria migrant worker. Of course, here, Bourdieu's theory of practice offers a familiar position for understanding human praxis, expressed, in this context: 'the relationship between external constraints which leave a very variable margin for choice, and dispositions which are the product of economic and social processes which are more or less completely reducible to these constraints, as defined at a particular moment' (*ibid.*).

Bourdieu takes a practical example, that of Howard Becker. Both Becker and Bourdieu had written about the 'cost' of having children. However, while Becker sees individuals acting according to 'norms' of calculated costs and profit, Bourdieu understands them in terms of *interests* (or more precisely the *illusio*) and *strategies*. In *La Noblesse d'État*, Bourdieu wrote: 'economists deserve credit for explicitly raising the question of the relationship between the profits ensured by educational investment and those ensured by economic investment' (1996b/1989: 275). However, he argued that such a relationship was not simply expressed in terms of explicit rational choices over the economic, but involved a configuration of *social, cultural* and *economic capital*, as well as a whole orientation to the past, present and future. Thus, Becker is criticized for not recognizing that social reproduction is involved – not simply individual monetary outlay and yield – in the example of educational investment. The nub of the argument is again epistemological and methodological. Bourdieu concludes:

> ... if one fails to recognize any form of action other than rational action or mechanical reaction, it is impossible to understand the logic of all the actions that are reasonable without being the product of reasoned design ... adjusted to the future without being the product of a project or a plan ... And, if one fails to see that the economy described by economic theory is a particular case of a whole universe of economies, that is, fields of struggle differing both in the stakes and the scarcities that are generated within them and in the forms of capital deployed in them, it is impossible to account for the specific forms, contents and leverage points thus imposed on the pursuit of maximum specific profits and on the very general optimizing strategies (of which economic strategies in the narrow sense are one form among others).
>
> (1990c/1980: 51)

Fin de Siècle Social Theory?

The introduction to this chapter suggested that the way social theory developed in the second half of the twentieth century can be seen as a cross-fertilization of academic disciplines, and of modernist and post-modernist discourses. This chapter now considers another form of philosophy and social theory with which Bourdieu's approach competed in the *fin de siècle* global intellectual market.

RCT and RAT theories can be understood as a positivist attempt to salvage social theory from the clutches of radical neo-Marxists, of whom Bourdieu was considered one. What is at stake, of course, is philosophy, the status of knowledge and reason, and its use in the social world. In many ways, RCT was underpinned by a desire to define a social organization which could lead to a less impoverished social life; one which was more lawful and in which greater wealth was enjoyed by the majority. This outcome was seen in terms analogous to free market conditions, where individuals were free to make choices which, by definition, would lead to greater wealth and happiness. In a sense, this approach was *against* the state and *for* the individual. Individuals' action is reasonable and rational because conscious, intentional choices are made. Bourdieu's objection to this is twofold: first, it does not take sufficient account of material conditions; second, it does not view social action as essentially 'strategic' and thus beyond consciousness. This latter point returns to the question of subjectivity on which so much post-modernist philosophy is based.

Post-modernism ruled the day for much of the second half of the twentieth century, and could be sensed in all aspects of living. In philosophy, writers such as Foucault, Lyotard, Barthes and Lacan were all 'infected' by some aspect of it, to a greater or lesser extent. Central to this project was a form of 'hyper-subjectivity' which could accept no external linguistic authority; for example, the conceptual terms of social theory. Indeed, reflexivity was seen as the way to proceed, but not a reflexivity based on preset terms, or even limits, but 'reflexivity' in its own terms and without limits. Such a project, for Bourdieu, led to two extremes: either a 'view from everywhere', 'a critique of foundations' which elides the question of the (social) foundation of critique, a 'deconstruction' which fails to 'deconstruct' the 'decon-structor' (2000a/1997: 107); or, partly as a response to this, a 'view from nowhere', where, due to post-modernist deference to offer no symbolic violence by avoiding any theoretical projection, nothing is said. Bourdieu argued that both positions committed the delusion of claiming to avoid transcendence while actually enacting an intellec-tual one.

It was to fellow Frenchman and former ENS pupil, the post-modernist Jacques Derrida, that Bourdieu took most exception. In *Distinction*, Bourdieu detailed his objection to Derrida's position. Der-rida had written his own commentary on Kant's *Critique of Judgement* (Derrida, 1978). Derrida can be seen very much as *the* post-modernist philosopher. His work focused not simply on philosophical issues but on the language of the discourse itself. The *signifier* and *signified* are forever separated in Derrida's own view of philosophy, and it is his intention is to bring them together. However, in order to do this, Derrida had to pay close attention to the form of his writing, which no longer conformed to conventional narrative structures. So, play, irony and ruse are all employed by him as means of generating effects which 'open up' the philosophical terrain. For Bourdieu, Derrida's attempt to break free from philosophical discourse, in this case with his critique of Kant, only ends by accomplishing the very opposite; its means actually assert the end itself in Kantian terms rather than breaking from it (see Bourdieu, 1984a/1979: 494ff).

Bourdieu begins his critique of Derrida by acknowledging that his reading of *Critique of Judgement* does indeed show up the opposition between 'pleasure' and 'enjoyment': 'agreeable arts which seduce by the "charm" of their sensuous content and the Fine Arts which offer pleasure but not enjoyment'. Enjoyment, simple 'sensations of the senses', are therefore contrasted with 'pure taste'. In a sense, this is the aspect of culture which is at the base of the separation of individuals into distinct levels of achievement in secondary schools. Bourgeois disgust with sensual pleasure is seen as rooted in 'pure' taste in that the latter separates one from attachment and provides the disinterestedness of existence or non-existence of an object. Working class (*sic*) desire 'ensnares' and, therefore, has to be kept at a distance. Bourdieu argues that, although these issues are present in Derrida's text, they are not explicit and that connections are left unmade. Bourdieu's point is that, by adopting this style, Derrida is in fact re-performing the separation he is criticizing Kant for making; namely, constructing a philosophical text whose only *raison d'être* is as a piece of philosophy, and that he does so by leaving out the socio-historical conditions both of its production and of the text it is addressing:

> To summarize a discourse which, as is shown by the attention Derrida devotes to the writing and typography, is the product of the intention of putting content into form, and which rejects in advance any summary aiming to separate content from form, to reduce the text to its simplest expression, is in fact to deny the most fundamental intention of the work and, by a sort of transcendental reduction which no critique has any thought of carrying out, to perform the *épochè* of everything by which the philosophical text affirms its existence as a philosophical text, i.e. its 'disinterestedness', its freedom, and hence its elevation, its distinction, its distance from all 'vulgar' discourse.
>
> (*ibid.*: 495)

In other words, what Derrida is doing is re-enacting Kant's own *prise de distance*: the masses from the bourgeoisie, the popular from the elite, the vulgar from the refined, the educated from the uneducated – ultimately the sociological from the philosophical. For Bourdieu, this amounts to an intellectual game:

> It is an exemplary form of denegration – you tell (yourself) the truth but in such a way that you don't tell it – which defines the objective truth of the philosophical text in its social use.

> Just as the pictorial rhetoric which continues to foist itself on every artist produces an inevitable aestheticization, so the philosophical way of talking about philosophy de-realizes everything that can be said about philosophy.
>
> (*ibid.*)

Bourdieu argues that this game allows the perpetrator to exist both in and outside the *field*; an intellectual space where, 'one can combine

the profits of transgression with the profits of membership' (*ibid.*).
The post-modern condition affects both philosopher and artists: 'Like
the religious nihilism of some mystic heresies, philosophical nihilism
too can find an ultimate path of salvation in the rituals of liberatory
transgression' (p. 496). He concludes by arguing that post-modernist
philosophy is itself a response to and avoidance of the destruction
of philosophy, 'when the very hope of radical reconstruction has
evaporated'. By radical, Bourdieu, of course, means a philosophy
which has been reconstructed according to his own epistemological
principles.

    The term 'Fin de siècle' was also used as the title of a book by Jeffrey
Alexander (1995), subtitled 'relativism, reduction and the problem
of reason'. He took as his premise the decline of reason in the modern age, and with it the loss of rationalist thinking and the principles
of human progress. He claims that, faced with this situation, there
have been two major responses: relativism and reduction. Relativism
is the response of post-modernism, and includes thinkers and artists
who intensified spontaneous acts of emotion (and sadism!) as a way
of opening up a space for a new humanity to be born. For relativists,
it was modernism itself, with its search for universals (grand narra-
tives), paradoxically which had resulted in dehumanization: 'Only
anti-foundationalism can create a climate in which, because nothing is demanded, everything is given in return' (p. 3). The second
response rested on an analytically ambitious social construction. Reason is not rejected but integrated into method, or approach, which
sees it as an epiphenomenon of social structures. This is the world
of reduction. For Alexander, neither response is satisfactory: 'relativism commits the *epistemological fallacy*, arguing from the presence
of subjectivity in reasoning to the absence in reasoning of any universal scope. Reductionism commits the *sociological fallacy*, arguing from
social sources of ideas to the absence in ideas of anything other than
social source' (p. 3)

    In a chapter entitled 'The Reality of Reduction; the Failed Syn-
thesis of Pierre Bourdieu', he takes Bourdieu to task. He accuses
Bourdieu of exaggerating the objectivist/determinist aspects of cultural theory in order to emphasize the subjectivist, voluntarist nature
of his own theory of practice. At the same time, he argues that, for
Bourdieu, *habitus* is constructed in terms which reflect, even replicate,

external structures. The term 'unconscious strategies' is an oxymoron for Alexander. Social *fields* are also less autonomous from economic structures than assumed. For Alexander, reductionism operates at both the macro and the micro level, with Bourdieu changing his theoretical perspective as he goes to make the 'habitus-strategy-field' amalgam operate; for example, when is a disposition a predisposition and vice versa? He goes on to set out his own reading of Bourdieu's thesis on education before criticizing it. Empirically, Alexander claims, Bourdieu's studies can be refuted: it is simply not true that educational attainment can be reduced to a father's occupation. Rather, achievement and social mobility are independent of social origin. However, it is not at the level of empirical analysis that Alexander is most concerned. He sums up his attack on Bourdieu: for 'the impoverished understanding of meaning, the caricature of motivation, the inability to conceptualize the interplay of sensible self and differentiated institution in contemporary society' (p. 171). Alexander accuses both Bourdieu and his 'enthusiastic readers' of not understanding what a 'multidimensional social theory' requires: namely, 'how individual action and its social environments can be interrelated without reduction; how ideal and material dimensions can be brought into play without sacrificing autonomy and reducing one to the other; how macro can be linked to micro without committing the fallacy of assuming that the fit between them is entirely neat' (p. 194). These are odd comments, since one might argue that what Bourdieu is doing is precisely aiming to achieve what Alexander calls for from a 'multi-dimensional social theory'. It is not good enough to quote Bourdieu – 'I wanted to reintroduce agents that Lévi-Strauss and the structuralists ... tended to abolish, making them simple epiphenomena of structure. And I mean agents, not subjects' (1990d/1987: 9) – and then asserting that he had failed because he is being too reductionist in his use of theoretical concepts; especially when such reductionism is claimed on the basis of Alexander's own misinterpretation of them. For example, at one point he writes: 'Like Bourdieu's other key concepts, habitus turns out not merely to be loosely defined – the critique so beloved of scientism – but to be ambiguous in what can be called a systematic way' (p. 136). However, much of what Bourdieu has done is to show his concepts 'work' with each other. They are not intended to be defined as independent categories;

indeed, this is precisely the (positivist) epistemological attitude he is wishing to avoid.

What is at stake, again, is the form and status of knowledge itself – how it is derived and how it is used. For Alexander, 'Present Reason' must be represented by a social scientific discourse based on pragmatic foundationalism, providing universal argument and, ultimately, a post-positivist objectivity. Leaving aside the issue of how such a discourse operates in practice, we might set this concept beside Bourdieu's own – 'Practical Reason'. For Bourdieu, the issue is one of theory and practice and the resultant knowledge his own method offers. He states, quoting Kant, that 'research without theory is blind, and theory without research is empty' (1992a: 162). And:

> 'This opposition between pure theory of the *lector* devoted to the hermeneutic cult of the scripture of the founding father ... on the one hand, and survey research and methodology on the other is an entirely *social* opposition. It is inscribed in the institutional and mental structures of the profession, rooted in the academic distribution of resources, positions, and competencies, as when whole schools (e.g conversational analysis or status attainment research) are based almost entirely on one particular method' (*ibid.*).

For Bourdieu, many of the oppositions of which he is accused represented divisions in the scientific *field*, expressed at a certain time and place. This is why his own version of *practical reason*, praxeological knowledge, sets such store on objectifying the subject of objectification; making their knowledge production contingent without being relative (see 2000a/1997: 28ff). Bourdieu saw such practical reason as being inherently reflexive since it turns back the epistemology *of* analysis *onto* the analysis and those who analyze. We might consider this alternative to Alexander's 'Present Reason' to be instead a form of 'historicist rationalism'.

Sociological Terrorism?

Part 4 of this book brings the impact and influence of Bourdieu up to date by considering publications appearing in the first few years of the twenty-first century. This part also discusses the potential applications of Bourdieu's approach in education and educational research. Part 3, however, now concludes with a broader consideration of the nature of what Bourdieu is attempting to do and the way it has been interpreted.

In 1983, Robert Connell, with one or two reservations, gave a more or less positive account of Bourdieu and *La Reproduction*. He writes that, 'he is one of the few systematic social theorists to have a way of talking about what living in the world is really like, its shadows and its sunlight' (p. 153). Indeed, it might be argued that because Bourdieu straddles theory and practice – practical theory and theoretical practice, subjectivity and objectivity, mental structures and materials conditions – it is possible to find something for everyone in Bourdieu. Connell saw *La Reproduction* as pointing the way to 'a realistic social psychology (which will be both a historical psychology and a depth psychology)' (*ibid.*).

In fact, Bourdieu himself always avoided confusing his sociology with the discipline of psychology. Nevertheless, in *La Misère du Monde* (1999a/1993), there are accounts which center on individual psychologies; for examples, of some of the 'victims' of society, of relations between men and women, of parents and their children. At one point (2000b), he even suggested that his method acts as a form of psychotherapy; that in some cases the interviews conducted for this book made the interviewees feel better about their lot. These observations seem a volte-face from a man who was always committed to 'scientific rigor'.

An apparent similar contradiction can be found over the matter of socio-political action. In 1995, Alexander was able to write that 'Bourdieu's writing about the public is impoverished', pointing out that, 'Bourdieu dismisses public struggles on behalf of 'the people' as merely symbolic strategies designed to profit the social movement leader himself' (1990d/1987: 150–5). However, even in 1995, this statement was already out of date. Bourdieu had moved on to a decade of involvement in social activism, including the publication of short pamphlet-like statements of the *Raisons d'Agir* series, presented as 'acts of resistance'. In this respect, it might be felt that Bourdieu wanted it all ways: to be both an academic and a public intellectual;

to command sociology while colonizing other disciplines; to be theoretical and practical; to be contra Marx, Durkheim and Weber – in short, to be all things to all men. This element of Bourdieu's work is at the heart of further criticisms of him. For example, Jenkins (1992) sums up his objection as follows: he seeks 'to transcend the objectivist-subjectivist dualism while remaining firmly rooted in objectivism. He vociferously rejects determinism while persistently producing deterministic models of social process. He perpetually reminds his readers that his accounts of social life should be only read as models of that social reality – "it all happens as if" – but is equally consistent in his use of the language of positivistic empiricism, which presents his analysis as a "real material world"' (p. 175). Jenkins is particularly critical of Bourdieu's use of language and his general style, which he finds unnecessarily complex.

However, Bourdieu's star was in the ascendant. By the end of the twentieth century, with a formidable collection of publications behind him, Bourdieu had created a space for himself as 'public intellectual', appearing regularly in the media and intervening in a series of social movements (see 2002b, Chapter 8). The French weekly news magazine *L'Événement* carried a special edition on him (1998) with the cover title: 'Bourdieu – the most important intellectual in France'. However, it also added the subtitle: 'and if his was the only way of thinking?' The implication behind this question was that Bourdieu offered a rather single-minded vision of the world. The theme was also taken up in a book by Jeannine Verdès-Leroux: *Le Savant et la politique* (The Scholar and Politics) (1998). The subtitle of this book says it all: 'essay on the sociological terrorism of Pierre Bourdieu'. Verdès-Leroux's thesis is that Bourdieu's vision of the world is imaginary and far from reality. What he offers is a caricature of society. His language is artificial and technical to the point where some of his texts are unreadable. His upbringing was not as unique as he makes it sound, and the talk of 'wounding' and being a 'victim' is simply being melodramatic. She charges him with not taking into account the changes that had occurred in French society over the previous 30 years, and claims that his theory was part 'extreme-Left' and part reactionary. She argues that he presented his work as science but, when he was attacked for the falsity of his method, 'invokes' resistance as a response. He takes advantage of the authority of his position and intervenes in anything. In short, his influence on the unemployed, undecided and young was dangerous.

Considering Bourdieu's work on education in particular, Verdès-Leroux claims that Bourdieu knew what he wanted to say before undertaking his empirical research, and therefore made the facts fit the storyline; especially so in *Homo Academicus* and his account of preparatory and training schools. In other words, he was methodologically lax. He took a part for the whole and saw himself as a 'militant'. But, Verdès-Leroux claims, what he offered in this book was actually quite conservative – a century out of date. His impressions were offered as 'scientific facts', and the grandiosity of his announced project – in a first chapter of 50 pages! – actually turned out to be small-scale: '*Homo Academicus = academica mediocritas*' (p. 154). Verdès-Leroux also takes several personal swipes at Bourdieu – his office, his emergence as a militant, his 'disciples' – before concluding that here is naïvity posing as something serious. His theory is a myth; his arguments offered as a single vision of the world in much the same way as a religion. If you are a 'non-believer', you are cast out. He acts as a 'preacher' delivering judgements on any subject. Actually, behind Bourdieu's theory there lay old-fashioned Marxism and Leninism acting as a game of bluff in order to impose his fantasies and opinion. The rationale behind Bourdieu's theory and his rhetoric of intimidation was, therefore, finally untenable. Verdès-Leroux believed that Bourdieu's sociology was absolutionist; he tolerated no modifications, least of all criticisms. In this respect, she saw Bourdieu as acting like the 'total intellectual', wishing to dominate everything in his field, in this society and the world at large.

Such an ambition, were it his, would indeed be totalitarian. It is true that Bourdieu was a harsh opponent when under attack. In 1989, Richard Jenkins had written a review essay on *Homo Academicus* in which he pokes fun at Bourdieu's use of language: 'Could someone pass Professor Bourdieu a copy of Gower's *Plain Words*'. Bourdieu took exception to the attitude Jenkins displays, asking whether he would write the same thing about Giddens, Parsons or Garfinkel? Here is his reply:

By reproaching my alleged attachment to what he mistakenly takes
to be a French tradition ... , Mr Jenkins betrays his undiscussed
adherence to a writing tradition that cannot itself be separated
from the *doxa* – since such is the word – which, better than any
oath, unites an academic body. Thus, for instance, when he goes so
far as to excoriate me for an expression such as 'the doxic modality
of utterances', he reveals not only his ignorance ('doxic modality'
is an expression of Husserl that has not been naturalized by ethno-
methodologists) but also and more significantly his ignorance of
his own ignorance and of the historical and social condition that
make it possible.

(1992a: 169)

Of course, this riposte exactly shows Bourdieu at his practical theoretical sharpest; taking an expressed idea and situating it in an individual's academic *habitus* as constituted by its own *field* context. Finally,
however, the degree to which any one takes or leaves Bourdieu's
work – and there is an all-or-nothing aspect to it – really depends
less on particular theoretical refinements and more on what might
be described as 'an attitude of being'. The next Part further considers the potential of such an attitude or position for education and
educational research.

Part 4

Bourdieu: Present and Future Relevance

Introduction

This part of the book begins with a look at the reception of Bourdieu's work in more recent times. (It is worth again recalling that Bourdieu dealt with a wide range of subjects; we will focus only on education.) Further, a number of special editions of journals have been published since Bourdieu's death in 2002, as a homage to him and his career, and we will look at some of these in this chapter, before the Part concludes with discussion of the ongoing relevance of Bourdieu's ideas for educational research.

Chapter 16

Millennium Critiques

Once again, it is important to begin by setting the context for Bourdieu's work. By the turn of the twenty-first century, it is arguable that the sociology of education was on the wane. In a sense, it had lost (at least some of) its *raison d'être*. The impact of the collapse of the Soviet bloc, and a increasingly liberal global economy, on radical thinking should not be underestimated. Under Ronald Reagan in the USA and Margaret Thatcher in the United Kingdom, latter-day Capitalism was given a boost through a rediscovery of the power of economic markets to distribute resources. It has been noted how the French government, after a brief fling with state socialism, also went much the same way. If this development led to rejuvenated economies in many Western countries, the effect on individuals was often catastrophic: many became unemployed as state subsidies were withdrawn, and the accent changed from one of social security to individual responsibility and accountability. The language of writers in and around the 'new' sociology of education – 'resistance', 'power', 'ideology', 'control' – was eclipsed by a new language of realism in education – of individual school management, organization and pupil achievement. The sociology of education, along with the other 'foundational disciplines' – psychology, philosophy and history – were now frequently withdrawn entirely from teacher education courses, both pre- and in-service, and replaced by training which was aimed at delivering the latest ministerial curriculum framework or strategy, in Britain at least. Many sociologists of education had to 'reinvent' themselves to survive: as policy evaluators, life-skill trainers, or simply departmental managers. Others increasingly took up the post-modernist torch and with it a denouncement of contemporary discourses, both theoretical and practical.

In this climate, the radicalism which had characterized the 1970s and early 1980s withered or went underground. Yet, the decades leading up to the millennium were also marked by a voluminous increase in educational research, often carried out in teacher-training departments. Such research was often practitioner focused and built up strong regional links between local teaching communities and institutions of higher education. Case-study became a dominant mode of process-orientated research; partly evaluative, partly investigative. This approach and other qualitative methodologies did much to develop the 'theory/practice' link, albeit in a climate of increasing state intervention in educational policy at all levels. However, by the mid-1990s, in England at least (and, it is necessary always to compare one national context with another in concluding where on the continuum a particular education system sits), sufficient state agencies had been created to mount a full-fronted attack on educational research per se. This attack was led by two agencies which had been set up to lead educational reform and training. First, the *Teacher Training Agency* (TTA) took charge of implementing all aspects of teacher training in the country (even its name was a political statement, expressing as it did, what many educationalists would consider a narrow view of teacher development – *training* – rather than the broader and more profound *education*. (Note: The TTA was later renamed the 'Teacher *Development* Agency' under the Blair government.) Second, the *Office for Standards in Education* (Ofsted), which was charged with the inspection of teaching and learning in schools and teacher training in higher education institutions and schools. Through the vociferous spokesmen and women of these agencies – for example, one time Director of Education, University Professor and Curriculum Director, David Hargreaves – the current state of educational research was called into question. Its methods were seen as being insufficiently rigorous, its data collection small-scale and therefore parochial, its findings often biased, and its conclusions unfounded (see Hillage *et al.*, 1998, and Tooley and Darby, 1998). The latter report singled out the work of Bourdieu for special criticism; or, at least, less Bourdieu himself than those who made use of his ideas, who were accused of 'adulating great thinkers'. As an alternative, there was a call for more 'evidence-based research', including 'random control trials' and a return to more quantitative research methods. What we need, Hargreaves argued, was more research of a type 'that if teachers change their practice from x to y there will be a significant and enduring improvement in teaching and learning' (1996: 5). Leaving aside the question of what sort of relation between theory and practice this argument implies, and indeed the issue of the relationship between teachers and/as researchers, our immediate concern is how Bourdieu might feature in such a climate.

Bourdieu, of course, it has been noted, mounted his own response to neo-liberal economics as a series of 'acts of resistance'. He also continued to address issues of education up until his death. However, much of this involvement was based in and around France, with its own particular social and political concerns. *La Misère du monde* offered a clarion call for all those who stood against modern state policies and the destructive side effects many of them had for individuals involved in the various public industries, of which education (for teachers, students and pupils) was a case in point. There is, obviously, a limit to what one man can do, even one with a large international media profile. Two important questions are: in what ways have Bourdieu's ideas been employed elsewhere outside of France, and what potential do they still hold?

In a sense, even a quick run-through the range of papers published in academic research journals of education that have used Bourdieu's ideas as a focus is demonstration of the way the *field* has changed over the last decade or so. The language used (of resistance, for example) in approaching education is far less radical, and a more pragmatic perspective is taken in discussions of the outcomes of research. For example, in 1993 Johannesson concluded a paper on 'principles of legitimation in educational discourses in Iceland' by arguing that the research framework based on Bourdieu's conceptual approach was a way of thinking about events but not necessarily a method for producing progress. Leaving aside the issue of what would be the nature of such progress, Johannesson discusses the conflicting philosophies apparent in teacher education in Iceland: for example, between technological perspectives on education (teaching as a science) and child-centered perspectives (teaching as a social relationship). This dichotomy is expressed in terms of the distinction between 'scientific' and 'progressive' educational knowledge.

It is argued that the principles of legitimation behind these modes compete in teacher education: on the one hand, there are academic conventions, (subject methodologies) in disciplines such as language and literature, history, theology, biology and chemistry; and, on the other hand, there are the approaches of educational and curriculum theory, psychology, etc. (pedagogical 'science'). Of course, in theory, such 'poles' of legitimation are arbitrary – they could exist in any form. However, what Johannesson argues is that the 'progressive' and 'educational science' poles are gaining legitimacy at the expense of subject-based methodologies through educational policy reforms, and that the consequence of this is that the structure, content and thus value of teacher education *capital* has changed. In other words, 'teacher knowledge' is being reformulated through policy. But, this change is driven by policy reformers who take for granted the notions of evolution and progress, thus adopting a non-reflective stance on the historical contingency of change, and resulting in an instrumental and utilitarian view of educational knowledge.

In 2000, Karl Maton also wrote about 'languages of legitimation' in academic *fields* in terms of their structuring principles. Integrating Bourdieu's theoretical perspective with that of Basil Bernstein, or the distinction between 'how' intellectual *fields* structure educational knowledge and the structuring significance of educational knowledge for intellectual *fields*, he makes a distinction between two 'modes' of legitimation: the 'knowledge mode', where legitimation is with reference to 'procedures appropriate to a discrete object of study'; and, the 'knower mode', where educational knowledge is legitimated in terms of the personal characteristics of the author or subject (p. 155). The distinction is an important one because Maton shows that even though the 'knower mode' can be understood in terms of Bourdieu's maximization of individual *capital* accumulation, it is in fact 'bought' by 'new' knowers declaring 'new' beginnings, redefinitions, even complete ruptures from the past. It is then necessary for one's own valuing in the intellectual *field* to declare distinction through originality. One way of doing this is to 'banish to the past' what has gone before. However, a major side effect of such a 'knower mode of legitimation' is the proliferation and even fragmentation of positions within the *field*, leading to segmented and schismatic knowledge structures. He concludes: 'The tendency of knower modes to insist upon multiplicity of truths and proclaim against the adjudication of competing knowledge claims renders them particularly vulnerable within the current educational climate, where policy-linked research funding and the market of student demand (characterized by credential inflation and, in Britain at least, rising student debt) are likely to induce increasingly utilitarian demands of subject areas' (p. 163). The paradox is, of course, that there is something inherent to relations to knowledge in the educational *field* which contributes to the structuring of institutional and intellectual trajectories of the *field*. Furthermore, the outcome is likely to render the intellectual community more, not less, open to attack, and thus prone to accommodate themselves to policies originating from outside of the *field*. This argument would seem to explain why, given Bourdieu's definition of 'science' as being dependent on the autonomy of the scientific *field*, intellectual products of the educational research *field* might be seen as fragmented and non-accumulative. The fact that in some ways educational research seems to be doing this 'to itself', but doing it in response to the political climate that surrounds it, only underlines its position of being a 'dominated faction within the dominant' *field*.

In various parts of this book, it has been noted that Bourdieu claimed to never actually 'theorize' as such, and that he worked by immersing himself in empirical data with a view to identifying the correspondences and links between processes at play within *fields*. One product of this undertaking has been the formulation of a set of thinking tools, which he encourages others to make use of in other practical contexts. It is, perhaps, therefore unsurprising that Bourdieu's theoretical concepts continue to be 'interrogated'. His world is a highly symbolic one – social reality as semiotic. This is expressed through his *field* theory and related concepts – *habitus*, *capital*, etc. These are each discussed in the following three examples.

The symbolic nature of Bourdieu's theory is probably best expressed through his concept of *capital*. *Capital*, it should be recalled, includes ideational as well as material actualizations. According to this theory, all *capital* is symbolic in that it accrues value in terms of power and 'purchases' practice in a range of *field* contexts. It has been shown how, according to Bourdieu, it exists in three primary

forms: *economic*, *social* and *cultural*. Rob Moore (2004) examines the
latter with particular respect to the way it 'transubstantiates' from and
to other forms of *capital*. He emphasizes that *cultural capital* has value
because, although it is in fact arbitrary, it is valued by the *field* according to the structure of the logic of practice of the *field*, which itself is
an expression of the structural morphology of the *field*. He concludes
that it therefore has a 'dual aspect': of appearance and reality. Moore
insists on the 'economic' derivation of such structural logic and the
power relations which underlie it. However, he also picks up on a
point originally noted by Bourdieu's contemporary, Basil Bernstein.
Bernstein (1990: 174–7) argues that Bourdieu is essentially concerned
with relations *to* legitimacy in a social context rather than relations
within it. In other words, Bourdieu is preoccupied with the causes
and consequences of social hierarchy, while what is needed is a shift
to a focus on the internal construction of legitimacy. What this perspective is inviting us to do is to look more closely at the internal
workings of the *field*. Moore reasons that the structural homology
between *economic capital* and *cultural capital* is most apparent between
social classes in the educational *field*. However, there are, within the
field, other sites where *capital* value, the arbitrary and legitimacy are
expressed in terms other than directly economic. For Moore, there
is the possibility, even within Bourdieu's theoretical analyses, for a
'degree of selection', which results in some individuals within a social
category surviving in education, while others are eliminated. Those
who do survive are ascribed 'manifest exceptional qualities', or 'particularities of their family', which interact with 'something or other' that
is not simply *cultural capital*. Moore concludes that: 'The "whatever
it is" of the more rigorous selection is a capacity to engage independently with those meanings that are not merely the cultural arbitrary
of the educational habitus, but the epistemological non-arbitrary of
real knowledge' (p. 454). This argument suggests that not all aspects
of knowledge are arbitrary and, even within a social theory of class
reproduction, there may be an autonomous site for individuals to
work for their own selection which is quite distinct from the one
determined for them by their position within the *field*.

Others writers have examined Bourdieu's conceptual tools. For
example, *habitus* continues to attract critical appraisal. Reay (2004), in

an otherwise positive discussion of its usefulness and the paradoxical ways in which its 'conceptual looseness also constitutes a potential strength' (p. 441), reminds us of the criticisms of *habitus* that arise from Bourdieu's emphasis on its unconscious aspects. She quotes Andrew Sayer in saying that Bourdieu neglects 'mundane everyday reflexivity' and our 'inner conversations'. Here, Bourdieu is again charged with determinism – that the way we act, think and act is pre-programmed. Reay also quotes Crossley's view that reflection and pre-reflection are collapsed into one concept and that *habitus* 'needs to recuperate the reflective and creative aspects of practice' (p. 437). There is the temptation in this type of discussion to get involved in a cycle of accusation and rebuttal. In response, one might note that Bourdieu himself stated:

> Husserl did indeed clearly establish that the *project* as a conscious aiming at the future in its reality as a contingent future must not be conflated with *protention*, a pre-reflexive aiming at a forthcoming which offers itself as a quasi-present in the visible ... the imminent forthcoming is present, immediately visible, as a present property of things, to the point of excluding the possibility that it will not come about, a possibility which exists theoretically so long as it has not come about.
>
> (2000a/1997: 207)

In sum, we are social agents 'whose sense of the game is immediately adjusted to the forthcoming of the game'. However, the example clearly shows that a delicate theoretical balance and socio-genetic awareness should be kept in mind. If Bourdieu is read without continually recalling that he was constructing a theory of practice against the 'rule following' of the structuralists and the conscious 'choices' of the rational action theorists, then *habitus* is indeed understood as overstating the unconscious. This mistake leads, rather ironically, to a kind of determinism, which the entire *raison d'être* of Bourdieu's work was seeking to avoid.

Naidoo (2004) takes up the issue of Bourdieu's concept of *field*. She states that it has received less attention than other concepts such as *habitus* and *cultural capital*, a curious statement, given the way

Bourdieu described his own public lectures as 'Explorations in Field Theory'. Naidoo employs the concept of *field* as a way of analyzing the changes in the South African higher education sector; in particular, the relationship between 'massification' and 'democratization', and the way various proportions of students originating from different regions in *social space* are subjected to subjective and objective acts of selection. This selection then establishes differences within institutions and across the higher-education field as a whole, creating positions at different levels and a relative hierarchy. Nevertheless, she finds two 'limitations' in Bourdieu's concept of *field*. First, she notes that his theory of practice cannot easily be applied in contexts characterized by conflict and change; this is because, here, the underlying *field* logics are themselves breaking down and being reformulated. In other words, Bourdieu focuses too much on existing 'dominant' principles. Second, she concludes (as in the case of Bernstein and Moore above) that Bourdieu's use of *field* pays insufficient attention to its 'internal content'; in particular, the intrinsic structuring of knowledge. In a sense, neither qualification refutes Bourdieu's concept of *field*, yet they indicate areas for further development. Naidoo nevertheless argues that Bourdieu's approach may be particularly useful in analyzing the changes which have taken place in higher education in recent years. Much of Bourdieu's own work was conducted at a time of relative collaboration between higher education, the state and society. However:

> Government perceptions of higher education as a lucrative service that can be sold in the global marketplace have begun to eclipse the social and cultural underpinnings of the social compact. Relatedly, the belief that universities require a relative independence from political and corporate influence to function optimally, which was in turn linked to the need for guaranteed state funding, academic tenure and professional autonomy, has been eroded.
>
> (Naidoo, 2004: 469)

In sum, what Naidoo is arguing is perfectly congruent with Bourdieu's own position – that the application of neoliberal economic principles and associated managerial practices to education has led to a reconfiguration of *capital* value between *cultural* and *economic capital*.

Moreover, much of this change has been implemented through changing structures: relationships between those involved both within the *field*, and between this *field* and other *fields*. Such changes can be understood in terms of the 'commodification' which now runs through the sector and applies to knowledge as a saleable resource, to students and, ultimately, to the place of institutions in league tables that separates out the elite from the rest, and rewards accordingly and explicitly. Inequality is therefore at the core of higher-education systems and, in part, acts as its generator. In this respect, higher education should not be seen as site of consensus but of ongoing conflict which will exert an influence on all its activities and products.

The morphology, or nature of the structure, of the *field* of education is also discussed by Deer (2003) in a comparative study between France and England. In a sense, these two countries have vastly different social backgrounds and ruling principles. How then might they differ or reflect each other over the course of reforms during the last decades of the twentieth century? While avoiding any analyses which lead to a declaration of universal homologies between France and England, Deer shows how both academic *fields* have been influenced by similar morphological tendencies. In one sense, both have suffered from a 'crisis in *habitus*' brought about by the large-scale increase in student populations, and the restructuring of the academic *field* according to the *capital* values now existent there. Furthermore, relationships with the state and other interest groups – both of the polity and populace – have been radically restructured, so that previous patterns of autonomy have been lost. In France, the relative closed nature of the political center meant that majorities could select which sections of the higher education *field* they were appealing to, at least from the 1970s until the first half of the 1980s. However, the *Loi Savary* (1984) and the *Devaquet Bill* (1986), together with political instability brought about when the socialists were obliged to 'cohabit' with other political factions, policies of decentralization, and a decline in the power of the trade unions all led to an increased heteronomy of the political *field*. The result, somewhat paradoxically, was a weakening of the influence that the political *field* wielded over the academic *field*. Deer sees that in France the political *field* has sought to relinquish part of its control over the academic *field*. However, while encouraging greater innovation and devolution, the resultant degree of functionalism and differentiation has been moderated by the continued dispositions of political elites to manipulate structural change. Further heteronomy of the academic *field* will paradoxically only occur if the political *field* chooses to relax part of its influence, leaving the former open to influence of other groups within the education *field* as a whole; that is, external interest groups (students and their families and other groups with specific economic interests) and the teaching professions, as well as the polity.

In England, on the other hand, Deer sees the changes in the quantities and configurations of *capital*, which have occurred and resulted in the loss of the traditional autonomy of the academic *field* and the way it gauged its activities to favor *capital* exchange rates with other dominant groups. The political *field* has in fact increasingly used its own resources to influence the academic *field* to operate according to its own values. It has acted on the financial independence of higher-education institutions by imposing funding patterns – the selection of funding for research and teaching – and by limiting academic employment protection. As an alternative to 'academic freedom', it has promoted an ideology of economic rationality in the academic *field* so that change and stasis cannot be managed in an autonomous way. Such moves have necessitated agents within the academic *field* to engage increasingly with agents in other *fields*; in particular, the *economic field*, which in turn has resulted in still further submission of the academic *field* to a discourse of economics. Academics have sought to restructure their activities and to exchange them against other external activities leading to greater *capital* accumulation and thus strengthening their position within the academic *field* itself. This increased heteronomy is part of a *field* which is now divided, 'epitomized by the introduction of new managerial institutional practice, centrifugal interests and a multiplicity of value discourses' (Deer, 2003: 203).

These changes need to be seen as the realization on the part of the political elite that higher education is in fact an economic commodity which can be bought and sold. They have then moved to create a competitive environment in higher education; for example, in Britain, the Research Assessment Exercise (a periodic audit of institutional research against which funding is set) and Teaching Quality Assessment (a public audit of systems of quality assurance and enhancement) in England, and contractual funding procedures and decentralized decision-making in France. For Deer, such changes show ways in which 'a community of discourses between various interest groups' has been promoted by the political elite with the aim of influencing its activities. These morphological changes 'illustrate how the political, the economic and the academic fields may undergo types of transformation that, although not directly correlated, can impinge on their further inter-relationship' (p. 205). Deer sees such an analysis as developing Bourdieu's *field* theory away from a straight application of 'heuristic' conceptual tools – *field*, *habitus*, *capital* – and undertaking instead an 'analytical dualistic' approach. This approach recognizes that, as the nature of the higher education *field* changes, so must the way we use Bourdieu's structuring concepts and hence our understanding of their explanatory dimensions. Of the *field* changes apparent, the rise of the European dimension and the growing internationalization of higher education are two significant developments. Both of these raise issues about the present nature of *fields* and highlight *field* structures as time dependent. The growth in new international legal structures has begun to build superordinate *field* structures above national *fields*. Such judicial frameworks, as well as statements of entitlement, inclusion, curriculum and training, result in *field* contexts with very different political principles and social interactions. For example, Lingard, Rawolle and Taylor (2005) argue that the influence of such documents as the OECD educational indicators, and the TIMMS and PISA studies, create a 'new social space' in educational policy. Faced with an international *field*, both students and academics work to position themselves at the international level. However, education and educational policy must still be seen in terms of local, national and international contexts.

Mann (2000) writes of the multilayered nature of the policy *field* in terms of 'socio-spatial networks': for example, local, national, international (between nations), transnational (passing through national boundaries) and global. It is therefore important to recognize that there are parts of higher education where relative autonomy has been granted and that small 'micro-fields' have emerged in the sector – what Bourdieu called '*microcosms*'. Both in terms of the micro and the macro, such *fields* can be understood in terms of their morphology and structural generating principles, or logics of practice.

Certainly, as other researchers work with Bourdieu's theory of practice and conceptual thinking tools, new language is called upon to describe what is presently occurring and the way this complements Bourdieu's own analyses. For example, Maton (2005) calls attention to the way Bourdieu's concept of *field* is defined in terms of relative autonomy, and that the structure of higher education as a whole acts 'like a prism' (Bourdieu, 1993b: 164), which refracts external influences according to its own *field* logic. In other words, wider social pressures are transformed in the process of *field* mediation between the external and the internal; while 'refraction' is constituted by the way forces of autonomy and heteronomy give rise to hierarchical structures: 'Thus, contrary to internalist approaches, macro-social influences cannot be confined to the status of contextual background but, against externalist accounts, how these wider pressures are played out within higher education depends on its "refraction coefficient"' (Maton, 2005: 690). Maton traces the development of UK higher education from the 1960s and argues that, in the current context, it has not been able to refract external pressures in terms of its pre-existing own logics of practice so that structural change has occurred. He extends the dimensions of 'autonomy', suggesting there is a need to make a distinction between 'positional' autonomy and 'relational' autonomy. The former is the primary *field* location of those with power over HE policy; while the latter refers to the 'origins' of the logics which inform the *field*. For Maton, there is still considerable 'positional' power in higher education; namely, control over policy is contained within the *field*. However, the logic of practice itself is now based on market economics and managerialism; 'relational' autonomy is therefore severely reduced. Indeed, one might well argue that the mechanisms of legitimation of the higher-education policy reforms depend on the separation of principles of practice (from without) and the agents of change (from within). Thomson (2005) demonstrates the way that this shift is actualized in practice through the 'codification' of knowledge and the way it is represented in language. For example, school administration is redefined in terms of 'leadership' and 'middle managers'. Moreover, a policy of 'equity' and 'inclusion' becomes rearticulated in terms of 'choice', 'access schemes' and 'value added' league tables, and a misrecognized return to vocationalism. The result is a perpetuation of social reproduction through 'a more explicitly codified symbolic economy of positions (schools, teachers and students) and capitals' (p. 747), not a genuine attempt to dismantle its mechanisms. Furthermore, such misrecognized forms of *doxa* can be seen to animate the whole of the public sector under new public management principles which redefine the activities of distinct *field* locations in terms of the same logics of practice. An example of this can be seen in England, in the move in local government from 'Education Services' to 'Children's Services'. The collusion of the private sector of the economy in this 'colonization' of discourses is exemplified by the 'mediatization' of *fields* such as education by the *field* of journalism; itself reconfigured in terms of neo-liberal economics through such ideas as the 'knowledge economy'. Rawolle (2005) shows how this occurs less in terms of a distortion of one *field* by another – education by the media – and more through a 'symbiotic though contested relationship between fields' (p. 723). For example, journalistic 'scoops' are used to set an agenda which is then followed up by others' articles, and events can be 'hijacked' where occasions are used by politicians to highlight a cause to which they attach other policies of their own.

Potential Applications

Of what relevance is Bourdieu's work today? This book has so far presented an account of his theory of practice and the subsequent applications that arose from a biographical trajectory that led him to connect a number of what, at the time, might have been regarded as disparate sectors of society: education, culture, politics, ex-colonies, peasant farmers. And, it was in the course of addressing the practical problems that he found in each of these that his conceptual thinking tools were developed. There is then the issue of how valid these tools are in contemporary educational settings and how applicable they might be when separated from Bourdieu's own personal perspective.

Both in Part 3 and in previous chapters of this book, the interpretations and misinterpretations of Bourdieu's work over the decades have been discussed. In his work, Bourdieu developed his own version of sociology, and indeed made a significant impact on the sociology of education, informing this discipline as it has evolved over the years. How might Bourdieu's 'sociology' help in understanding topics in education? The articles quoted above give some indication of the way thinking about aspects of contemporary education can be informed by Bourdieu's work. The final chapter of this book will return to the radical and critical nature of Bourdieu's work, and where it is likely to take us. But before this, we should further address the ways in which Bourdieu's writing might also elucidate other educational research topics.

Bourdieu's approach combines two equally important aspects: practical theory and theoretical practice. His theory is indeed based around terms carrying complex and sophisticated epistemological matrices. It is not enough simply to 'define' *habitus* as agency and *field* as context; or to equate 'reflexivity' with being self-aware; or to acknowledge that cultural and linguistic differences are relatively arbitrary and thus should be seen in terms of *cultural capital* for the positions it allows those holding it to achieve. Bourdieu's approach is also about the researcher, their motives, the way they position themselves with respect to what they research, and the status of the resulting knowledge.

So, how seriously should we take Bourdieu and the project he is urging us to undertake? There is little doubt that many individuals involved in a wide range of activities in education have found their encounter with Bourdieu's ideas to be insightful. Even a commenter such as Jenkins, who, as we noted, Bourdieu found to be 'ignorant of his own ignorance', concludes that he is 'good to think with' (1992: 176). In an earlier commentary on 'Bourdieu and Education', the conclusion was rather more positive: 'whilst we do not wish to insist that a Bourdieuian approach is always automatically the best way to research educational phenomena . . . (our conviction is that it) offers insights and understandings not readily visible in other approaches' (Grenfell *et al.*, 1998d: 2). Finally, it is probably less important whether Bourdieu was, or was not, a realist or a phenomenologist; or essentially

Jacobin and thus dictatorial; or whether he was a Marxist, Weberian or Durkheimian; or if he really was a sociologist of education. In a sense, he was all of these and none, and it is worth reiterating once again that Bourdieu was essentially addressing practical problems, often in an empirical way. He saw that solutions to such problems were difficult to come by, so entwined were the mechanisms for reform with the malady itself. However, there was a modernist project at the heart of Bourdieu's work, one which insisted that if the legitimate claims and outcomes of educational systems were at odds, and actual processes were misrecognized, then, at the very least, it was better to know this than not to know it. In some cases, he offered no solutions – quite stubbornly so – and would not be tempted to say how things should be organized differently. Yet, at other times, he did venture out into the political arena and offered ideas and principles on the future of schooling. And, as his own sense of deception within the political machinery grew, he eventually did launch a more overt series of 'acts of resistance'. To this end, we cannot conclude anything other than that Bourdieu's approach was essentially critical in its search for emancipation and empowerment for all those involved in education: pupils, students, teachers, university lecturers and researchers.

This line of thinking is pertinent in looking at language: both *in* and *of* education. Bourdieu offered his own specialized language and encouraged others to make use of it as a way of elucidating the various aspects of education and educational research. Nevertheless, a sustained commenter such as Nash asks, in considering the concept *habitus*, whether it 'is all worth the candle?' (1999: 185). His response is to argue that if it takes the best part of a decade to make sense of it as a concept, then perhaps not. He does, however, concede that in the process of this 'making sense', there is a deeper and truer appreciation of the educational system, and a world without Bourdieu – and Lyotard and Foucault – would be the poorer. This perspective would seem to be part of a reception and application of his work which comes under the 'useful to have around' title. Useful indeed but it might be argued that a more direct application is still waiting to be undertaken. Such a project would have the philosophy of language at its core.

Chapter 17

The Language of Educational Research

In one interview article Bourdieu warned the would-be researcher to 'beware of words' (1989b: 54). 'Common' language, he argued, is the repository of 'common' sense; that is, a historical accumulation of orthodox meaning – names, groups, concepts, taxonomies and categories. In practical educational terms, these might include such concepts as 'achievement', 'class', 'young and old'. Unsurprisingly, Bourdieu continued by inviting researchers to reveal the *misrecognitions* which are apparent in such commonly accepted terms, and to uncover both their historical construction and their present applications as a way of 'breaking' with the dominant *doxa*. And, of course, when talking about language, Bourdieu had in mind not only everyday usage but the actual technical terms used by researchers. In fact, one of the principal phenomena of the post-modernist age is the way language has been 'colonized', that is, conquered and put to use on behalf of the dominant discourses. In an article with Loïc Wacquant, published in *Le Monde* in 2000, he listed vocabulary which had passed into the common parlance of bureaucrats and the media without due reflection on its provenance and effects: 'globalization', 'flexibility', 'governance', 'employability', 'exclusion', 'under class', 'new economies', 'zero tolerance', 'community', 'multiculturalism' (2000b: 6). The point is that an entire philosophy – often of neo-liberal economics – is itself imported when such language is used, which defines certain actions and behaviors and thus establishes the logic of practice that generated them in individuals' subsequent activities – a kind of epistemological Trojan Horse. If this is true of everyday life, it is equally true of the world of research. And, indeed, it is consequently unthinkable that the researcher should not interrogate the problems, concepts and objects of their enquiry in terms of the collective work that was undertaken to constitute them in the first place: 'For the sociologist, more than any other thinker, to leave one's own thought in a state of unthought (*impensé*) is to condemn oneself to be nothing more than the instrument of what one claims to think' (*op.cit.*: p. 55). Part of the process of 'objectivation of the objectifying subject', which is so central to Bourdieu's project, is not only to position oneself in the *field* of inquiry, but also to examine the language used in conducting research in drawing inferences from it. Such an undertaking is possible at any stage in any educational research project, not simply one involving a critical sociology looking at issues of class, gender, inequality and nationality. What follows are examples where an existing research area is reconsidered in terms of Bourdieu's approach.

Chapter 18

Teacher Education

There is extensive research literature on the professionalism of teachers. Much of this takes its lead either from objectivist or subjectivist approaches to the topic. For example, there is a tradition of looking at teacher professionalism in terms of processes of socialization towards a given state of vocationalism. This work involves considering the stages that teachers go through in the course of gaining professional competence and the dilemmas they face: between theory and practice; classroom management; the institutionalization of schools; curriculum control, etc. It is essentially an 'objective' mode of inquiry (see, for example, Lacey, 1977; Ginsburg, 1988). Another tradition reflects a more 'subjective' approach to professionalism. The roots of this tradition lay in 'trait theory'; that is, individuals are born with particular 'traits' which make one or another profession the most suitable for them. A more recent version of this approach is the examination of 'teacher knowledge' or craft with a view to edification as a part of defining professional competence (see, for example, Calderhead, 1987). Of course, both of these traditions use techniques which tell us a lot about teacher training, professionalism and education. However, a study using Bourdieu's theory of practice would approach the topic in its epistemological sense and examine the very language we use to talk and write about teachers and professions. Bourdieu stated:

> The notion of profession is dangerous because it has all the appearance of false neutrality in its favour. Profession is a folk concept which has been uncritically smuggled into scientific language and which imports with it a whole social unconscious. It is the product of a historical work of construction and representation of a group which has slipped into the very science of this group. This is why this concept works so well, or too well: the category of profession

refers to realities that are, in a sense, 'too real' to be true, since it grasps at once a *mental* category and a *social* category, socially produced only by superseding or obliterating all kinds of differences and contradictions.

(1989b: 37–8)

Because of this, the very term 'profession' itself has to be treated as an 'object' rather than an 'instrument' of analysis, and reconfigured in terms of Bourdieu's own conceptual thinking tools: *habitus*, *field*, *capital*, etc. The *field* of teacher professionalism – from pre-service to in-service – is open to the kind of 3-level analysis suggested in Part 2, Chapter 7. This method would bring together the structure of teachers' professional life, both in terms of material conditions and the ideational discourse which direct their work. The latter are represented in curricula, assessment procedures and official pedagogies – not to mention management principles – all of which have their logic of practice in establishing an ideational *field*. However, teachers are also physically located, and each of these theories and practices are spread across and congregate in specific points of their everyday activities: teacher–pupil interactions, lessons, classes, classrooms, school departments, schools and the education profession. The *field* that is the education profession necessarily exists as a *field* within *fields* and shares this space in terms of specific relational structures. In other words, all these interact – more or less – at any one particular instance. What occurs does not just depend on the *field* and the local contexts (the *microcosms*) of educational practice; it also results from the interaction between all these with individual teacher dispositions and predispositions, which have been formed in the course of the teachers' biography – in other words, *habitus*.

It is indeed possible to explain teachers' professional practice in terms of the interaction between their *field* contexts and their own *habitus* (see, for example, Grenfell, 1996). What is found is that teachers are often caught in a space where 'who' they are and 'what' they are obliged to do in terms of the dominant discourse sometimes clashes. There is then a *double bind*, in Bourdieu's terms, when they are asked to operate double structures: theory and practice; personal knowledge based on experience and the official pedagogies of curricula; institutional norms – school and other agencies (government, training, local authorities). In this space, they can be *nowhere* and experience it as a deep experiential dilemma: for example, teaching/learning principles based on past experiences that have apparently proved successful, and a new approach which has not; personal views versus salient models of the training course; teaching technique and individual personality; planning versus flexibility. Such 'dilemmas' are managed by all sorts of strategies, including one of *misrecognition*; thus, a kind of cognitive dissonance is present which may silence or mask its own truth by sanctioning the official logic of practice and its practical consequences – a kind of pragmatic bad faith. Thus, Bourdieu's approach reveals a *field* mechanism and a structural positioning, all while recognizing the actual experiences of teachers and trainees. A similar analysis could be undertaken specifically on teacher educators (see Johannesson, 1993).

There is, therefore, a potential in Bourdieu's work to apply his conceptual thinking tools to the topics of educational research other than the major issues of sociological research. The way to do this is to replace one language with another: the first based on 'common sense', forced neutrality and thus historically constitutive recognitions (*doxa*); the second coming from an epistemology which integrates subject and object into a dynamic structural method for analysis of educational practice. The move is therefore more than simply a linguistic or technical modification. It involves a fundamental shift in understanding about knowledge formation and practice in actual real-life contexts.

Researching Classroom Language

Language is the medium of education: all classrooms must have language to work. What does a Bourdieusian approach to the language of classroom discourse look like?

Bourdieu's thesis of academic discourse is clear:

• The linguistic background of the family influences the student's ability to deal with both the content and form of scholastic language.

- There is an implied interest in perpetuating this misunderstanding as it shores up social selectivity, misrecognized as such as a collective act of *mauvaise foi*.
- The way we think and speak betrays a whole relationship to language and conceptual modes of thought.
- The location of particular disciplines in the institutional hierarchy of studies is a structural homology of these differences most apparent in differentials of performance according to social class. (see 1977a/1970; 1979b/1964; 1994c/1965)

Early research on real classroom language took a broadly ethnographic approach by unpicking the structure and content of the medium of learning. For example, Sinclair and Coultard (1975) showed how the structure of classroom knowledge was built on I-R-F exchanges – initiation, feedback and response – that two-thirds of classroom language was talk, two-thirds of it was teacher talk, and two-thirds of this was based on lecturing and questioning, thus giving rise to the 'law of two-thirds'. Others (for example, Barnes, 1976, and Barnes and Todd, 1977) examined the nature of group work as opposed to teacher-focused language, and the power of *open* and *closed* questioning.

Those working in this tradition later took up the theories of the Soviet psychologist Lev Vygotsky in order to account for what is happening in classroom discourse (see Part 2, Chapter 10). Vygotsky died in 1934 but his work became increasingly influential from the 1960s when his major book was first published in English (Vygotsky, 1962). In opposition to the Piagetian notion of the learner as a 'lone-explorer' passing through sequential stages of cognitive development, Vygotsky set out a model of psychology as a collective process. For him, the early learner mediates between themselves and the world around them, both physical and social, and, in this mediation, gains control over *objects*, *self* and *others*. What results is a process of 'self-regulation' where knowledge means control. Vygotsky concluded in a similar way to Durkheim, that 'nothing appears in the psychological plane without first appearing in the social plane'; in other words, the *intra*-psychological must be understood as a product of the *inter*-psychological.

Vygotskyan psycholinguistics has impacted on analyses of classroom discourse and the theoretical terms used to describe it. Given Vygotsky's situation, it is perhaps unsurprising that his was essentially a positive account of the social background to individual knowledge formation. It is the social that supports and informs individual learners. And it is the social that is the source of individual enrichment. Writers on classroom discourse who have taken Vygotsky as their point of departure often focus on 'common knowledge' rather than 'mutual misunderstanding' (cf. Edwards and Mercer, 1987, and Taylor, 1992). They take the Vygotskyan concept of the 'Zone of Proximal Development' (ZPD): 'the distance between the actual developmental level as determined by independent problem solving and the level of potential development as determined through problem solving under adult guidance or in collaboration with more capable peers' (Vygotsky, 1978: 86). The ZPD offers a way of conceptualizing classroom discourse and language in learning as a structure which needs to be shaped and *scaffolded* (see Wood *et al.*, 1976), so that the learner is supported at the point of handover where knowledge becomes their own. The research task is then to identify and explain what constitutes this 'scaffolding' and 'handover' in order to understand how to maximize its effectiveness in pedagogic discourse. It provides pedagogic edification of the processes and strategies available to teachers: for example, reworking knowledge, demonstration, the dynamics of explanation, styles of explaining, etc. (see Ogborn *et al.*, 1996). Mercer (1995: 75–6) offers an explicit example of 'scaffolding' where a pupil is brought back on track after offering an apparently 'wild-card' answer to a mathematics problem. In this example, the teacher is supporting the pupil as he works with a logarithm. In the first part he discusses a difficult sum and receives affirmative responses from the teacher. The discussion continues and he appears to make progress until he comes out with the surprising conclusion. At this point, the teacher talks him through the method until he is *back on line*. She also uses another pupil for support. Mercer concludes that this is an example of 'scaffolding' and informs us that the pupil went on to do this type of sums without assistance.

This is true. However, there is a deeper question about what was happening at the critical point when he makes a wild-card guess. From a Bourdieusian perspective, to call what happened 'scaffolding' might indeed be to indulge in a kind of 'scholastic fallacy', which confuses the 'things of logic with the logic of things'. In attempting to represent both a mental and social process, 'scaffolding' becomes perhaps more real than the thing it is supposed to represent, and follows its own logic of practice. Writers in the Vygotskyan tradition admit that they are emphasizing continuity, co-operation and sharing over conflict and disfunctionality (Mercer, 1995: 121). However, it is difficult not to see two world views – two *habitus* – often colliding at critical points within classroom discourses, as teachers talk pupils through according to their own (legitimate) way of thinking based on the official pedagogy. What, of course, gets left out is the pupils' own cognition: what thinking produced this surprising answer/solution? The point is that by pursuing the pupil's own method, a more enhanced interpretative understanding might result rather than the exclusion of one way of thinking by another. To reconstitute the analysis in terms of *habitus* and *field* is to see the context in terms of the hierarchy of teaching methods within discipline discourses, the curriculum and the language used to transmit legitimated procedures; and, the individual teacher–pupil relationship in terms of their past and present experiences and the schemes of thought these have given rise to; further, the way underlying principles of thought impact on classroom discussions. It is difficult not to see such examples as instances where *pedagogic authority* is a form of *symbolic violence*; in other words, 'the power to impose (or even inculcate) the arbitrary instruments of knowledge and expression (taxonomies) of society' (Bourdieu, 1991a/1982: 168). It is constituted within a *field* and is expressed and impacts on individual *habitus*. What occurs might therefore be seen as less supportive than the 'scaffolding' metaphor would seem to suggest. From a Bourdieusian perspective, both the language of pedagogic discourse and the language used to discuss that discourse are interrogated epistemologically in order to grasp something of the full reality that is taking place (see Grenfell, 1998: 72–88).

A further example will show how the structure of classroom discourse can actually carry dominant pedagogic principles in a covert way, which misrecognizes the consequences of their resultant practice. The short extract of classroom dialogue below illustrates these principles in terms of dimensions of authority in classroom discourse and how they operate in practice. The example is taken from a lesson in England in which the tenets of the National Literacy Strategy (NLS) are being applied. The NLS was initiated by governmental decree in 1998 (DfEE, 1998), with the expressed aim of raising the standards of literacy skills of pupils in England and Wales. Teachers were trained in a prescribed approach, which included a set lesson structure and a particular language taxonomy. Lessons were designated 'the literacy hour' and divided into four parts: the first two and final parts involve whole-class instruction. The third part was for 'independent reading, writing or word work, while the teacher works with at least two ability groups each on guided text work'. During this third part, pupils not working with the teacher were to be trained 'not to interrupt the teacher and there should be sufficient resources and alternative strategies for them to fall back on if they get stuck' (DfEE, 1998: 9–12).

Alexander (2000) carried out a large international comparative study of primary education classrooms. He argues that the teachers' language in the classroom often originates in the educational discourse of a particular country. For example, he offers an extract of an NLS lesson where 'child-centeredness' is identified in the classroom language and is seen as being symptomatic of a particular approach to pedagogy:

> (*Tables 1 and 2 have prominent signs announcing 'We are working with the teacher'.*)
> Teacher (*To tables 3, 4 and 5*): Right, I'm closing the magic curtain. (*Mimes closing a curtain. Some pupils laugh. The teacher smiles and puts finger to lips.*) Now, if it's a curtain I can still hear you. And I'm going to try and work with these two tables and you're trying (*frowns at pupil who is talking loudly*) to work on your own. (*Goes to table 1.*)
>
> (Alexander, 2000: 482f)

An example of such 'child-centeredness' is the teacher's oblique formula for commanding silence ('I'm going to close the magic curtain') or class control ('Now if it's a curtain I can still hear you'). Later in the lesson:

G: Miss Newton, Miss Newton, can you spell 'what'?

Teacher (*Leaning towards G with her hands resting on the table*): 'What'? There's a hat in 'what'. (*Picking up G's wordbook, moves round to stand behind him*) Shall we see if it is in here?

G (*Nods*)

T (*Notices F is not working, but staring at the teacher's radio microphone*): Hello F, shall we get on with the third word?

Here, the same pedagogical approach is noticeable in the inclusive use of 'we' as a way of blurring the oppositional (I, you); indirect in the management of turns ('Hello F, shall we get on with the third word'); and in a tone which is gentle and approachable.

These characteristics of the culture of the classroom, as expressed in and through language, are telling. However, if a Bourdieusian perspective is adopted, a number of other features become visible. First, this personal teaching disposition must be seen as a *cultural psychobiography*, which develops into a specific *pedagogic habitus* characteristic of the teacher-training *field* in the 1970s and 1980s (see also Grenfell, 1996). Furthermore, the teacher's methodological principles need to be seen as a form of *cultural capital* (symbolic and valued with a specific underlying logic of practice), enacted in a practical *field* site of the classroom. In other words, what the teacher does is bring her own professional *habitus* into the classroom, which characterizes her language and shapes the classroom discourse. What the National Literacy Strategy tried to do in fact was to change pedagogical *habitus* (those aspects of *habitus* gained in life experience/training which result in 'recognizable' practice in the education *field*) by altering the valuing of *capital* constituents. The pedagogy of the NLS values something else – it has a different logic of practice. In place of 'child-centeredness' was put 'instruction'; in the case of the NLS, children are required to be inducted into the formal terminology of language. This technical discourse of the NLS breaks through in the following extract in the teacher's focus on phonemes (for example, 'f', 'v' and 'w' sounds):

F (*Pointing to the microphone*): I've seen that on television on 'Count Me In'.

Teacher (*Smiling*): It's listening to you, F. (*Continues to scan G's wordbook. To G*) We're looking for 'w'. Help me find 'w'. (To F) No you are. 'w'. 'w', 'w', 'w', what! It's the 'w' – 'h' page. Sh-sh (*To F, while walking towards her*) Come on now, the best thing you can do would be . . .

Later, the teacher also uses the term 'phoneme', albeit in a rather self-conscious way. How would such a pedagogic *habitus* contrast with a teacher trained more recently? Alexander offers an example. Here, in place of the inclusive language, the teacher is more direct and instructional: 'Have a look. . .'; 'No, it's not in that one . . .'; 'Is it the right word . . . ?'; 'See if it's in the other book'; 'Don't you even have the letter in that one?'; 'How do you know that then?'; 'What do you think she did . . . ?' (p. 478). Such differences come from different generating principles (logic of practice), developed in the course of acquiring a different professional *habitus*; one formed in response to the full force of criticism leveled at previous progressive and inclusive approaches.

The differences in *habitus* between the two teachers above are themselves the product of the *field*, or the *social space*, of education. In the 1970s and 1980s, this space was relatively protected and teachers were relatively autonomous. However, enormous restructuring in teacher education occurred in the 1990s, which radically changed relationships – managerial, intellectual and financial – between institutions and individuals in education. These changes were brought about by governmental edict. What is valued (*cultural capital*) has been redefined. This change of product has occurred as a result of changing processes in the *field* by restructuring it. There is then a consequential impact on the professional *habitus* of those involved. From a Bourdieusian perspective, education is ruled by *capital* values, which take their legitimacy from governmental intentions to shape policy in line with economic exigencies. It is not surprising, therefore, to see *cultural capital*, the language of pedagogy, and the valuing of scholastic content defined in terms congruent with an economic discourse. Indeed, there may be tensions – a *double bind*, as referred to above – between teacher knowledge, gained through previous experience and training, and the principles of the new pedagogy; especially when the latter is expressed in terms of 'achievement', 'performance', etc. Alexander also notes this: 'This lesson reveals an albeit gentle collision of discourses which manifests a sharper underlying collision of educational values' (p. 486).

The example shows differences in pedagogic culture and the interaction at one time between different *field* structures as expressed in the classroom discourse, the teacher's pedagogic *habitus*, and the impact it has on pupils' own language and learning. *Cultural capital* is always relative and only possesses value to the extent to which it is legitimized within the larger *field*. It is not surprising therefore that there are differences in the pedagogic discourse (*field* and thus *habitus*) of systems from different national cultures. Without designating them in Bourdieusian terms, Alexander sums these up: rote learning (India), democratic pedagogy (United States), readiness (England and United States), acceleration (Russia) and conciseness and rapidity (continental Europe) (p. 429). From a Bourdieusian perspective, these features can be seen as operating in *fields* and through *habitus* in terms of expectations, dispositions and orthodoxy. They are present and brought into being in the organization of education – managerially, physically and intellectually – and so can be seen as an expression of *cultural capital* brought to life.

Further Examples

Bourdieu's theory of practice is therefore of use in elucidating the language of education at various levels and focusing on the principles of practice underlying a range of methodologies and policies. As always, these need to be understood at the micro- and macro-levels, as well as structural relations within *fields* and between *fields*. There is clearly great potential in Bourdieu's approach for considering the overall principled structure of the education *field* and its sub-fields. For further examples, Thomson and Holdsworth (2003) challenge the implication in much of the educational change literature that institutional structures and habitual ways of doing things can be shifted by 'free and autonomous' individuals who know what they are doing. They consider the changing policy landscape in Australia; in particular, policy reform in the late twentieth century, which led to wider student participation in the decisions that were made about teaching and learning. Using Bourdieu, they conceptualize the education *field* as 'stratified vertically' in terms of levels of schooling and training. However, they argue that there is a 'horizontal' as well as a vertical organization, with the possibilities of populist, more equitable and democratic education on one side, and, a highly categorized, selective education with pronounced elite forms on the other (p. 385). The horizontal options are available at each of the vertical levels. They then take this *field* model into the context of changes in the Australian educational *field*, which, in particular, underwent a policy to increase school retention in the latter part of the twentieth century. They make the point that those who traditionally had the upper school 'to themselves' found they were now part of the masses. When there are greater numbers, competition intensifies as the privileged few fight to retain or restore their advantage in schools. In this climate, everything that distinguishes between courses, pedagogies and schools becomes acutely important in the struggle to define the currency value of various forms of *capital*. They conclude: 'The intense period of struggle was short lived, and the field was re-stratified horizontally with a new regime of common certification and training programs. Democratic activists found themselves out-maneuvered and their practices incorporated as part of a new official structure and system. Student participation became a matter of attendance and representation of an elite of student leaders (p. 387). Thomson and Holdsworth conclude that this 'principal opposition' between democratization and hierarchization is now part of the generating logic of institutions, policies institutions and educators' actions; a principle of contestation which makes the field unstable. They find some optimism in the fact that spaces have been opened up and made available where 'participatory players' can represent a sense of equity that things might be different.

Taylor and Singh (2005) also show the potential of Bourdieu's work to open up the *field* workings of education. They take as their *point de départ* a major policy initiative – the Queensland State Education 2010 – on social justice. They conducted interviews in three key sections of the bureaucratic system implementing the policy:

workforce and professional development; curriculum and assessment; and strategic direction, performance and measurement. What they found was that there were important differences in the language used in each of these sections, and that these differences represented different roles and priorities in implementing the policies. The study confirms the theoretical suggestion that subfields can exist as quasi-autonomous sites – *microcosms* – which operate according to their own logic of practice which partly represents and partly overrides – in its own interests – the superordinate *field* logic and structure. In such conditions, poor communication can exist between the various sub-fields, or even policy-makers and those on the frontline of practice. Changes in *field* structure – for example, through a policy of greater decentralizasation – reconfigure the whole *field* as the relationship between the center and the periphery is redefined. There is therefore a value in tracking the taxonomic shifts, and what produced them, within and between *fields*, in terms of both the logic of practice which defines and legitimates practice and its outcomes.

These research projects show different ways in which Bourdieu's theory of practice has been applied and developed. However, they are more than an alternative methodology as they focus equally on the object and the subject of research. In a way, what Bourdieu's concepts give us is a language to reveal the active principles present in other languages used to describe processes. Since he understood much of this language to be 'colonized' by other (often economic) discourses, his own thinking tools offer both a revelatory and emancipatory potential: to reveal underlying generating structures – both material and ideational – and to offer the possibility of gaining some freedom from the meanings and actions they impose.

Chapter 19

Knowledge and Education

Part 4 now concludes by returning to one further important aspect of Bourdieu's approach to education: what he called a process of 'objectivation of the objectifying subject'. What does this mean in terms of the potential for future educational research?

The last chapters have referred to some of the changes that have taken place in educational research in Britain over the past decade or so, often in response to fierce criticism from both other educational researchers and government representatives. In fact, it is necessary to regard educational research itself as a *field* and therefore open to all the *field* processes referred to in the course of discussion of Bourdieu, education and training in this text. To treat educational research as a *field* is ultimately to objectify not only the mechanisms of the *field* of knowledge production, but to situate the individual researcher within it. Bourdieu criticized scholastic reason for the way it was expressed unreflexively and without acknowledgement of the biases such reasoning contained. He writes:

> It is ... from the social history of educational institutions ... and from the history of our singular relationship to these institutions that we can expect some real revelations about the objective and subjective structures (classifications, hierarchies, problematics, etc.) that, in spite of ourselves, orient our thought.
>
> (2000a/1997: 9)

Bourdieu wrote extensively about how to conceptualize a *field* and conduct a *field* analysis. In particular, in *The Rules of Art* he showed how *fields* – in this case, the art *field*, but in fact any knowledge *field* – exist in terms of series of morphological generations stretched out over time. But, time is defined not simply in terms of real-time – days, weeks, months and year – but also as time associated with individual trajectories and also as social time. Some *field* phenomena have longer lifespans than others; some outlive the individuals who established them; others come and go. He constructed a *field* diagram to show this condition of the *field* (see 1996a/1992: 159). A major generating force within the *field* is the 'avant-garde': a kind of vanguard movement which replaces the presiding ruling generation, itself the consecrated product of a previous avant-garde. In the case of art, which *Rules* addressed, Bourdieu saw that in 'heroic times' avant-garde artists do indeed represent a kind of sweeping away of the old by the new, as something that is genuinely different and needed is produced (see Grenfell and Hardy, 2007). The case of the nineteenth-century French pre-Impressionist painter, Edouard Manet, is a perfect example. Here, the 'avant-garde' asserted their autonomy from the status quo and developed a new representation of art. Such change was of course resisted, since it meant the death of one generation as another defined its own field leadership: 'To impose a new producer, a new product and a new system of taste on the market at a given moment means to relegate to the past a whole set of producers, products and system of tastes, all hierarchized in relation to their degree of legitimacy' (1996a/1992: 160).

It must be recalled that what is do-able and not do-able, what is 'thinkable' and 'unthinkable', is defined by the *field* which sets its own limits. A *field* is responsible for its own products to the extent to which it is autonomous. In an ideal, fully autonomous *field*, only the *field* mechanisms themselves would determine their product, independently from any influence of other *fields*. In an ideal heteronomous *field*, the *field* product would in fact be more a product of other *fields* than the *field* itself. In a sense, what is at stake here is the extent to which a *field* can operate according to its own logic of practice. The logic of this line of reasoning is that a scientific *field* can be more scientific to the degree to which it is autonomous, since in an ideal state it will act as an ideal critical community holding up the products of its own activities for validation from those within the *field* who define the actualization of its logic of practice. In other words, a scientific *field* is objective to the extent to which it is autonomous. The same could be argued for a social scientific field: it will be more objectively

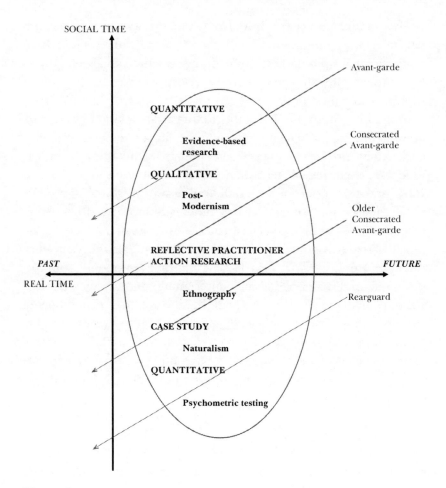

Figure 1

scientific to the degree to which it is autonomous. Of course, this is a theoretical supposition which would never exist in its ideal state. However, what is probably more common and equally true is that a *field* is less scientific, according to its own practical logic, to the extent to which it is open to influences from outside of the field.

If we take these arguments to the *field* of educational research, we see that it is possible to conceptualize the various methodological shifts in terms of structural generational movements over the past 40 years or so (see Figure 1).

This figure is a schematic depiction of the way methodological trends have developed in the course of the growth in educational research. Crudely expressed, it shows that a largely quantitative and positivistic paradigm was displaced by successive generations of naturalistic or qualitative methods, which included case study, ethnography, reflexive practitioner and post-modernist approaches. However, in recent years, there has been a return to quantitative and more positivistic methods through calls for 'evidence-based research' and quasi-experimental techniques. This would not be a problem if such moves arose from the dynamics within the *field* itself, and thus were objective and autonomous. However, in the case of the 'return' to quantitative methods, this has occurred in the UK through sustained influence and regulation from government agencies such as the Teacher Training Agency (TTA) and the Office for Standards in Education (Ofsted) and their sponsored agents. Many of these state institutions were influenced themselves by a technicist model of educational research dominant in the United States, which itself operates according to the principles of the neo-liberal economics so prevalent there. What is defined as 'good' research and good methodological principles are defined from outside of the *field*. Educational research could therefore be charged with not being 'scientific' enough since, theoretically at least, the degree of autonomy it possesses and its mechanisms of critical validation are undermined by external influences from outside of the *field*, which oblige it to behave in a certain way. If recent educational research is found to be lacking, it may be because it is not sufficiently independent. This is not a question simply of methodological preferences. If the way science is conducted in the educational research *field* produces findings which yield disappointing results when applied to practice, it may be that it is because its science is being impeded by influences with preset agendas of *what* the outcomes should be and *how* they should be; namely, in line with the already decided political discourse and its legitimated values and consecrated knowledge systems. Bourdieu's theory of practice offers the possibility of this objectification of the educational research *field* in a way which provides a radical critique of its systems of knowledge formation as part of a reflexive methodology. It calls on researchers to objectify their *field* and their own position within it at each stage of the research process. The implication here is that if this occurs, then the *field* will sufficiently reconstitute itself; that its own science will necessarily become more objective. This argument is part of a radical critique both of the existent educational research *field* and its processes and products. It also forms part of an alternative epistemological approach to educational research, which will lead to a form of knowledge which might be termed *reflexive objectivity* (see Grenfell and James, 2004 for further discussion).

Furthermore, it is not sufficient for the researcher to objectify their science *field*, they must also objectify themselves. However, such an objectification is a long way from a self-reflexivity, or self-awareness, in which the researcher attempts to hold to account their own subjective biases and blind spots. Indeed, Bourdieu was scornful of those who suggested this was possible. For Bourdieu, *misrecognition* simply went too deep. He was therefore suspicious of those who proclaimed the virtues of the 'epistemology of practice' of Schön's 'reflective practitioner' (see Schön, 1983). He was still more critical of the language of 'poetics and politics' to be found in criticisms of ethnography made by such writers as Clifford and Marcus (1986). As stated previously, for Bourdieu, neo-post-modernist texts were dangerous because they relativized everything and thus destabilized the modernist project of science and progress. In fact, Bourdieu claimed that his own 'reflexive sociology' had very little to do with any of these, and still less with the 'rational action theorists'. So, how else do we 'objectify the objectifying subject'?

Bourdieu stated that research should 'turn back onto itself the same scientific weapons it produces' (1989b: 55). However, besides the sort of *field* positioning described above, there is also the need to employ the conceptual terms developed in the course of the Bourdieusian project: namely, *habitus, field, capital*, etc. Yet, these terms are not used simply as descriptive options, but for the epistemological spotlight they throw on both the researcher and the researched. They are, as stated above, epistemological matrices carrying an explanatory dynamic, which acts as a medium between the researcher and the researched – a link between explanation and understanding, object and subjective, and theory and practice. Indeed, it is almost as if Bourdieu was arguing that in using these terms – *habitus, field, capital* –

reflexivity was necessarily present. They are ever present in the process of scientific enquiry: 'sociologists need to convert reflexivity into a constitutive disposition of their *habitus*' (*ibid*.: 174). Bourdieu's theory of practice, as represented by its conceptual terms, was internalized to form a kind of mordant between *habitus* and *field* in a way in which neither individual cognitive structures and their resultant dispositions, nor contextual forces, could act as determinants of thought and action (see Grenfell, 2004b, Chapter 7). Moreover, such a process is available to everyone in education; the teacher, the research, the student and the policy-maker. Acquiring this world view gave access to a kind of universality, expressed through Bourdieu's thinking tools to gain access to 'reflexive objectivity' and 'universal truths'. This is a radical project. The struggle for sociological rationality, as defined by Bourdieu's approach, is ultimately a political act as it offers an alternative view of society in the name of truth and reason. The latter were the products of history, of the work of *fields*, which had been employed in the service of society. That truth and reason in the knowledge *field* – in this case educational research – had been hijacked by those who acted to assert and protect their interests was, for Bourdieu, a threat to science itself. His method is not therefore based on cause and effect, but is one which aims to establish the 'conditions' for a new way of seeing the world. It could also be seen as a *realpolitik of reason* (1998c/1994: 139). Bourdieu asserted that this exercise in promoting and defending the social conditions for such rational discourse could only occur in contexts in which it was hotly contested. Liberation from the *misrecognition* and *symbolic violence* present in our deepest dispositions was therefore both a personal and social struggle. Because this theory of practice is not a commonsense way of knowing the world, it is, as it were, a stranger in it. It is therefore presented in the face of opposition and resistance. This new way of viewing the world is the *metanoia*, or at least a 'new gaze' (see 1992a: 252), as referred to in Part 2. That such a new way of seeing is offered in terms of 'science' and 'truth' and 'universals', as well as an 'act of resistance', is probably the final testament of Bourdieu's work on education and points to the greatest potential for its further development and application.

Afterword

The aims of this book have been to offer an account of Bourdieu in terms of both his biography and his work, to discuss some of the main issues arising from his ideas, and to address the issue of their continuing relevance. Part 1 looked at Bourdieu's own socio-historical background, as well as ideas that surrounded him in his formative years. At different points in the book, I have insisted that there is a need to understand both Bourdieu's work and the reception of it in terms of the climate – social, political, intellectual – of the day. Part 1 also showed how Bourdieu shaped his ideas both in response to his own academic training and personal experiences in the Béarn and Algeria.

Part 2 set out Bourdieu's theory of practice. It attempted to give an account that balanced two countervailing views of his basic approach: first, that it arrived in a fully developed form; second, that it changed radically over the years of its formation. In fact, the main tenets of Bourdieu's basic epistemology arrived early in his career. However, there were numerous later developments, stylistic trends, orientation and practical applications. As noted above, the essential point was that Bourdieu never theorized for the sake of theorizing. Rather, he immersed himself in practical situations and wrote theoretically about the links and connections between individuals and the contexts they found themselves in. Concepts of *habitus*, *field* and *capital* enabled him to highlight the relationship between the logic of practice of *fields* and the individual dispositions of those who passed through them, as well as relations within and between *fields*. Part 2 also gave an account of Bourdieu's key texts on education. Two points should be stressed here. First, education, in one form or another, occupied Bourdieu for most of his career, and, to a general academic public, he was probably best known as a 'sociologist of education'. Certainly, it is unthinkable that any present day sociologist of education could undertake their work without addressing both the methodological and substantive issues which arise in books such as *The Inheritors*, *Reproduction*, *Homo Academicus*, and *The State Nobility*. Second, it should again be emphasized that this book has dealt only with Bourdieu's work on education. There are equally challenging texts on taste and culture, art, economics, politics, philosophy, language and history. It is as well to recall that Bourdieu was an anthropologist first and, in many ways, his interests included practically all aspects of communities, societies and the cultures emergent from them. In all these cases, the same issues of theory and practice are at their core.

Bourdieu's own studies did vary in terms of the extent to which empirical data analysis underpinned each work. Education sees him at his most empirical. Part 2 took a chronological journey through his main educational texts showing what he found out, what interpretations he gave to these discoveries, and how his thinking on education developed in the course of this work. It was shown how Bourdieu's early reluctance to become involved in the world of policy and politics changed to a more direct personal engagement in policy formation. This engagement then in turn led to a further withdrawal from official avenues within the political discourse and a more over opposition to what was occurring in terms of educational reform.

Part 3 considered the ways in which Bourdieu's work was received. The discussion situated Bourdieu within the new 'sociology of education' which emerged in the 1970s, and showed the way his ideas formed part of this movement. The initial response to Bourdieu's views on education was discussed, as well as the problems that some commentators had with the implications of Bourdieu's arguments. The question was also asked: to what extent does Bourdieu's explanation of the education system in France give rise to an account which is applicable, or has relevance, to other national systems? Once again, the emerging issues are both theoretical, in terms of the interpretations made and the implications drawn, and practical, in terms of the empirical evidence used to support conclusions and the policy reforms suggested by them. Such debates involve political philosophy and the way it has shaped, and is shaping, educational policy and practice, and sociology itself, and the dominant paradigms that emerged in the second half of the twentieth century. Bourdieu's own words were used to answer many of the issues and objections that were raised.

Finally, Part 4 addressed the ways in which Bourdieu's perspective continues to be used in education; both in the sociology of education and its possible applications as a methodological approach to more general educational research topics.

It would be pertinent to emphasize that Bourdieu both came from and wrote about a world very different from our present one, and to question the continued relevance of his work. Certainly, he was the youngest and last of a generation which included the likes of Lévi-Strauss, Althusser, Sartre, De Beauvoir, Lacan, Foucault, Barthes, Lyotard and Derrida; in other words, some of the world's foremost intellectual leaders of the second half of the twentieth century. The scale and magnitude of his achievement should not be underestimated. Initially, Bourdieu was heading for the traditional route of the French academic elite, but he seemingly turned his back on philosophy and embraced sociology – a discipline of low prestige and which was hardly taught in universities. This itself can be seen as a 'high-risk' *field* strategy. Institutionally, he worked constantly to create a space that was distinct, and therefore somewhat liberated from, the official university dominance – most noticeably of *La Sorbonne*. Yet, he also challenged French politicians and policy-makers – indeed, the ruling elites of France itself – in showing up the misrecognitions of their systems. Equally, he attacked intellectuals and academics – especially philosophers and sociologists – for their 'scholastic fallacies' in imagining things in their own terms rather than as they were. Finally, he abandoned his reservations about public action and threw himself into a program of 'acts of resistance' against what he saw as the pernicious consequences of ruling political philosophy – neoliberal economics. Moreover, Bourdieu increasingly saw the potential that his ideas had for individuals at a personal level. In this case, the 'thinking tools' he provided could be used as a way for individuals to objectify the social forces which acted upon them and, in doing so, liberate themselves from them. Bourdieu's later statements became increasingly biographical and, while explicitly avoiding any autobiography, his work can be seen very much in terms of a personal trajectory to explain the climate of the times. This was a project that put 'reflexivity' at its core, which should be understood as the practical application of his epistemological perspective to every action of what might be called the 'empirical' and 'scientific' subject.

It is difficult to imagine someone else like Bourdieu emerging and operating in a similar fashion in our contemporary society. In the twenty-first century world of international communications, it is unlikely that anyone would act in a similar manner. Issues of colonialism have given way to the pressing exigencies of combating international terrorism. With the collapse of the Soviet bloc, communism is no longer considered a viable alternative to Capitalism; and even socialism has lost much of its appetite for social reform. Rather, successive national governments are obliged to act with the international and global stage in mind in terms of both economics and politics. In a post-modern world of extreme relativity and with access linked by the World Wide Web, few now talk of 'resistance'. Instead, the public discourse is one of achievement and accountability. The 'new' world view of neoliberal economics was anathema to Bourdieu, and yet so was post-modernism. He deplored the way that post-modernist philosophies had taken over the philosophical debate, which he saw as particularly dangerous because of the reactionary backlash that followed in their wake. However, he also railed against the way that education had been taken over by the law of the market; whether applied to individual pupils, school achievement, or indeed, the output of educational researchers themselves. In the course of the developments listed, sociology itself has had to change. It is no longer the fashionable subject it once was. A student is now more likely to take a course in Business or Business Studies, while once a radicalized student body clamored for social science degrees. The 'sociology of education', once a foundation discipline for educational theory and an ever-present part of teacher-training courses, now has to struggle to hold its own in an academic *field* calling for research which impacts directly on pupil achievement. This is also a world of constant reform in education. Bourdieu argued that it is sometimes better to do a lot of little things, 'because those little things generate changes that generate changes' (2000g: 19). He consequently urged that France, at least, should abandon notions of sweeping reforms – for example, of education – in favor of cultivating a culture of change. Gigantic changes often create more problems than they solve and often lead to reactionary backlashes. An alternative culture of change, he argued, comes about through more people – academic, politicians and the public – understanding society and the way it works; in other words, adopting his sociology as a guiding discipline in effecting change. This is a long process and one unlikely to be popular among politicians who see their careers evaluated in the short term, and look to achieve results after just a few months. The implication of Bourdieu's work is, however, that the theoretical tools he provided allow for considerable insight which can impact directly on national and global policy. To this extent, the issues which Bourdieu addressed, as much as the methodology he adopted to approach them, will continue to offer useful insights for educationalists, researchers, teachers and students.

Bibliography

The bibliography gives details of all the references cited in the book. It also includes some publications not addressed explicitly in the text, but still of pertinence to the theme of 'Bourdieu, Education and Training'. In order to aid an English-speaking reader, I have used English translations of Bourdieu's works wherever possible. These are cited and listed below with two dates: the first refers to the English publication; the second to the French publication. Occasionally, the French publication is a reprint of an earlier work. In these cases, I have given the original publication as a third date. Bourdieu always argued that his work should be read in terms of its 'socio-genesis'; namely, the context in which it appeared. I therefore feel it is important to make time of publication details as explicit as possible. Where the reference is cited in French only, the translation in the text is my own.

Accardo, A. (1983), *Initiation à la sociologie de l'illusionnisme social*. Paris: Le Mascaret.

Accardo, A. and Corcuff, P. (1986), *La Sociologie de Bourdieu: textes choisis et commentés*. Paris: Le Mascaret.

Alexander, J. (1995), *Fin de Siècle Social Theory*. London: Verso.

Alexander, R. (2000), *Culture and Pedagogy: International Comparisons in Primary Education*. Oxford: Blackwell.

Althusser, L. (1969/1965), *For Marx* (trans. B. Brewster). Harmondsworth: Penguin.

— (1970), 'Idéologie et appareils idéologiques d'État', in *Positions*. Paris: Éditions sociales (1976) pp 79–137.

— (1975/1968), *Reading Capital* (trans. E. Balibar). London: New Left Books.

Archer, M. (1983), 'Process without system', *Archives Européennes de Sociologie*, 24, 1, 196–221.

The Insurgent Sociologist, 8, 2–3 (Fall) 126–146.

Aronowitz, S. and Giroux, H. (1986), *Education Under Siege: The Conservative, Liberal and Radical Debate over Schooling*. London: Routledge and Kegan Paul.

Banks, O. (1968), *The Sociology of Education*. London: Batsford.

Barnes, D. (1976), *From Communication to Curriculum*. Harmondsworth: Penguin.

Barnes, D. and Todd, F. (1977), *Communication and Learning in Small Groups*. London: Routledge and Kegan Paul.

Barton, L. and Meighan, R. (eds) (1978), *Sociological Interpretations of Schools and Classrooms: A Reappraisal*. Nafferton: Nafferton Books.

Bates, R. (1980), 'New developments in the new sociology of education', *British Journal of the Sociology of Education*, 1, 1, 67–79.

Baudelot, C. and Establet, R. (1971), *L'École capitaliste en France*. Paris: Éditions Maspero.

del Bayle, L. (1969) *Les Non-conformists des Années 30: Une Tentative de Renouvellement de la pensée Politique Française*. Paris: Seuil.

Berger, P. L. and Luckmann, T. (1971/1967), *The Social Construction of Reality*. Harmondsworth, Middlesex: Penguin.

Bernstein, B. (1990), *The Structuring of Pedagogic Discourse: Class, Codes and Control, Vol. 4*. London: Routledge and Kegan Paul.

Bidet, J. (1979), 'Questions to Pierre Bourdieu', *Critique of Anthropology*, 13–14, 203–8.

Bonnewitz, P. (1998), *La Sociologie de Pierre Bourdieu*. Paris: PUF.

— (2002) *Pierre Bourdieu: Vie, oeuvres, concepts*. Paris: Ellipses.

Bourdieu, P. (1958), *Sociologie de l'Algérie*. (New Revised and Corrected Edition, 1961.) Paris: Que sais-je?

— (1961), 'Révolution dans la révolution', *Esprit*, Jan., 27–40.

— (1962a), *The Algerians* (trans. A. C. M. Ross). Boston: Beacon Press.

— (1962b), 'Célibat et condition paysanne', *Etudes rurales*, 5–6, 32–136.

— (1962c), 'De la guerre révolutionnaire à la révolution', in F. Perroux (ed.), *L'Algérie de demain*. Paris: PUF.

— (with Darbel, A., Rivet, J. P. and Seibel, C.) (1963), *Travail et travailleurs en Algérie*. Paris, The Hague: Mouton.

— (with Sayad, A.) (1964a), *Le Déracinement, la crise de l'agriculture tradionelle en Algérie*. Paris: Les Editions de Minuit.

— (with Passeron, J.-C.) (1964b), *Les Étudiants et leurs études*. Paris, The Hague, Mouton, Cahiers du Centre de Sociologie Européenne.

— (1966), 'L'Idéologie jacobine', *Démocatie et Liberté*, 167–73.

— (1968), 'Structuralism and theory of sociological knowledge', *Social Research*, 35, 4, 68–706.

— (1971a/1967), 'Systems of education and systems of thought', in M. F. D. Young (ed.) *Knowledge and Control: New Directions for the Sociology of Education*. London: Collier Macmillan. 'Systèmes d'enseignement et systèmes de pensée', *Revue Internationale des Sciences Sociales*, XIX, 3, 338–88.

— (1971b), 'The Thinkable and the Unthinkable', *The Times Literary Supplement*, 15 October, 1255–6.

— (1971c/1966), 'Intellectuel field and creative projet', in M. F. D. Young (ed.) *Knowledge and Control: New Directions for the Sociology of Education*. London: Collier Macmillan. 'Champ intellectuel et projet créateur', *Les Temps Modernes*, Nov., 865–906.

— (1972), 'Les doxosophes', *Minuit*, 1, 26–45.

— (1974/1966), 'The school as conservative force: scholastic and cultural inequalities' (trans. J. C. Whitehouse) in J. Eggleton (ed.) *Contemporary Research in the Sociology of Education*. London: Methuen. 'L'école conservatrice, les inégalités devant l'école et devant la culture', *Revue Française de Sociologie*, VII, 3, 325–47.

— (with Passeron, J.-C.) (1977a/1970), *Reproduction in Education, Society and Culture* (trans. R. Nice). London: Sage. *La Reproduction. Eléments pour une théorie du système d'enseignement*. Paris: Editions de Minuit.

— (1977b/1972), *Outline of a Theory of Practice* (trans. R. Nice). Cambridge: CUP. *Esquisse d'une théorie de la pratique. Précédé de trois études d'ethnologie kabyle*. Geneva: Droz.

— (1977c), 'The economics of linguistic exchanges' (trans. R. Nice), *Social Science Information*, XVI, 6, 645–68.

— (1979a/1977), *Algeria 1960* (trans. R. Nice). Cambridge: CUP. *Algérie 60. Structures économiques et structures temporelles*. Paris: Editions de Minuit.

— (with Passeron, J.-C.) (1979b/1964), *The Inheritors, French Students and their Relation to Culture* (trans. R. Nice). Chicago: The University of Chicago Press. *Les Héritiers. Les étudiants et la culture*. Paris: Les Editions de Minuit.

— (1982), *Leçon sur une leçon*. Paris: Les Editions de Minuit.

— (1984a/1979), *Distinction* (trans. R. Nice). Oxford: Polity. *La Distinction. Critique sociale du jugement*. Paris: Editions de Minuit.

— (with Eribon, D.) (1984b), 'Université: les rois sont nus', *Le Nouvel Observateur*, 2–8 November, 86–90.

— (with Salgas, J.-P.) (1985a), 'Le rapport du Collège de France. Pierre Bourdieu s'explique', *La Quinzaine Littéraire*, 445, 8–10.

— (1985b), 'Les intellectuels et les pouvoirs. Retour sur notre soutien à Solidarnosc', in *Michel Foucault, une histoire de la vérité*. Paris: Syros.

— (with Honneth, A., Kocyba, H. and Schwibs, B.) (1986a), 'The struggle for symbolic order. An interview with Pierre Bourdieu', *Theory, Culture and Society*, 3, 3, 35–51.

— (1986b), 'The forms of capital', in J. Richardson (ed.) *Handbook of Theory and Research for the Sociology of Education*. New York: Greenwood Press.

— (with deGaudemar, A.) (1986c), 'A quand un lycée Bernard Tapie', *Libération*, 4.

— (1988/1984), *Homo Academicus* (trans. P. Collier). Oxford: Polity. *Homo Academicus*. Paris: Les Editions de Minuit.

— (1989a), 'Social space and symbolic power', *Sociological Theory*, 7, 14–25.

— (with Wacquant, L.) (1989b), 'Towards a reflexive sociology: a workshop with Pierre Bourdieu', *Sociological Theory*, 7, 1, 26–63.

— (with Boltanski, L., Castel, R. and Chamboredon, J. C.) (1990a/1965), *Photography. A Middle-brow Art* (trans. S. Whiteside). Oxford: Polity. *Un Art moyen, essai sur les usages sociaux de la photographie*. Paris: Les Editions de Minuit.

— (with Darbel, A. and Schnapper, D.) (1990b/1966), *The Love of Art. European Art Museums and their Public* (trans. C. Beattie and N. Merriman). Oxford: Polity Press. *L'Amour de l'art, les musées d'art et leur public*. Paris: Les Editions de Minuit.

— (1990c/1980), *The Logic of Practice* (trans. R. Nice). Oxford: Polity. *Le Sens pratique*. Paris: Les Editions de Minuit.

— (1990d/1987), *In Other Words: Essays Towards a Reflexive Sociology* (trans. M. Adamson). Oxford: Polity. *Choses dites.* Paris: Les Editions de Minuit.

— (1991a/1982), *Language and Symbolic Power* (trans. G. Raymond and M. Adamson). Oxford: Polity Press. *Ce que parler veut dire: L'économie des échanges linguistiques.* Paris: Fayard.

— (with Chamboredon, J.-C. and Passeron, J.-C.) (1991b/1968), *The Craft of Sociology* (trans. R. Nice). New York: Walter de Gruyter. *Le Métier de sociologue.* Paris: Mouton-Bordas.

— (1991c/1988), *The Political Ontology of Martin Heidegger* (trans. P. Collier). Oxford: Polity Press. *L'Ontologie politique de Martin Heidegger.* Paris: Les Editions de Minuit.

— (with Wacquant, L.) (1992a), *An Invitation to Reflexive Sociology* (trans. L. Wacquant). Oxford: Polity Press. *Réponses. Pour une anthropologie réflexive.* Paris: Seuil.

— (1992b/1989), 'Principles for reflecting on the curriculum', *The Curriculum Journal*, 1, 3, 307–14. *Principes pour une réflexion sur les contenus d'enseignement.*

— (1992c), 'Pour une Internationale des intellectuels', *Politis*, 1, 9–15.

— (1993a/1980), *Sociology in Question* (trans. R. Nice). London: Sage. *Questions de sociologie.* Paris: Les Editions de Minuit.

— (1993b), *The Field of Cultural Production: Essays on Art and Literature.* Oxford: Polity Press.

— (1993c), 'Concluding remarks: For a sociogenetic understanding of intellectual works', in C. Calhoun, E. LiPuma and M. Postone, *Bourdieu: Critical Perspectives.* Oxford: Polity Press.

— (1994a), 'Un parlement des écrivains pour quoi faire?', *Libération*, 3 November.

— (1994b), 'Comment sortir du cercle de la peur?', *Liber*, 17, 22–3.

— (with Passeron, J.-C. and de Saint Martin, M.) (1994c/1965), *Academic Discourse.* Oxford: Polity. *Rapport Pédagogique et Communication.* The Hague: Mouton.

— (with Haake, H.) (1995a/1994), *Free Exchange* (trans. I. Utz and H. Haake). Oxford: Polity Press. *Libre-échange.* Paris: Seuil.

— (with Grenfell, M.) (1995b), *Entretiens.* CLE Papers 37: University of Southampton.

— (1996a/1992), *The Rules of Art* (trans. S. Emanuel). Oxford: Polity Press. *Les Règles de l'art. Genèse et structure du champ littéraire.* Paris: Seuil.

— (1996b/1989), *The State Nobility. Elite Schools in the Field of Power* (trans. L. C. Clough). Oxford: Polity Press. *La Noblesse d'État. Grandes écoles et esprit de corps.* Paris: Les Editions de Minuit.

— (with Derrida, J., Eribon, D., Perrot, M., Veyne, P. and Vidal-Naquet, P.) (1996c), 'Pour une reconnaissance du couple homo-sexuel', *Le Monde*, 1 March.

— (1998a), *Acts of Resistance. Against the New Myths of our Time* (trans. R. Nice). Oxford: Polity Press. *Contre-feux.* Paris: Raisons d'Agir.

— (1998b/1996), *On Television and Journalism.* London: Pluto Press. *Sur la télévision, suivi de L'Emprise du journalisme.* Paris: Raison d'Agir.

— (1998c/1994), *Practical Reason.* Oxford: Polity Press. *Raisons pratiques. Sur la théorie de l'action.* Paris: Seuil.

— (with Charle, C., Lebaron, F., Mauger, G. and Lacroix, B.) (1998d), 'Pour une gauche de gauche', *Le Monde*, 8 April.

— (1999a/1993), *The Weight of the World. Social Suffering in Contemporary Society* (trans. P. Parkhurst Ferguson, S. Emanuel, J. Johnson, S. T. Waryn). Oxford: Polity Press. *La Misère du monde.* Paris: Seuil.

— (1999b), 'Questions aux vrais maîtres du monde', *Le Monde*, 14 October, 18.

— (2000a/1997), *Pascalian Meditations* (trans. R. Nice). Oxford: Polity Press. *Méditations pascaliennes.* Paris: Seuil.

— (with Wacquant, L.) (2000b), 'La nouvelle vulgate planétaire', *Le Monde Diplomatique*, May, 6–7.

— (2000c), *Les Structures sociales de l'économie.* Paris: Seuil.

— (2000d), ' Entre amis', *AWAL: Cahiers d'Etudes Berbères*, 5–10.

— (2000e), 'Making the economic habitus. Algerian workers revisited' (trans. R. Nice and L. Wacquant), *Ethnography*, 1, 1, 17–41.

— (2000f), 'Manifeste pour des états généreux du mouvement européen, *Le Monde*, 7.

— (with Swain, H.) (2000g), 'Move over, shrinks', *Times Higher Educational Supplement*, 14 April, 19.

— (2000h), 'Participant Objectivation', address given in receipt of the Aldous Huxley Medal for Anthroplogy, University of London, 12 November.

— (2001a/1998), *Masculine Domination*. Oxford: Polity Press. *La Domination masculine*. Paris: Seuil.

— (2001b), *Contre-feux 2. Pour un mouvement social européen*. Paris: Raisons d'Agir.

— (2001c), *Science de la science et réflexivité*. Paris: Raisons d'Agir.

— (2002a), *Le bal des célibataires. Cris de la société en Béarn*. Paris: Seuil.

— (eds. Discepolo and F. Poupeau) (2002b), *Interventions (1961–2001)*. Marseille: Agone.

— (2003), *Images d'Algérie*. Paris: Actes Sud.

— (2004), *Esquisse pour une auto-analyse*. Paris: Raisons d'Agir.

Bredo, E. and Feinberg, W. (1979), 'Meaning, power, and pedagogy: Pierre Bourdieu and Jean-Claude Passeron, Reproduction in Education, Society and Culture: Essay Review', *Journal of Curriculum Studies*, 11, 4, 315–32.

Brubaker, R. (1985), 'Rethinking classical sociology: The sociological vision of Pierre Bourdieu', *Theory and Society*, 14, 6, 745–75.

Calderhead, J. (ed.) (1987), *Exploring Teacher's Thinking*. London: Cassell.

Calhoun, C., Lipuma, L. and Postone, M. (eds) (1993), *Bourdieu: Critical Perspectives*. Oxford: Polity Press.

Castel, R. and Passeron, J.- C. (eds.) (1967), *Education, développement et démocratie*. Paris, The Hague: Mouton.

Chauviré, C. and Fontaine, O. (2003), *Le Vocabulaire de Bourdieu*. Paris: Ellipses.

Clifford, J. and Marcus, G. (eds) (1986), *Writing Culture*. Berkeley: University of California Press.

Coleman, J. S. (1986), *Foundations of Social Theory*. Cambridge, MA: Belknap Press of Harvard University Press.

— (1990) *Foundations of Social Theory*. Cambridge, MA: Cambridge University Press.

Collins, R. (1989), 'Review of *Homo Academicus*', *American Journal of Sociology*, 95, 2, 460–3.

Connell, R. W. (1983), 'The Black Box of habit on the wings of history: Reflections on the theory of reproduction', in *Which Way Up?: Essays on Class, Sex and Culture*. London: Allen and Unwin.

Corcuff, P. (1995), *Les nouvelles sociologies*. Paris: Éditions Nathan.

— (2003) *Bourdieu Autrement. Fragilités d'un Sociologue de Combat.* Paris: Textual.

Darras, (1966), *Le partage des bénéfices, expansion et inégalités en France.* Paris: Editions de Minuit.

Davies, B. (1977), 'Phenomenological sociology and education: radical return or magic moment?' in D. Gleeson (ed.), 189–204.

Deer, C. (2003), 'Bourdieu on Higher Education: the meaning of the growing integration of educational systems and self-reflective practice', *British Journal of Sociology of Education*, 24, 2, 195–207.

Department for Education and Employment (DfEE) (1998), *The National Literacy Strategy.* London: HMSO.

Derrida, J. (1978), *La Vérité en peinture.* Paris: Flammarion.

Deslaut, Y. and Rivière, M.-C. (2002), *Bibliographie des travaux de Pierre Bourdieu: suivi d'un entretien sur l'esprit de la recherche.* Pantin: Le Temps des Cerises.

DiMaggio, P. (1979), 'Review essay on Pierre Bourdieu', *American Journal of Sociology*, 84, 6, 1460–74.

Dreyfus, H. and Rabinow, P. (1993), 'Can there be a science of existential structure and social meaning?' in C. Calhoun *et al. Bourdieu: Critical perspectives.* Oxford: Polity Press, pp 35–44.

Durkheim, E. (1952/1897), *Suicide: A Study in Sociology* (trans. J. A. Spauding and G. Simpson). London: Routledge.

— (1964/1933), *The Division of Labour in Society.* London: Macmillan.

Edwards, D. and Mercer, N. (1987), *Common Knowledge.* London: Routledge.

Elster, J. (ed.) (1986), *Rational Choice.* Oxford: Blackwell.

Elster, J. (1990), 'Marxism, functionalism, and game theory'' in S. Zukin and P. DiMaggio (eds), 87–118.

Fanon, F. (1961), *Les Damnés de la Terre.* Paris: Gallimard.

Gartman, D. (1991), 'Culture as class symbolization or mass reification: a critique of Bourdieu's *Distinction*', *American Journal of Sociology*, 97, 2, 421–47.

Gay, P. (ed.) (1973), *The Enlightenment: A Comprehensive Anthology.* New York: Simon and Schuster.

Ginsburg, M. B. (1988), *Contradictions in Teacher Education: A Critical Perspective.* Lewes: Falmer Press.

Giroux, H. (1980), 'Understanding School Knowledge: a Critical reappraisal of Basil Bernstein and Pierre Bourdieu,' *Educational Theory*, 30, 4, 335–346.

— (1981), *Ideology, Culture and the Process of School*. Lewes: Falmer Press.

— (1983a), *Theory and Resistance in Education: A Pedagogy for the Opposition*. London: Heinemann.

— (1983b), 'Theories of reproduction and resistance in the new sociology of education. A critical analysis', *Harvard Educational Review*, 53, 257–93.

Gleeson, D. (ed.) (1977), *Identity and Structure: Issues in the Sociology of Education*. Nafferton: Nafferton Books.

Gorder, K. (1980), 'Understanding school knowledge: a critical reappraisal of Basil Bernstein and Pierre Bourdieu', *Educational Theory*, 30, 4, 335–46.

Gramsci, A. (1971), *Selections from the Prison Notebooks*. London: Lawrence and Wishart.

Grenfell, M. (1996), 'Bourdieu and the initial training of modern language teachers', *British Educational Research Journal*, 22, 3, 287–303.

— (1998), 'Language and the Classroom', in M. Grenfell and D. James *Bourdieu and Education: Acts of Practical Theory*. London: Falmer.

— (2004a), 'Bourdieu in the Classroom', in M. Olssen *Language and Culture*. New York: Greenwood Press.

— (2004b), *Pierre Bourdieu: Agent Provocateur*. London: Continuum.

— (2006), 'Bourdieu in the field: from the Béarn to Algeria – a timely response', *French Cultural Studies*, 17, 2, 223–39.

Grenfell, M. and Hardy, C. (2003), 'Field manoeuvres: Bourdieu and the Young British Artists', *Space and Culture*, 6, 1, 19–34.

Grenfell, M. and Hardy, C. (2007), *Art Rules. Pierre Bourdieu and the Visual Arts*. Oxford: Berg.

Grenfell, M. and James, D. (1998), *Bourdieu and Education: Acts of Practical Theory*. London: Falmer.

Grenfell, M. and James, D. (2004), 'Change in the field – changing the field: Bourdieu and the methodological practice of educational research', *British Journal of the Sociology of Education*, 25, 4, 507–24.

Hanley, D. L., Kerr, A. P. and Waites, N. H. (1979), *Contemporary France: Politics and Society since 1945*. London: Routledge.

Hargreaves, D. (1996), *Teaching as a Research-based Profession: possibilities and prospects*. London: Teacher Training Agency.

Harker, R. (1984), 'On reproduction, habitus and education', *British Journal of Sociology of Education*, 5, 2, 117–27.

Hillage, J., Pearson, R., Anderson, A. and Tamkin, P. (1998), *Excellence in Research in Schools*. London: Department for Education and Employment.

Hirst, P. H. (1966), 'Educational Theory', in J. W. Tibble (ed.) *The Study of Education*. London: Routledge and Kegan Paul.

Jenkins, R. (1989), 'Language, symbolic power and communication: Bourdieu's "Homo Academicus"', *Sociology*, 23, 4, 639–45.

— (1992), *Pierre Bourdieu*. London: Routledge.

Johannesson, I. (1993), 'Professionalization of progress and expertise among teacher educators in Iceland: A Bourdieusean interpretation', *Teacher and Teacher Education*, 9, 3, 269– 81.

Karabel, J. and Halsey, A. (1977), *Power and Ideology in Education*. New York: Oxford University Press.

Kennett, J. (1973), 'The sociology of Pierre Bourdieu', *Educational Review*, 25, 3, 237–49.

Lacey, C. (1977), *The Socialisation of Teachers*. London: Methuen.

Lane, J. (2000), *Pierre Bourdieu: A Critical Introduction*. London: Pluto Press.

Lingard, R., Rawolle, S. and Taylor, S. (2005), 'Globalizing policy sociology in education: working with Bourdieu', *Journal of Educational Policy*, 20, 6, 759–77.

Loubet del Bayle, J.-L. (1969), *Les Non-conformistes des années 30: Une tentative de renouvellement de la pensée française*. Paris: Seuil.

Lukes, S. (1973), *Émile Durkheim: his Life and Work: A Historical Critical Study*. Harmondsworth: Penguin.

Mann, M. (2000), 'Has globalization ended the rise and rise of the nation-state?', in D. Held and A. McGrew (eds) *The Global Transformation Reader*. Cambridge: Polity Press.

Martin, B. and Szelényi, I. (1987), 'Beyond cultural capital: Towards a theory of symbolic domination', in R. Eyerman, T. Svensson and

T. Söderquist (eds) *Intellectuals, Universities and the State.* Los Angeles: University of California Press.

Maton, K. (2000), 'Language of legitimation: the structuring significance for intellectual fields of strategic knowledge claims', *British Journal of Sociology of Education,* 21, 2, 147–67.

— (2005), 'A question of autonomy: Bourdieu's field approach and Higher Education policy', *Journal of Educational Policy,* 20, 6, 687–704.

Mercer, N. (1995), *The Guided Construction of Knowledge.* Clevedon: Multilingual Matters.

Moore, R. (2004), 'Cultural capital: objective probability and cultural arbitrary', *British Journal of Sociology of Education,* 25, 4, 445–55.

Musgrave, P. (1966), *The Sociology of Education.* London: Methuen.

Naidoo, B. (2004), 'Fields and institutional strategy: Bourdieu on the relationship between Higher Education, inequality and society', *British Journal of Sociology of Education,* 25, 4, 457–72.

Nash, R. (1999), 'Bourdieu, *habitus* and educational research: is it all worth the candle?', *British Journal of Sociology of Education,* 20, 2, 175–87.

Nice, R. (1978), 'Bourdieu: a vulgar materialist in the sociology of culture', *Screen Education,* 28, 23–33.

O'Connor, D. (1957), *An Introduction to the Philosophy of Education.* London: Routledge.

Ogborn, J., Kress, G., Martins, I. and McGillicuddy, K. (1996), *Explaining Science in the Classroom.* Milton Keynes: Open University Press.

Ostrow, J. (1981), 'Culture as a fundamental dimension of experience: a discussion of Pierre Bourdieu's theory of human habitus', *Human Studies,* 4, 3, 279–97.

Passeron, J.-C. (1986), 'La signification des théories de la reproduction socio-culturelle', *International Social Science Journal,* 38, 4, 619–26.

Peuple et Culture (1945), *Un Peuple: Une Culture.* Paris: PEC.

Pinto, L. (1998), *Pierre Bourdieu et la théorie du monde social.* Paris: Albin Michel.

Popkewitz, T. S. (1987), *Critical Studies in Teacher Education.* Lewes: Falmer Press.

Prost, A. (1980), 'Une sociologie stérile: *La Reproduction*', *Esprit*, 3, 851–61.

Rawolle, S. (2005), 'Cross-field effects and temporary social fields: a case study of the mediazation of recent Australian knowledge economy policies', *Journal of Educational Policy*, 20, 6, 705–25.

Raynaud, P. (1980), 'Le sociologue contre le droit', *Esprit*, 3, 82–93.

Reay, D. (2004), '"It's all becoming habitus": beyond habitual use of habitus in educational research', *British Journal of Sociology of Education*, 25, 4, 431–44.

Reed-Danahay, D. (2005), *Locating Bourdieu*. Bloomington: Indiana University Press.

Robbins, D. (1991), *The Work of Pierre Bourdieu*. Milton Keynes: Open University Press.

— (1998), 'The need for an epistemological break', in M. Grenfell and D. James *Bourdieu and Education: Acts of Practical Theory*. London: Falmer.

Sartre, J.-P. (1963/1960), *The Problem of Method* (trans. H. E. Barnes). London: Methuen.

Schön, D. (1983), *The Reflective Practitioner: How Professionals Think in Action*. London: Temple Smith.

Sinclair, J. and Coultard, R. (1975), *Towards an Analysis of Discourse: The Language used by Teachers and Pupils*. Oxford: Oxford University Press.

Swartz, D. (1977), 'Pierre Bourdieu: the cultural transmission of social inequality', *Harvard Educational Review*, 47, 4, 545–55.

Taylor, S. and Singh, P. (2005), 'The logic of equity practice in Queensland state education – 2010', *Journal of Educational Policy*, 20, 6, 725–40.

Taylor, T. J. (1992), *Mutual Misunderstanding: Scepticism and the theorising of language and interpretation*. London: Routledge.

Thomson, P. (2005), 'Bringing Bourdieu to policy sociology: codification, misrecognition and exchange value in the UK context', *Journal of Educational Policy*, 20, 6, 741–58.

Thomson, P. and Holdsworth, R. (2003), 'Theorising change in the "educational field": re-readings of students' participation projects', *International Journal of Leadership in Education*, 6, 4, 371–91.

Tomusk, V. (2000), 'Reproduction of the "State Nobility" in Eastern Europe: past patterns and new practices', *British Journal of Sociology of Education*, 21, 2, 269–82.

Tooley, J. and Darby, D. (1998), *Educational Research: A Critique*. London, OfSTED.

Touraine, A. (1968), *Le Mouvement de mai et le communisme utopique*. Paris: Seuil.

Verdès-Leroux, J. (1998), *Le savant et la politique: essai sur le terrorisme sociologique de Pierre Bourdieu*. Paris: Grasset.

Vygotsky, L. (1962), *Thought and Language*. Cambridge, MA: MIT Press.

— (1978), *Mind in Society: The Development of Higher Psychological Processes*. London: Harvard University Press.

Wacquant, L. (1987), 'Symbolic violence and the making of the French agriculturalist: An inquiry into Pierre Bourdieu's sociology', *Australian and New Zealand Journal of Sociology*, 23, 1, 65–88.

— (1993), 'On the tracks of symbolic power: Prefatory notes to Bourdieu's "State Nobility"', *Theory, Culture and Society*, 10, 1–17.

Weill, N. (2001), 'Pierre Bourdieu, sujet du dernier cours de Pierre Bourdieu', *Le Monde Interactif*, 29 March.

Willis, P. (1977), *Learning to Labour*. London: Kogan Page

Wood, D., Bruner, J. and Ross, G. (1976), 'The role of tutoring in problem solving', *Journal of Child Psychiatry*, 17, 89–100.

Young, M. F. D. (ed.) (1971), *Knowledge and Control: New Directions for the Sociology of Education*. London: Collier Macmillan.

Zukin, S. and DiMaggio, P. (eds) (1990), *Structures of Capital: The Social Organization of the Economy*. Cambridge: Cambridge University Press.

Index

and the structure of higher
education and the field of
power 143–8
state patronage 135–7
strikes 107, 117, 120
structuralism 37, 38–9, 42, 175,
179
  anthropological 202
  constructivist 52–3, 131
  criticisms of Bourdieu's
    structuralist tendencies 177
  versus existentialism 131
  pre post-structuralism 37, 42
  and the relational mode of
    thinking 50–1
  structured structures *see habitus*
  subjectivism and 51–2
students
  and the academic field *see*
    academic field
  Bourdieu's research on
    students and studying 82–91
  rise in student population 122,
    127
  student protests 95, 117–18,
    119–20
subjectivism 42, 51–2, 62
  'hyper-subjectivity' 205
  versus objectivism 131
  research methodology
    and 82–3
substantialism 35–6, 50, 57
Swartz, David 180
symbolic capital 61, 221–2
symbolic power 102, 146
symbolic violence 112, 239, 251
  in *Knowledge and Control* 117

in *La Reproduction* 102, 103,
  177, 181, 191
post-modernist avoidance
  of 206
'Systems of Education and
  Systems of Thought' 97–101,
  111

Taylor, S. and Singh, P. 244–5
teacher education 115, 188, 190
  educational research
    and 218–19, 234–45
  principles of legitimation
    219–21
  researching classroom
    language 236–43
Teacher Trading Agency (TTA)
  218, 249
Teaching Quality Assessment
  227
Thatcher, Margaret 163, 217
theory of practice 47–64
  Bourdieu and social
    theory 201–14
  capital 60–1
  contemporary relevance of
    Bourdieu 229–31
  criticisms of 181–3
  dispositions 57–8
  as an epistemological third
    way 53
  field theory 54–7, 59, 60–1, 62,
    113 *see also* field theory
  habitus 58–9, 62, 113 see also
    habitus
  internalized 251
  origins of 27, 42